No Joke
Todd Phillips's *Joker* and American Culture

No Joke

Todd Phillips's *Joker*
and American Culture

M. Keith Booker

First published 2023 by
Liverpool University Press
4 Cambridge Street
Liverpool
L69 7ZU

© M. Keith Booker

M. Keith Booker has asserted the right to be identified as the editor of this book in accordance with the Copyright, Designs and Patents Act 1988.

All rights reserved. No part of this book may be reproduced, stored in a retrieval system, or transmitted, in any form or by any means, electronic, mechanical, photocopying, recording, or otherwise, without the prior written permission of the publisher.

British Library Cataloguing-in-Publication data
A British Library CIP record is available

ISBN 978-1-80085-645-5

Typeset by Carnegie Book Production, Lancaster
Printed and bound by CPI Group (UK) Ltd, Croydon CR0 4YY

Contents

List of Figures	vii
Introduction	1

I *Joker* and Cultural History

1	"Wait'll They Get a Load of Arthur Fleck": *Joker* and the Batman Franchise	11
2	The Cultural Logic of Early Neoliberalism: *Joker* as Postmodern Art	33
3	"You Talkin' to Me?": *Joker* and the Films of the 1970s and 1980s	63
4	Arthur, Portrait of a Serial Killer: *Joker* and Horror Film	87
5	"That's Life": The Music of *Joker*	109

II *Joker* and Political History

6	"How Can a President Not Be an Actor?": *Joker* and the Reagan Era	127
7	"Clowns Can Get Away with Murder": *Joker* and the Golden Age of American Serial Killing	151
8	*Joker*, Performance, and the Society of the Spectacle	175
9	"Kill the Rich": *Joker* and the Politics of Rebellion	199
10	The Politics of *Joker* and the Age of Trump	219

Conclusion	241
Works Cited	247
Films and Television Series Cited	259
Index	263

Figures

All screenshots from *Joker* (Warner Bros.)

1. Arthur Fleck suddenly becomes a formidable killer on the subway — 51
2. Fleck brutally stabs his co-worker Randall in the eye with scissors — 54
3. Fleck runs down a garbage-strewn sidewalk, pursued by police — 56
4. The movie screen is suddenly overwhelmed by television screens — 57
5. Fleck, in full Joker costume, dances down the stone steps near his apartment, accompanied by Gary Glitter's "Rock and Roll Part 2" — 112
6. Fleck shoots his hero Murray Franklin on live TV — 152
7. Fleck performs as a clown in a children's hospital — 154
8. Fleck performs his comedy routine at Pogo's Comedy Club — 155
9. Fleck grabs Alfred Pennyworth through the iron gate that separates Wayne Manor from the rest of Gotham City — 159
10. Fleck dances in a grimy public restroom — 188
11. Fleck dances alone in his apartment, accompanied by Frank Sinatra singing "That's Life" — 189
12. Fleck overlooks a riotous crowd of his admirers, who have taken over the streets of Gotham City — 212
13. The pained face of Arthur Fleck — 223

Introduction

Todd Phillips's *Joker* was one of the most striking cinematic events of the first two decades of the twenty-first century. For one thing, it was the surprise international box-office hit of 2019, with a billion-dollar-plus worldwide gross that far exceeded the expectations of Warner Bros., its parent studio. After all, while the film was marketed as a superhero film about the origins of the most important enemy of the superhero Batman, it includes no superheroes and none of the high-action computer-generated sequences that we have come to associate with such films. Meanwhile, the film was rated R in the United States (15 in the United Kingdom), primarily because of its graphic violence, and R-rated films have traditionally failed to achieve top-level box-office numbers. Thus, while the PG-13 superhero extravaganza *Avengers: Endgame* had broken all-time box-office records with nearly $2.8 billion in worldwide receipts earlier in 2019, the all-time box-office champ among R-rated films was the 2018 superhero film *Deadpool 2*, which took in $785 million, aided by the fact that it featured an actual superhero, albeit a somewhat vulgar one. *Joker* easily blew past that film, becoming the highest-grossing R-rated film of all time. By some measures, *Joker* was even more profitable than *Avengers: Endgame*, given that it was much less expensive to make.

What was perhaps even more surprising about *Joker* than its box-office success was the critical respect that it received. Many critics dismissed the film rather harshly as a crude and violent bit of exploitation that might actually encourage some impressionable audience members to commit violence of their own. At the same time, the film also received a number of accolades, beginning with its surprise win of the prestigious Golden Lion Award as the best film to screen at the 2019 Venice Film Festival, beating out an international array of rivals from such respected directors as Roman Polanski, Atom Egoyan, Olivier Assayas, Steven Soderbergh, and Noah Baumbach. In contrast, Phillips—the director, co-producer, and co-writer of *Joker*—was previously best known as the director of the trilogy of *Hangover* films from 2009, 2011, and 2013, rudely raucous comedies that achieved significant commercial success but were not exactly highly regarded as works of art. Given this background and given the nature of *Joker* as a film, many saw the Golden Lion win as something of a shocker. However, partly because of this win, many critics began to take a closer look at the film. Objections remained to its graphically violent content, but this closer look also brought more appreciation to the artistry of the film, well beyond the initial focus on star Joaquin Phoenix's spectacular performance in the title role. For example, the film's cinematographer Lawrence Sher (who had shot all three of Phillips's *Hangover* films and was just coming off the special effects extravaganza of *Godzilla: King of the Monsters*) gained significant attention for his work on the film. Indeed, in the interest of conventional visual artistry, both Sher and Phillips originally wanted to shoot *Joker* on 70 mm film, although the idea was nixed by Warner Bros. in favor of the now-conventional digital video (Sharf, "Cinematographer"). In addition, the music of the film drew serious critical attention. *Joker* features a particularly compelling score by Icelandic composer and musician Hildur Guðnadóttir, who was just coming off her work on the HBO miniseries *Chernobyl*, the score for which won her both a Primetime Emmy and a Grammy. But the soundtrack of *Joker* also makes especially important use of well-known popular tunes from American musical history, ranging from songs derived from Charlie Chaplin's 1936 film *Modern Times* to standards performed by American music legend Frank Sinatra, to a glam-rock hit from Britain's Gary Glitter.

By the time the 2020 Oscars rolled around, *Joker* had already piled up an array of other awards, including a BAFTA Award, a Screen Actors Guild Award, and a Golden Globe for Best Actor for Phoenix and a BAFTA Award and Golden Globe for Best Score for Guðnadóttir. Nevertheless, it was still something of a surprise that *Joker* garnered 11 Oscar nominations, more than any other film of the year. Though the film won only in the categories of Best Performance by an Actor in a Leading Role (Phoenix) and Best Achievement in Music Written for Motion Pictures (Guðnadóttir), it was nominated in most of the major categories, including Best Motion Picture, Best Achievement in Direction, Best Adapted Screenplay, and Best Achievement in Cinematography.[1]

In short, despite the dismissive attitude taken toward the film by some critics, *Joker* has also received significant attention as a work of cinematic art. I will argue extensively in the coming chapters that the film is, in fact, a complex and intricately constructed postmodern text that defeats final, definitive interpretations while generating a rich array of competing meanings. In addition, *Joker* engages in dialogues with an extensive array of extratextual materials, including not only the obvious connections with the long history of the Batman superhero franchise, but also film, television, music, and other forms of American popular culture over roughly a half century leading up to the 2019 release of the film. But *Joker* also engages in dialogues with material history over this same period, producing in the process a surprisingly sophisticated commentary on American society and politics from the beginning of the Nixon presidency in 1969 to the late years of the Trump presidency 50 years later, a period that marked the rise and then consolidation of the global power of neoliberal ideologies. All of these intertextual dialogues not only enrich the creation of meaning within *Joker* but help the film to produce a meaningful commentary on more than a half century of American cultural and political history.

The Basic Narrative of *Joker*

On the surface, *Joker* tells a fairly straightforward story, at least in terms of what we actually see on the screen. As the film begins, Arthur Fleck (Phoenix) is a troubled young man who lives in a shabby apartment with his aging mother, Penny Fleck (Frances Conroy), while working part-time as a rent-a-clown. He dreams, however, of becoming a successful stand-up comedian and thus transforming his life, ascending to a position of wealth and fame somewhat analogous to that occupied by his show-business hero and role model, television talk-show host Murray Franklin (Robert De Niro). In reality, though, Fleck has little talent and little hope of making it in show business. This fact, combined with his pre-existing mental illness, eventually drives Fleck over the edge and into a killing spree, the victims of which ostensibly include both his own mother and Franklin, leading eventually to his commitment to a mental health facility. Along the way, Fleck begins to call himself "Joker," thus explaining the title of the film.

Joker and Cultural History

Beginning with a consideration of *Joker*'s dialogue with the tradition of Batman comics, Part I of this study examines *Joker*'s dialogue with American cultural history, mostly between the 1970s and the 2010s, but reaching back even further into the twentieth century. The film includes a wide variety of clues that allow us to locate its action fairly precisely in the fall of 1981, while numerous visual indicators suggest that the action is taking place in a fictionalized version of New York City. This entire situation is complicated, however, by the fact that the city in which all of this occurs is explicitly identified, not as New York, but as Gotham City, the fictional home of Batman, whose most important criminal foe in the comics tradition happens to be called "the Joker." Further, the rich mayoral candidate who is murdered near the end of the film is none other than Thomas Wayne (Brett Cullen), a character who has traditionally been identified as the father of Bruce Wayne, the young boy who will go on to become Batman. Indeed, the scene in which Thomas Wayne and his wife Martha (Carrie Louise Putrello) are shot down, with their horrified son (Dante Pereira-Olson) looking on, closely replicates the widely known primal scene that sets young Bruce on the road to becoming Batman.

Thus, despite the style of gritty realism with which most of the film is presented, we are clearly asked to view all the events of the film within the context of what we know as the tradition of Batman narratives. That association was clearly a key to the remarkable commercial success of *Joker*, while also adding a vast array of cultural texts (including previous films) that enrich the meaning of the film by adding decades of background information. However, it is also the case that not all this information is internally consistent, not to mention the fact that *Joker* differs in important ways from anything of the other texts in the Batman universe. The first chapter of this study examines some of these background texts, from the first appearance of Joker in Batman comics in 1940 to the revisionary Batman comics of the 1980s, from the first Batman film of Tim Burton in 1989 to the "Dark Knight" films of Christopher Nolan from 2005 to 2012, from the campy Batman television series of the 1960s to the *Gotham* television series that concluded only months before the release of *Joker*.

Having established the nature of the connection between *Joker* and the Batman franchise in Chapter 1, Chapter 2 moves on to a consideration of just what sort of text *Joker* really is, thus laying the groundwork for a detailed reading of the film in the succeeding chapters. In particular, this chapter begins with a consideration of what it means, in general, to be "postmodern" and then moves on to a discussion of the some of the basic characteristics of *Joker* that establish it as a postmodern text. This chapter draws most centrally upon the seminal theorization of postmodernism by Fredric Jameson, especially in his 1991 book *Postmodernism, or the Cultural Logic of Late Capitalism*. It adopts Jameson's insistence on viewing postmodernism within the historical process in which it occurs and therefore considering the rise of postmodernism to be a natural consequence of the long historical process of capitalist modernization. On this view, postmodernism is the sort of culture that one would expect to arise at a time in history when this process is essentially complete, resulting

INTRODUCTION

in the essential incorporation of all aspects of society (including culture) within the capitalist economic system.

Chapter 3 follows with an in-depth exploration of *Joker*'s engagement with a number of films of the 1970s and 1980s, particularly the early films of Martin Scorsese, which were among the most important works that helped to establish the New Hollywood movement. The most important of these are *Taxi Driver*, from 1976, and *The King of Comedy*, from 1982, although *Mean Streets* (1973) is significant as well. Chapter 3 details exactly what these connections are, including both specific intertextual references and more general spiritual kinships. This heavy reliance on earlier films illustrates the way in which so much of *Joker* is constructed in a mode of postmodern pastiche. In addition, by establishing such close connections with the films of a period roughly 40 years before its own release, *Joker* makes it clear that there is significant continuity between the culture of roughly 1981 and that of roughly 2019, while at the same time indicating its own postmodern difficulties with establishing a coherent historical narrative.

Joker establishes significant intertextual connections to some of the most important mainstream films in American cinematic history, from the groundbreaking New Hollywood films of the 1970s and 1980s to the record-smashing superhero films that were such huge box-office hits in the 2010s. But, as Chapter 4 discusses, *Joker* also has much in common with important strains in the more marginal genre of the American horror film. Once again, this intertextual connection involves a dialogue with dual time periods: in this case with both the horror films of the 1970s/1980s and the "prestige" horror films of the 2010s. Indeed, *Joker* contains so many elements that are normally associated with horror films that it easily qualifies as a horror film in its own right, thus inviting readings in that context.

Chapter 5 completes the examination of the cultural background of *Joker* by looking at its use of music. One of the ways in which *Joker* establishes itself as a serious work of cinematic art is through its Oscar-winning score, which has received almost universal acclaim and which was clearly composed in a mode of high seriousness. Combining orchestral string instruments with electronics, this haunting score seeks to convey the depths of Arthur's psychic pain and makes a powerful contribution to the emotional impact of the film. At the same time, the music of *Joker* (like most aspects of the film) combines high cultural seriousness with pop cultural familiarity. Indeed, one of the most important ways in which *Joker* engages in a dialogue with the cultural past is through its prominent use of well-known popular music, again roughly from the time period of the film's action (and all from that period or earlier), so that Fleck and other characters in the film might be expected to be familiar with it.

No Joke: Todd Phillips's *Joker* and American Culture

Joker and Political History

Part II of this study examines *Joker*'s dialogue with American political history over roughly the same time period as its dialogue with cultural history. This period is particular crucial because it marks the rise to dominance of a new form of radical free market capitalism that has been widely referred to as "neoliberalism," a phenomenon that is closely congruent with what is also often referred to as "late capitalism," although the term "neoliberalism" places particular emphasis on the political implications of this stage of capitalism. The term "neoliberalism" has a long history but was first widely used in its contemporary sense to describe the economic reorganization of Chile under the regime of Augusto Pinochet in the 1980s. However, the pro-market policies of the Thatcher government in the United Kingdom and the Reagan administration in the United States also marked the movement of neoliberalism into the global capitalist mainstream during this same decade. Based on the work of economists such as Friedrich Hayek and Milton Friedman, but reaching to the laissez-faire capitalism of the nineteenth century, the rise of neoliberalism in the 1980s had roots that went back further. Moreover, the rise of neoliberalism was importantly accompanied by the unprecedented dominance of Republican administrations in the United States between 1969 and 1992, although the period since 1992 has seen even further growth and consolidation in the global power of neoliberalism.

Chapter 6 explores some of the ways in which *Joker* engages with and comments upon the specific historical context of the early 1980s, when its action takes place (even if it takes place in an alternate reality that is not quite the same world as our own). While the events of *Joker* are definitively linked to the fall of 1981 in numerous ways, the film also involves a blurring of historical context by drawing upon events that occurred (in our reality) over more than a decade before and after 1981, from roughly 1969 to roughly 1992, the period during which the domination of American politics by Republican Party presidents greatly facilitated the rise and spread of neoliberalism (although one might also suggest that the spread of neoliberalism facilitated the unprecedented period of Republican dominance in presidential politics during this period). But *Joker*, as a film of 2019, also reminds us that the period between 1992 and 2019, which was *not* dominated by Republican presidents, did very little to curb the continuing growth of the neoliberal agenda around the world.

Chapter 7 further establishes the significance of the setting of *Joker* in the fall of 1981 by noting that this year is directly in the midst of a historical period in which serial killers first became prominent in the public consciousness of Americans, both because there was an unprecedented number of serial killings during this period and because these killings received an unprecedented amount of attention in the popular media. *Joker* clearly depicts Arthur Fleck as a serial killer, or at least as a would-be serial killer, leaving open the possibility that his killings occur only in his fevered imagination. Moreover, some characteristics of Fleck as a serial killer appear to have been directly influenced by the careers of real-world serial killers, especially John Wayne Gacy, aka the "Killer Clown."

The period from roughly 1969 (with the notorious Manson murders) to 1992 (with the conviction of Jeffrey Dahmer) was a sort of "Golden Age" of American serial killers. Understanding this fact suggests that the dark and violent texture of *Joker* is well motivated by its connection to the American historical past. Meanwhile, this understanding is particularly significant due to the fact that *Joker* was released in the midst of a period in which American popular culture was informed by a wave of nostalgic representations of the 1980s as a simpler, happier, and more innocent time—and especially of the popular culture of the 1980s as a culture informed by lighthearted youthful exuberance.

Chapter 8 of this study grows out of an awareness that the rise of neoliberalism can be seen as the culmination of the evolution of the "society of the spectacle," as famously outlined by Guy Debord in 1967. One of the crucial themes of *Joker* has to do with the way performance and performativity are central to the texture of neoliberalism, under which all of us present ourselves to the world as if marketing a product. Arthur Fleck is a man who lacks a stable identity, and one of the ways in which he attempts to cope with this lack is through the performance of a series of assumed, perhaps fantasized, identities. As the film begins, he works as a rent-a-clown; as it proceeds, he attempts to pursue a career as a stand-up comedian. Both of these roles allow him to adopt an identity, but to remain shielded behind different kinds of masks. He also imagines himself playing roles such as lover to his neighbor Sophie (Zazie Beetz) or son to Thomas Wayne. And, finally, he assumes the identity of "Joker," who might or might not be a psychopathic killer. Chapter 8 argues that the focus on performance and spectacle in *Joker* does a great deal to tell us what kind of film we are watching, identifying the film as a postmodern esthetic artifact.

Joker is not overtly political, in that it puts forth no specific political agenda. It is, however, a film that says a great deal about a number of political issues in both of its dual time frames. Moreover, the plot of the film itself involves an all-out popular rebellion that erupts in the streets of Gotham. Chapter 9 continues the themes of Chapter 8 by arguing that the rebellion in *Joker* is informed by a performative aspect that links it to certain strains that informed the countercultural politics of the 1960s. The French version of those politics, of course, were the central impetus behind Debord's original formulation of the society of the spectacle. In the case of *Joker*, meanwhile, there is a way in which the performativity of Arthur Fleck is (inadvertently) transferred to the crowds in the streets of Gotham. Inspired partly by reports of a clown-masked avenger in their midst, the rebels don clown masks of their own. In so doing, they give their rebellion a carnivalesque aspect, but is a dark-hearted carnival for which the malicious Joker from the Batman comics would seem to be an apt symbol. *Joker* makes no final statement about this rebellion, leaving it to viewers to draw their own conclusions about the meaning and the ultimate outcome of the uprising.

Finally, Chapter 10 discusses the specific relevance of the political content to the historical context of the late 2010s, when the film was made and released. For example, the popular rebellion depicted in *Joker* began to appear eerily prescient in the summer of 2020, when protests over racial injustice swept across America, in the wake of several shocking killings of African Americans, especially the death of George Floyd at the hands of Minneapolis police. These protests seemed to suggest a widespread dissatisfaction with the status quo, potentially giving the rebellion in *Joker* new resonance. Then, that resonance changed again on January 6, 2021, as a violent mob assaulted the U.S. Capitol—and in a mood that clearly corresponded more closely to that of the rebels in *Joker* than had the Black Lives Matter protests of the previous summer. The link between the popular rebellion in *Joker* and the Capitol insurrection of January 6, 2021, provides a direct connection between the politics of the film and the politics of the time of the film's release. However, this chapter also discusses the ways in which the film suggests a continuity in history between the Trump administration and earlier Republican administrations going all the way back to Nixon (but especially to Reagan), while at the same time suggesting that all of these Republican administrations were key landmarks along the road to the historical development of neoliberalism.

Note

1 According to the Internet Movie Database (IMDb.com), *Joker* received a total of 218 award nominations overall, winning 104 of them.

Part I
Joker and Cultural History

CHAPTER ONE

"Wait'll They Get a Load of Arthur Fleck"
Joker and the Batman Franchise

Most reviews of *Joker* transparently refer to the film as the story of the evolution of its protagonist, Arthur Fleck, into the supervillain Joker, arch-enemy of Batman. Some have noted that the Joker into whom Fleck evolves might not actually be the same Joker who has harassed Batman for more than three-quarters of a century, but the marketing of the film itself—no doubt influenced by the huge box-office success of superhero films—did nothing to discourage the equation of Fleck with the famous comic book supervillain. Indeed, the closing credits of the film contain the overt designation that the film is "based on characters created by Bob Kane, Bill Finger and Jerry Robinson" the creators of the Joker character in the Batman comics. The closing credits are then followed by a series of company logos of those involved in producing the film, one of which is the logo of DC Comics, publishers of the Batman comic books. It seems clear, then, that the entire legacy of Batman comics, including their expansion into television and film, is a crucial part of the background to *Joker*, something that is clearly indicated by the content of the film.

Thomas Wayne in *Joker* and in the Batman Franchise

Of course, the very fact that *Joker* is set in Gotham City should make this point fairly obvious, given that this city does not actually exist in the real world as we know it but instead is a fictional creation (although transparently based on New York City) designed to give Batman and his foes a suitable setting in which to wage their battles against one another. It is also the case that, without mentioning Batman at all, the film introduces the ultra-wealthy Wayne family, including Thomas Wayne, his wife Martha, and his son Bruce. These figures are so prominent in American

No Joke: Todd Phillips's *Joker* and American Culture

cultural history that anyone with even a passing familiarity with the story of Batman will know that "Bruce Wayne" is the name of a Gotham City billionaire who becomes the superhero Batman. Most will also know that "Thomas Wayne" and "Martha Wayne" were the names of Bruce's ultra-wealthy parents in the comics.

It seems natural to assume that the Wayne family depicted in *Joker* is the same as the one known from Batman comics and previous Batman films. Meanwhile, probably the most widely known fact about the parents of Bruce Wayne is that they were both killed in a violent mugging, with a terrified Bruce looking on, ultimately to be inspired by that experience to fight crime as Batman. Seemingly sealing the notion that the Gotham City and the Wayne family in *Joker* are meant to be taken as the same as those in the Batman comics, we even see this famous scene re-enacted near the end of *Joker*, up to and including a moment in which the mugger rips a pearl necklace from the neck of Martha Wayne, sending pearls flying across the pavement—a specific iconic action that has been portrayed in a number of Batman comics as well as in the first major *Batman* film from 1989 and *Batman Begins* from 2005. These flying pearls are also particularly prominent in the opening moments of the pilot episode of the television series *Gotham*, which ran on the Fox network for five seasons from 2014 to 2019, making it an immediate predecessor to *Joker*.

This moment in the film, then, seems to have been carefully constructed to link *Joker* to the legacy of earlier Batman stories. As I will discuss in more detail in the next chapter (and throughout the rest of this volume), almost everything is open to interpretation in *Joker*, largely because most of the events are filtered through the unstable consciousness of Arthur Fleck, who seems to have a great deal of trouble distinguishing between fantasy and reality. Tellingly, though, the murder of the Waynes, is *not* related to us through Fleck's perception of it, because Fleck is apparently lying unconscious when that event occurs. As a result, the death of the Waynes would appear to be one of the few things in *Joker* that is to be taken at face value, so that this connection to the Batman franchise would appear to be unequivocal.

At the same time, the depiction of Thomas Wayne himself is one of the aspects of *Joker* that differs most radically from the Batman tradition. In that tradition, Wayne is typically a very positive figure. Though details vary, Wayne is generally seen as a highly virtuous model citizen (not to mention, in most versions, a gifted surgeon); in particular, he is a generous philanthropist, one of the few bright spots in the dark city of Gotham. He is looked up to and admired by the general population, who see him as a ray of hope in a city on the verge of collapse into anarchy. In *Joker*, however, Wayne is depicted as a cynical opportunist who sees the people of Gotham as a resource from which to fill his considerable coffers. He is also an ambitious politician who announces a run for mayor in the course of the film, perhaps for the corrupt purpose of using his position to make himself even richer.

We first encounter Thomas Wayne in *Joker* indirectly, as Penny Fleck complains to her son that Wayne must not be getting the letters she has been writing to him, given that he has never answered any of them. More skeptical, Arthur suggests that Thomas Wayne is a busy man, but Penny reminds him that she worked for the Wayne family for years, so that he could surely find time to write her back. The real story of the relationship (or lack thereof) between Penny and Thomas Wayne will never become absolutely clear in the film. It does seem certain that Penny worked in domestic service to the Waynes for a time roughly 30 years before the events related in the film. Penny also consistently claims (and appears to believe) that she and Wayne had been involved in a romantic relationship and that he is, in fact, Arthur's biological father. Wayne, however, vehemently denies that there was any such relationship—and certainly denies that he is Arthur's father. Indeed, there does seem to be evidence (which I will discuss in more detail in the next chapter) that Penny is deluded and that Arthur is, in fact, adopted, the biological son of neither Penny nor Wayne. But the film leaves open the possibility that Wayne might be unscrupulous (and powerful) enough to fabricate evidence to cover up the facts concerning his relationship with Penny.

It is certainly the case that, in the one scene in which we see a direct confrontation between Wayne and Arthur Fleck, Wayne treats Fleck quite cruelly. Soon after having gone to the Wayne estate and making overtures to young Bruce, Fleck (apparently) corners Wayne in a posh restroom in Wayne Hall and asks him to show a little decency to him. Wayne responds by insisting that Penny is "crazy" and that he never slept with her. When Arthur responds with one of his laughing attacks, Wayne punches him in the face and threatens to kill him if he ever comes near Bruce again. Wayne clearly comes off as something of a bully here, even though his reaction might not seem all that extreme, assuming he is telling the truth (which we don't unequivocally know to be the case). As I will discuss more in the next chapter, there is also reason to believe that Fleck might have imagined this whole encounter, in which case what we learn here is that Fleck *imagines* Wayne to be a bully.

Most of what we see of Wayne involves the public persona that he puts forth, usually on television. But then almost everyone in this film seems to be performing inauthentic identities—for cameras or otherwise. The first time we actually see him in the film, Wayne is appearing on a morning television program to discuss the subway shootings that supposedly initiated Fleck's career as a killer, noting that the three victims had been employees of Wayne Investments. Wayne attempts to sound as if he is grieving for those victims, noting that all "Wayne employees" are "family." Watching this performance on TV, Penny seems thrilled, feeling that, as a former employee, she must also be regarded as family by Wayne. Of course, Wayne also admits that he didn't actually know the men who were killed, which already makes his expression of family feeling for them a bit suspect. Then, he turns his expression of grief into a self-serving political statement. When his interviewer notes that a "groundswell of anti-rich sentiment" is currently sweeping Gotham, almost as if "our less fortunate residents are taking the side of the killer," Wayne responds by noting that this situation is one reason why he is considering a run for mayor, so that he can help to set the city back on a proper course. When asked about reports that the killer had been wearing a clown mask, Wayne says that it makes total sense that the killer would be wearing a mask, because he was obviously a coward who would want to hide behind such a disguise.[1] He goes on: "And until those kind of people change for the better, those of us who have made something of our lives will always look at those who haven't as nothing but clowns."

Wayne's contempt here for the "less fortunate" (read "lazy" and "shiftless") people of Gotham is palpable. A bit later (shortly before his encounter with Fleck at Wayne Hall), we again see Wayne on television, now having officially announced his run for mayor. Being interviewed about the increasing unrest in Gotham's streets, Wayne shows contempt for the increasingly angry (but still mostly peaceful) protestors who are filling the streets, declaring that "there's something wrong with those people." Envisioning himself as the city's savior, Wayne claims that he is running for mayor to help people, to "lift them out of poverty." Then, going full-on demagogue, he declares that, while the people of Gotham might not realize it, "I'm their only hope."

The politics of *Joker* are a bit muddled, as I will explore more fully in Chapters 8 through 10 of this study. It seems very clear, though, that Wayne is presented in the film as anything but a potential savior for the people of Gotham. I will discuss in Chapter 10 of this study the fact that multiple observers have suggested that he bears many similarities to Donald J. Trump, the highly problematic president who was still in office when *Joker* was made and released. Wayne is, in any case, clearly depicted as a pompous, blustering windbag who doesn't seem to care about anyone but himself (and possibly Bruce). Given his presentation in the film (aided

JOKER AND THE BATMAN FRANCHISE

by the performance of Brett Cullen) as such a negative figure, it is clear that Wayne is not the solution for Gotham. He is, in fact, a very big part of the problem, clearly feeling that his great wealth (which seems to have been inherited, given that he was already wealthy 30 years earlier) entitles him to a position of power and makes him more valuable as a person than the "clowns" that he sees around him in the streets of Gotham.

We can, of course, go to the extreme of questioning whether this "Thomas Wayne" is meant to be the same Thomas Wayne who is the father of the same "Bruce Wayne" who will become Batman. But, in order to talk about this film at all (especially in relation to the Batman franchise) it seems necessary to make at least a few assumptions, such as the fact that the film's "Gotham City" is meant to be taken as the same city in which Batman battles crime throughout his career. Moreover, the fact that this Thomas Wayne seems so different from the usual versions of Thomas Wayne is not necessarily a big surprise. Of all of the major superhero franchises, the Batman franchise has, over the more than 80 years of its existence, probably had the most inconsistent continuity, in terms of both style and content. There have, in fact, essentially been completely different Batman universes, in some of which various characters have been depicted quite differently than in others. The Batman of the original comics was a much darker figure than the more light-hearted Batman who emerged in the 1950s and 1960s, as DC Comics attempted to negotiate the constraints imposed by the new Comics Code. Then, the pendulum swung back in the other direction, and the new Batman who emerged in the comics of the 1980s was even darker than in the original comics of the 1930s and 1940s. The same can be said of other media. One need only compare the campy representation of Batman in the well-known 1960s television series to the dark and brooding Batman of the "Dark Knight" film trilogy to see how widely different representations of the character have been in film and television.

Even Thomas Wayne has been depicted quite differently at different times, especially in recent years. For example, the 2016 *Batman* videogame released by Telltale Games presents us with a Thomas Wayne who is a ruthless criminal and a member of the Falcone crime syndicate. In the limited comics series *Batman: Damned*, which ran from September 2018 to June 2019 and took the Batman story into supernatural horror territory, Wayne is also less a paragon than usual. For one thing, it is revealed that he has cheated on his wife and might have fathered an illegitimate son, a suggestion that is, of course, highly relevant to *Joker*. The most prominent example of a villainous Thomas Wayne appears in an alternate run of the *Batman* comic written by Tom King as part of

15

the *DC Rebirth* event that rebooted many DC comics in 2016. Here, Thomas Wayne is a key villain who becomes an ally of Bane, another of Batman's key enemies.

In the 2011 *Flashpoint* story arc, we are presented with an alternate world in which young Bruce Wayne is killed by a mugger, causing his father to become a particularly brutal version of Batman, driven by a desire to avenge his son. To add still another wrinkle, in this storyline Martha Wayne is driven insane by her son's killing and goes on to become the Joker! The Joker character has, in fact, also varied widely over time, although the title character of *Joker* has very little in common with any of the versions of the character from the history of the franchise, other than superficial similarities, such as his clown make-up, his laugh, and a mental illness that drives him to murder. But Arthur Fleck's Joker is very much a lone wolf, and it is hard to see him functioning as the criminal mastermind that we typically see in the Batman franchise. Numerous theories concerning the relationship of Fleck's Joker to the well-known Batman Joker can be proposed—for example, that Fleck's Joker merely serves as an inspiration for the more formidable Joker who would battle Batman, or, less likely, that Batman's Joker actually serves as inspiration for Fleck's fantasies of being Joker. However, while I do not think that *Joker* contains the evidence to enable a final conclusion to be drawn about this question, it is a key question nevertheless, worth pondering via a careful comparison between Fleck's Joker and the Joker with whom we are familiar from other works in the Batman franchise.

The Joker in Batman Comics

The Joker is unquestionably the most important member of the colorful rogues' gallery of Batman's foes.[2] In fact, he is arguably the greatest comic book villain of all time. In 2008, for example, *Wizard Magazine* placed the Joker fifth (and first among all villains) on its list of "The 200 Greatest Comic Book Characters of All Time," while *Empire* magazine placed the Joker eighth on its list of "The 50 Greatest Comic-Book Characters" (the highest-ranked villain on both lists). In a list of greatest comics villains compiled by Fred Blunden for the "Screen Rant" website in 2017, the Joker was again ranked first. The character has been named the greatest of all comic book villains in several other publications as well. If one wanted to make a film about a comic book villain, the Joker would be the obvious choice.[3] The Joker, as a character, has also received a surprising amount of serious critical attention, even before the high-profile 2019 film.[4]

The Joker first appeared in *Batman* #1, the first issue of Batman's self-titled comic, with a cover date of March 1940. This issue contains the first origin story of the evolution of Bruce Wayne into Batman (including the famous murder of his parents), although the Batman character had actually been appearing since *Detective Comics* #27 (May 1939). Batman was an immediate hit; he continued to be featured in every issue of *Detective Comics* until the appearance of *Batman*, then continued to be featured in both titles going forward. Joker would also become a regular feature of the Batman world. Originally, a grim and ruthless killer, Joker gradually evolved into a more humorous figure who, while still dangerous, loved to employ gags and practical jokes to wreak havoc, gaining him nicknames such as "The Clown Prince of Crime." Dennis O'Neil, a comics writer who helped to revitalize the Joker character in the 1970s, suggests that the Joker "is, arguably, the most perfect modern embodiment of what mythologists call 'the trickster archetype,' a figure in many of the world's mythologies whose main motivation is simply to raise hell."

This comparison with the trickster figure suggests that the Joker taps into archetypal energies, helping to explain the success of the character, although it is also the case that the traditional trickster (often a figure of great power) has little in common with the downtrodden Arthur Fleck. Despite pursuing careers as both a party clown and a stand-up comedian, Fleck has virtually no conventional sense of humor, although he does seem to enjoy the chaos we see in Gotham's streets near the end of the film. The Joker from Batman comics, though, would be much more likely to have the archetypal energy to cause Gotham's rebellion directly, which might help to explain why, over time, the Joker clearly became the most important of Batman's many colorful antagonists. Joker, in fact, has often been seen as Batman's complementary Other, the antithesis of all that Batman represents, but also a figure without whom Batman could not take on his full meaning. As Johan Nilsson puts it, Joker is the "yang" to Batman's "yin," an "agent of chaos" who stands opposed to Batman's "need for order" (165)

That an origin story for Batman would appear so early in the evolution of the Batman franchise points toward the way in which origin stories would go on to become a mainstay of superhero comics in general. Almost all major superheroes have been provided with detailed origin stories over the years, although it is also the case that many of them have been provided with multiple such stories, some of which vary widely from others. The vague outlines of Batman's origin have remained relatively stable, even though the secondary details have changed from one version to another. Meanwhile, the origins of Batman's rogues' gallery of criminal

No Joke: Todd Phillips's *Joker* and American Culture

foes have received more attention than most villains over the years. For example, *Detective Comics* #168 (1951) introduced the first full-fledged explanation of Joker's origins: a criminal known as Red Hood leaps into a vat of chemicals while attempting to escape from Batman and subsequently suffers the disfigurement that gives him the characteristic grinning Joker face. In this story, the name "Joker" is adopted because the Joker on playing cards typically bears a similar grin.

The prevalence of origin stories in the Batman franchise can perhaps best be seen in the recent *Gotham* television series, which is essentially an extended five-season story of the origins of Batman, beginning with the murder of the Waynes in the first scene of the series and ending with a finale in which Bruce has finally become Batman. But this story essentially takes place in the background; the real substance of *Gotham* is a series of origin stories of various Batman foes. In this case, unusual for the franchise, Oswald Cobblepot (aka Penguin, played by Robin Lord Taylor) takes the most prominent role, with figures such as Edward Nygma (aka Riddler, played by Cory Michael Smith) playing important roles as well. Joker, meanwhile, probably takes the least prominent role, though it is also the most enigmatic.

In fact, the name "Joker" is never applied to any character in *Gotham*, apparently because DC wanted to reserve that character name for movies. (It should be noted that the name "Batman" is never actually used either, even in the season finale.) But a character named Jerome Valeska (Cameron Monaghan) appears destined to become the Joker as early as his initial appearance in the first-season episode "The Blind Fortune Teller." This character continues to evolve, spreading anarchy and chaos until the fourth season, when he is suddenly and unexpectedly killed, only to be replaced by his twin brother Jeremiah (also played by Monaghan), who then seems headed toward becoming the Joker, but never quite does. Both Jerome and Jeremiah have been described as proto-Jokers who might possibly have inspired a later "true" Joker character, which obviously resonates with the situation of Arthur Fleck in *Joker*, who might evolve into the true Joker or might instead simply serve as an inspiration for the criminal who becomes the true Joker.

The Joker receded in importance for a time after the implementation of the Comics Code Authority in 1954. This attempt at industry self-censorship, modeled on the Motion Picture Production Code, grew out of widely publicized concerns that violent comics were having a negative psychological impact on their young readers.[5] Many of the early Joker stories (not to mention the recent *Joker* film) contained exactly the sort of material that the Code was meant to exclude, so that the limitations imposed by the Code made it much more difficult to produce effective Joker stories. Joker stories that did appear between the mid-1950s and mid-1960s tended toward comical silliness that lacked the impact of the earlier stories featuring this character. The character did, however, make a significant comeback thanks to his prominent presence in the spoofy *Batman* that ran for three seasons in 1966–1968. As portrayed by Cesar Romero, this TV Joker appeared in 18 different episodes, matching Burgess Meredith's Penguin as the villain with the most appearances in the series. This character still tended toward silliness, specializing in the construction of elaborate, gimmicky deathtraps for Batman and Robin (who, of course, always escaped). Nevertheless, the Joker was a clear favorite with television audiences, encouraging DC Comics to try to increase his prominence in the comics, which they did in the 1970s, thanks to the work of writers such as O'Neil.

By the beginning of the 1980s, the Comics Code was in a state of collapse, and the Joker was once again emerging as a darker and more dangerous figure. It was not, however, until 1986 when another truly landmark Joker story would appear. Emphasizing the fact that the Batman comics themselves were getting a bit long in the tooth, Frank Miller's *The Dark Knight Returns* (1986) features a 55-year-old Bruce Wayne, who returns from retirement, creaky bones and all, once again becoming Batman in the face of a crisis of crime confronting Gotham. A four-issue miniseries drawn by Miller and Klaus Janson, *The Dark Knight Returns*, is very much Batman's story, but it does include Joker as a significant figure, at the same time taking the character in a darker direction as a deranged mass killer, willing to do anything and everything to strike blows against Batman. As Ayres notes, in this miniseries, "Miller depicts Joker as a relentless homicidal maniac with a (problematic) homoerotic obsession with Batman. In the third chapter, Joker massacres hundreds of innocent people primarily to gain the attention of Batman. Reinforcing the homoeroticism of the Joker/Batman dynamic, Miller stages their final confrontation in a Tunnel of Love carnival attraction" (Ayres, vol. 3 1097).

In *The Dark Knight Returns*, the Joker quickly becomes a factor in the crisis enveloping Gotham, escaping from Arkham Asylum to renew his vendetta against Batman. Importantly, for my purposes, the Joker's escape is carried out when he convinces his caretakers at Arkham to allow him to appear on a late-night talk show, where he murders everyone in the studio with poison gas, fleeing the scene in the consequent chaos. Given that Arthur Fleck's killing spree in *Joker* culminates in his own appearance as a murderous talk show guest, Joker's activities in *The Dark Knight Returns* surely make that comic an important forerunner to the 2019 film.

No Joke: Todd Phillips's *Joker* and American Culture

Indeed, if there were any question that the talk show murders in *The Dark Knight Returns* were an important inspiration for the talk show scene in *Joker*, it should be recalled that the other guest on the talk show in the comic is a middle-aged lady sex therapist, clearly based on Dr. Ruth Westheimer, a talk show staple during the 1980s. The Joker, although portrayed in this comic in ways that clearly suggest that he is gay, grabs the sex therapist and starts aggressively kissing her, in the process delivering a deadly toxin (via his poison lipstick) that kills her. In *Joker*, when Fleck appears on *Live with Murray Franklin*, the other guest is also a middle-aged lady sex therapist, whom Fleck also immediately grabs and kisses, stunning her (although, in this case, not killing her). It seems obvious that the inclusion of this woman in the scene is an intentional nod to *The Dark Knight Returns*, which is thus identified as an important source for *Joker*.

In addition to such direct echoes in content, the overall dark and cynical tone of *The Dark Knight Returns* also makes it an important predecessor to *Joker*. For one thing, Batman himself, in the comic, decides to kill the Joker in order to put an end to his career once and for all. He ultimately pulls up short, at which the Joker brings about his own death in an attempt to incriminate Batman as a murderer. Subsequently, Batman must battle against the police and the authorities as much as against Gotham's criminals, making very clear a suggestion that runs through *The Dark Knight Returns* that the government and the police cannot be counted on as forces of virtue and rectitude. This situation ultimately leads Batman into direct conflict with Superman, who remains aligned with the forces of official power. In particular, Superman is brought into the fray by a president who is quite obviously designed to resemble Ronald Reagan himself, even though this president is not named in the text.

That a Reagan figure appears as the ultimate symbol of authority is no surprise in a text published in 1986, although his appearance as an actual character in *The Dark Knight Returns* does serve to make the series' action (and Gotham City) seem as if they reside in a version of the real world of 1980s America, rather than in a purely fictional comic book universe. At the same time, the Reagan of this comic is something of a caricature, a doddering, bumbling figure who wraps himself in the American flag but is able to do little other than spout folksy clichés while passing on most responsibilities to others. He makes authoritarian gestures—such as threatening to invoke martial law in order to deal with looters—but he hardly seems up to dealing with the major Cold War crisis that arises in the course of the narrative, leading to a national disaster, even with Superman intervening on the side of the United States.

Reagan's inclusion in *The Dark Knight Returns* is clearly satirical—and it is satire of a sort that remains relevant to *Joker*, given that the exaggerated president we see in the comic would seem almost like a realistic portrayal of the real president of 2019. It is certainly not accidental that Shant Eghian entitles a four-part online discussion of the ongoing relevance of the political satire of *The Dark Knight Returns*, "Making Gotham Great Again"—echoing the famed slogan that helped bring Donald Trump a victory in the 2016 presidential election. Eghian, however, suggests that it is not Reagan, but Batman himself who mirrors Trump.[6] In the third installment of his series, which focuses on Reagan, Eghian notes Miller's negative treatment of Reagan but argues that Miller's Batman is a right-wing figure who foreshadows the right-wing populism of Trump, a point he makes even more extensively in Part 1, which focuses on Miller's satire of the news media.

Indeed, one of the most telling narrative innovations in *The Dark Knight Returns* involves the frequent replacement of conventional comics frames by television screens, relating and commenting upon the events of the story via the (somewhat vacuous and facile) television coverage of them. As a result, the miniseries is able to add television news to the list of its objects of satire, while at the same time delivering a commentary on the mediatization of experience in the contemporary world and on the penetration of television into the innermost reaches of the American consciousness. In this, of course, *The Dark Knight Returns* prefigures *Joker*, which is frequently punctuated by television news coverage of its events and in which television is clearly such an important part of the daily life of Arthur Fleck.

One of the programs we see in *The Dark Knight Returns* is called *Good Morning, Gotham*, a program that we also see in *Joker*, suggesting that the connection might be quite direct. But, whether or not the use of television in *Joker* was directly inspired by *The Dark Knight Returns*, the parallel remains nevertheless, suggesting certain similarities between the projects of these two important texts, while also suggesting certain spiritual similarities between *Joker* and the tradition of Batman comics, especially during the dark turn taken by those comics in the 1980s. Indeed, the other truly major Batman story of the 1980s is an origin story for the character Joker, as most observers have assumed the film *Joker* to be, thus establishing what would appear to be an especially important connection between these two texts.

That comic, *Batman: The Killing Joke* (1988), written by Alan Moore and illustrated by Brian Bolland, continues the tendency toward darker and more adult-oriented Batman stories in the 1980s, although it is loosely based on a 1951 story entitled "The Man Behind the Red Hood!" In this story the Joker starts out as an ordinary chemical engineer but leaves that job in order to pursue his dream of being a stand-up comedian. He fails miserably, of course, then turns to a life of crime in an effort to support his pregnant wife Jeannie, agreeing to guide some criminals through the chemical plant where he previously worked so that they can rob the playing card company next door. Then, the engineer is informed that Jeannie and their unborn child have died in an accident. Despondent, he attempts to withdraw from the planned heist, but is strong-armed by the criminals into continuing. Batman interrupts the robbery, however, leading the engineer to be exposed to chemical waste in an attempt to escape. As a result, he is disfigured and discolored, emerging with the white skin, green hair, and grinning red lips that are associated with the Joker in the tradition of Batman comics. The combination of this chemical exposure and the death of his family also drives him insane, completing his transition into the Joker.

Perhaps the most important link between *The Killing Joke* and *Joker* is that the former, rather than depicting the Joker as driven by pure malice, takes seriously the notion that he was driven to supercrime by genuine suffering as the result of mental illness. At one point, the text even suggests that Joker's descent into madness was the result of "one bad day," which is apparently referenced in *Joker* in a key moment when Fleck, having just apparently made a key discovery about his past, breaks into the apartment of his neighbor Sophie, explaining his presence by saying, "I had a bad day."

If this moment is indeed a reference to *The Killing Joke*, then that would seem to imply that Fleck's discovery that his mother lied about his background was the key moment in his fall into insanity. It would also seem to support the notion that the Joker into whom Fleck evolves really is the Joker from the Batman universe. In any case, Valentino Zullo sums up *The Killing Joke* in a way that might apply to *Joker* as well:

> By placing *The Killing Joke* in the context of discussions of mental health, Moore and Bolland's text complicates questions of evil as well as empathy through the depiction of the villainous Joker in pain. The reader's identification with and connection to the character facilitates opportunities for both clinicians and laypeople to listen to and to witness the story of a villain, to know what he is, and to contend with the ambivalent feelings that emerge from such a situation of knowing both his sad history and his violent actions. (196)

The Joker in Batman Films

One year after *The Killing Joke*, the Batman franchise would take another major turn when its world became the setting of a major motion picture with the release of Tim Burton's *Batman*.[7] In this film, the first thing we see after the opening credits sequence is a shot of the Gotham City skyline at night. It's a skyline that is definitely reminiscent of New York City, but with just a slightly Expressionistic, Gothic twist that gives it the suggestion of something dark and sinister, a suggestion that will be reinforced in the following nighttime street scenes, which (within seconds) introduce us to garbage, bums, hookers, and a bewildered tourist family lost in the city. They soon get mugged, of course, after which Batman (Michael Keaton), looking as Gothic and sinister as the city itself, appears and makes short work of the muggers, commanding them to tell all their criminal friends about him. It's clear that Gotham is a high-crime, decaying city, much as in *Joker*. Only seconds later, we are introduced to gangster Jack Napier (Jack Nicholson), a key lieutenant to Jack Palance's menacing Carl Grissom, Gotham's top criminal kingpin. Napier, of course, will eventually do away with Grissom after becoming the Joker (his face disfigured into a permanent macabre grin as a result of falling into a vat of toxic chemicals in a battle with Batman). Subsequently, Napier/Joker will pursue his grudge against Batman as the hero's principal antagonist in the film—with the added twist that we ultimately discover in this case that a young Napier was the mugger who killed Bruce Wayne's parents.

Nicholson, of course, is the film's biggest star—at the time, he was perhaps still *Hollywood*'s biggest star, even if slightly past his peak. Little wonder, then, that he actually gets top billing in those opening credits, his name displayed right before Keaton's. And there is a reason why Burton felt it advisable to cast such a huge star in the Joker role, because Joker is in a very real sense the highlight of the film, Nicholson's campily evil cackling hijinks adding energy to a film that might otherwise have been rendered flat by Batman's taciturn demeanor and a lackluster story line (Burton being a filmmaker always more interested in creating interesting visual images than in telling compelling stories).[8] Of course, Joker's crucial role in the film also makes it seem more comical, less serious, and more like what broad audiences of 1989 would have associated with comic books, despite the dark turn some Batman comics had recently taken, a dark turn that clearly influenced the film as well, especially in its visual style.

Burton's follow-up, *Batman Returns* (1992), has much the same tone and visual style as *Batman* but is much less successful as a film, mostly because Danny DeVito's Penguin is simply a less entertaining villain than

Nicholson's Joker had been. Nicholson's cartoonish Joker remains the most memorable movie supervillain of his era, although that character has very little in common with *Joker*'s Arthur Fleck. He's totally insane, he's deadly, he laughs a lot, and he even occasionally dances, but otherwise, this brilliant, articulate, wise-cracking criminal mastermind is far from the tortured soul that we see in Fleck, although he is highly reminiscent of the prancing trickster who became known as the Clown Prince of Crime in the comics.

After *Batman Returns*, the Batman franchise, now missing not only the Joker, but Burton and Keaton, descended into silliness and helped to virtually kill off the big-budget superhero film for the rest of the decade. It should be noted, though, that important Batman stories continued to be produced, particularly in the highly regarded *Batman: The Animated Series*, which ran for 85 episodes from 1992 to 1994 and which was highlighted by Mark Hamill's voice work as the Joker.[9] Indeed, one of the most striking and successful aspects of this series was its figuration of the Joker, who is the most important villain in the series.[10] Among other things, the representation of the Joker in this series emphasizes his multiplicity and the fact that he has had a number of different purported origins over the years, something that seems to have been an intentional strategy on the part of the Joker. Indeed, one of the most telling aspects of the Joker is that accounts of his background have varied widely over the years, in keeping with this chameleonic nature. He has also perhaps had more nicknames and more alter egos than any other comics villain. As the Joker himself puts it in *The Killing Joke* (where he continually thwarts Batman's attempts to gain knowledge about him and understand who he is), "If I'm going to have a past, I prefer it to be multiple choice" (*Batman: The Killing Joke, The Deluxe Edition* 40).

Of course, the 1989 *Batman* has a special status as a forerunner to *Joker*, simply because it is a film of the 1980s (and thus a film from roughly the same time period as the events depicted in *Joker*). Indeed, despite its cartoonish (and even comical) elements, *Batman*, especially in its portrayal of Gotham City itself, has a decidedly dark visual style that was clearly influenced by the dark developments in Batman comics in the course of the 1980s. Batman, of course, had always had a darker edge than that of his counterpart, the squeaky-clean, all-American (although extraterrestrial) Superman. Indeed, the contrast between America's two most historically prominent superheroes could not be more clear than in the contrast between the bright and shiny visual style of Richard Donner's *Superman* (1978) and the dark, almost Expressionist visuals of Burton's Batman films.

One of the reasons for this contrast was the difference between the characters Superman and Batman, a difference with a long legacy, culminating in their battle in *The Dark Knight Returns*. The contrasts between these two heroes, of course, are centrally related to the fact that Batman has no superhuman powers and, from the beginning, unlike Superman, was endowed with human limitations and flaws, opening the way for more realistic stories. One could also argue that the confrontation between Batman and Superman in *The Dark Knight Returns* can be taken as an indication of the contrasts and contradictions that marked the whole decade of the 1980s, which perhaps helps to explain the fact that the years of the Reagan presidency have recently become the focus of much cultural and political nostalgia, even though these same years were, at the time, informed by a great deal of cynicism, selfishness, and greed. Despite the prominence today of memories of the pop culture of the 1980s as bright, bouncy, and innocent, this dark side of the 1980s was reflected in a number of films of the era, with Oliver Stone's *Wall Street* (1987) serving as a sort of summary cinematic exploration of certain tendencies of the Reagan era, and with Gordon Gekko's unironic "greed is good" declaring a crucial element of the ethos of the era.

Batman films would make a rousing comeback with Christopher Nolan's *Batman Begins* (2005), now with Christian Bale in the title role. As the title indicates, this film is a Batman origin story. By tracing the development of billionaire Bruce Wayne into the Caped Crusader, this film endows the character with a bit more humanity, although Bale's whisper-voiced Batman is still a rather grim figure. Perhaps it is not surprising, then, that the most memorable of Nolan's Batman films was the second one, *The Dark Knight* (2008), largely because it is once again enlivened by the presence of the Joker as the antagonist to Batman. In a now-legendary Oscar-winning performance (made more so by the actor's death while the film was still being edited), Heath Ledger portrays a Joker who is much darker and more serious than Nicholson's Joker, much more dangerously deranged. An anarchist misanthrope who robs and kills largely for the sadistic pleasure of creating suffering and chaos, Ledger's over-the-top Joker also has the ability to bring out both the best and the worst in Batman. Indeed, this version of the Joker character is notable, not just for Ledger's unhinged performance, but also for the way in which it makes clear the real reason why the Joker is the greatest of Batman's antagonists: because he is a sort of dark alter ego of Batman himself.

The depiction of the Joker in *The Dark Knight* was clearly influenced by *The Killing Joke*. Indeed, Ledger was quoted in interviews as saying that he was asked to read that comic when preparing for his role as the Joker

(Collura). Ledger, of course, certainly put his own stamp on the character with his bravura performance, although certain elements do seem to have been derived fairly directly from the comic. For my purposes, perhaps the most important of these is the Joker's declaration in *The Killing Joke* of his preference for a multiple-choice past, which is enacted in *The Dark Knight* via a running gag in which Ledger's Joker repeatedly reveals the source of the scars that give him the permanent grin that was so central to his transformation into the Joker.

Of course, the changing narrative provided by Ledger's Joker can also be taken as a reference to the fact that the Joker character has had so many different origin stories in the comics over the years—as can the "multiple-choice" declaration in *The Killing Joke*. It could also simply be a sign of another tradition derived from years of comics: that any information gleaned directly from the Joker tends to be spectacularly unreliable, a tradition that is also reflected in *Joker*, which makes clear that much of the action we see on the screen cannot be trusted to be "real" simply because it is filtered through the consciousness of an Arthur Fleck whose grip on reality is so tenuous.

Given all of this background, making a movie whose central point is to provide an origin story for the Joker—*and one that does not include Batman as a factor*—would seem a rather perilous enterprise. In fact, there have been numerous reports that even the executives at Warner Bros. were not optimistic that such a film could really be a success.[11] They were wrong, of course, and the film became one of the great success stories of 2019, grossing almost exactly the same amount worldwide as *Star Wars: The Rise of Skywalker*, a film released only a couple of months later (and with much higher commercial expectations). Meanwhile, although it would be difficult to quantify the exact source of the tremendous box-office appeal of *Joker*, it is surely the case that a great deal of its success had to do with the fact it was identified by audiences as a "superhero" film, even though it includes no superheroes whatsoever.

That the "brand recognition" of the Batman franchise was key to the success of *Joker* can perhaps be seen in the distribution of its box office, with over 69 percent of the receipts ($739 million) coming from outside the United States and Canada (where it combined for $335 million). By comparison, the top-grossing film of 2019 (and of all time) was the Marvel Cinematic Universe (MCU) film *Avengers: Endgame*, which took in a colossal $859 million in the United States and Canada and over $1.9 *billion* in the rest of the world. Interestingly, then, *Avengers: Endgame* also took in roughly 69 percent of its total receipts outside the United States and Canada. Of the other *Avengers* films (all grossing more than

1 billion dollars), *Avengers: Age of Ultron* (2015) and *Avengers: Infinity War* (2018) each took in 67 percent of their receipts overseas, while *The Avengers* (2012) took in 59 percent of its receipts overseas. In comparison, the MCU films *Spider-Man: Far from Home* and *Captain Marvel*, both of which were also billion-dollar-plus megahits in 2019, respectively took in 66 percent and 62 percent of their receipts from outside the United States and Canada. *Iron Man* (2008), the first MCU film, took in only 45 percent of its total gross overseas, suggesting a time-dependent effect, with the percentage of gross receipts taken in by MCU films from outside the United States and Canada having grown slowly from 2008 to 2015, then leveling off at around two-thirds of the total coming from overseas.

Similar trends can be observed in other superhero films. For example, *The Dark Knight* (2008), perhaps the superhero film that is most directly related to *Joker*, took in only about 47 percent of its gross overseas, roughly the same as *Iron Man* in the same year. Of the top ten grossing superhero films of all time, eight (including the top five) were recent MCU films, while another, the animated film *Incredibles 2* (2018), was released by Pixar and thus also had the Disney marketing machine at its back, although it took in only some 51 percent of its gross overseas, partly because it grossed almost twice as much in the United States as did *Joker*. The only film in the top ten based on a character from DC comics was *Aquaman* (2018), which took in slightly more overall than *Joker*, with 71 percent coming from outside the United States and Canada. Of other superhero films inspired by DC Comics characters (but falling just outside the top ten), *Batman v. Superman* (2016) took in 62 percent of its $873 million worldwide gross from outside the United States and Canada. Meanwhile, *Wonder Woman* (2017), which took in roughly 50 percent of its $822 million worldwide gross from outside the United States and Canada, would appear to be something of an outlier.

One should be careful not to attempt to draw too many conclusions from all of these numbers. For one thing, there are multiple factors that influence the box-office success of any given film. For another thing, I am not necessarily comparing apples to apples in all of these cases. *Incredibles 2*, for example, obviously appeals to a different demographic than the other top-grossing superhero films, while the enormous success of *Avengers: Endgame* was partly fueled by an impressive take of over $600 million in China, while *Joker* was not approved for release in China at all, due to its excessive violence. The *Avengers* films are, of course, far more violent than *Joker*, with vastly higher body counts—in *Infinity War*, half of the life in the universe is wiped out, for example. But the violence is those films is much more like *comic book* violence, with little graphic

27

bloodshed, as opposed to *Joker*, in which the violence shown on the screen is much more graphic and realistic (even if much—or even all—of it might be occurring only in Fleck's fantasies).

Still, despite all the differences in style and tone between *Joker* and more conventional superhero films, the box office statistics I have cited here tend to support the notion that the huge commercial success of *Joker* can be largely attributed to the fact that fans of superhero films largely treated *Joker* as such a film and attended it accordingly. Even Slavoj Žižek, after congratulating Hollywood for making such a film and lauding audiences for attending it, notes that "the reason for the film's popularity" is the perception of its connection to the Batman universe ("More on *Joker*"). Of course, this perception is not surprising, given that so much of the considerable hype surrounding the release of the film characterized it precisely as a film whose title character is, in fact, Batman's arch-enemy. Granted, the official trailers for the film did not particularly emphasize this aspect of the film, but they didn't dispute it, either, ending with acknowledgements to DC Comics, either via a simple display of the logo or via the even more overt notation "BASED ON CHARACTERS FROM DC."

One could argue, of course, that *Joker*'s title character could be "based on" the Joker from the Batman franchise without actually *being* that character. Indeed, it seems clear that Warner Bros. never intended this film to be part of the continuity that constitutes the "DC Extended Universe" (DCEU), their version of the MCU. Indeed, if anything, *Joker* exists in a sort of DC *Alternate* Universe, alternate universes, in fact, being a well-established feature of the Batman franchise and of superhero comics in general.[12] Thus, among the many rumors about possible *Joker* sequels, one of the most intriguing is that a sequel might include the origins of Batman, but that this Batman would actually be a *different* Batman than the one in DC mainstream continuity, thus confirming the notion that the title character of *Joker* is a different character than the one who has been featured for so long in the Batman franchise. Meanwhile, the very fact that multiple sequels have apparently been discussed suggests that DC regards the series of films surrounding the Arthur Fleck Joker to exist in an alternate timeline of its own.

Looking at *Joker* in the context of previous texts in the Batman franchise, it seems clear that we are intended to view the film in that context in order to add another dimension to the narrative. It is certainly the case that the story of Arthur Fleck could potentially be a compelling realistic drama on its own, set in New York City and with no comic-book connections. At the same time, it also seems unlikely that the film would have had anywhere near the same commercial appeal under those conditions.[13] One might compare, for example, the dark thriller *You Were Never Really Here* (2017), which also features a compelling performance by Joaquin Phoenix as a troubled and violent protagonist. That film has much the same texture that *Joker* might have had without the Batman connections, including the fact that multiple critics saw the film as a sort of "update" of *Taxi Driver*.[14] Yet, despite widespread critical acclaim (it received much more consistently positive reviews than did *Joker*), this film (directed by noted Scottish filmmaker Lynne Ramsey) took in a total of less than $10 million in worldwide box-office receipts, or less than 1 percent of the gross of *Joker*. Much of that difference no doubt has to do with marketing, but surely a great deal of it has to do with the extra box-office appeal added to *Joker* by the fact that moviegoers viewed it in light of its connections with the Batman franchise.

Given the history of the Batman franchise in general and the Joker character in particular, it is not particularly surprising that a strikingly new version of the Joker might appear, especially in a film that is clearly intended to reside outside the mainstream continuity of the DCEU. Whether Fleck would ultimately evolve into the very Joker who is so familiar to fans of the Batman franchise is not a question that can be answered from the contents of *Joker*, partly because there is no *one* Joker in the franchise. Of course, it is never really possible to project events in fictional texts beyond the bounds of those texts, other than by sheer conjecture. To see what "happens" next in the fictional world of *Joker*, we can only wait for the anticipated sequels. But, as I will discuss in the next chapter, *Joker* is a declaredly postmodern work that continually defeats definitive interpretation even *within* the bounds of the text, which makes any attempt to extrapolate *beyond* the text particularly fruitless. It is best, I think, simply to note that *Joker* establishes a productive dialogue with the Batman franchise and that this dialogue potentially enriches the meanings that are generated by the film.

Notes

1   This comment, of course, takes on extra meaning because of the way in which Wayne's son Bruce will presumably grow up to become Batman, a hero who also hides his identity with a mask.

2   For a concise history of the Joker in Batman comics, see the four entries on the character by Charles Coletta and by Jackson Ayres in the encyclopedia *Comics through Time*, to which my account is greatly indebted.

3 Interestingly, the Batman comics of 2020, in the wake of the success of *Joker*, placed a special emphasis on the Joker character, via the "Joker War" storyline. Here, Joker mounts a particularly serious assault on Gotham City and on Bruce Wayne, whose fortune is stolen via a Joker-conceived plot. (Catwoman steals it back, although it is not restored directly to Wayne).
4 See, for example, the collection of scholarly essays edited by Peaslee and Weiner.
5 These concerns were expressed most famously in the work of psychiatrist Fredric Wertham, especially in his 1954 book *Seduction of the Innocent*. See Hajdu for a discussion of this entire affair.
6 I might also note that, in Season 3 of the television series *Gotham*, Oswald Cobblepot (aka Penguin) wages a campaign to become mayor of Gotham City, employing the Trumpian slogan "Make Gotham Safe Again."
7 A film adaptation of the 1960s *Batman* television series had appeared in 1966, but it was a relatively minor work that made little contribution to the overall Batman franchise. Indeed, it was largely conceived as a promotion for the TV show. It features the Joker, the Penguin, and the Riddler (the three most important villains in the TV series) as the foes of Batman and Robin, all played by the same actors as in the series.
8 In a contemporary review of the film, Roger Ebert suggested that Nicholson's Joker is "the most important character in the film," noting that it is difficult to root for the "monosyllabic and impenetrable" Batman in his battles with the Joker.
9 This series was supplemented by an animated theatrical film entitled *Batman: Mask of the Phantasm* (1993), also featuring Hamill as the voice of the Joker.
10 This series is an important part of the Batman franchise and made important contributions to its mythos. For example, the episode "Joker's Favor," first broadcast on September 11, 1992, introduced the character of Harley Quinn as Batman's love interest. Quinn would go on to become an important DC character, appearing in a variety of places, including two feature films (so far) in which she is a major character: *Suicide Squad* (2016) and *Birds of Prey* (2020).
11 See, for example, Augustine.
12 Various stories in DC Comics, over the years, have attempted to explain certain discrepancies in the continuities of their narratives by positing that different stories take place in different parallel worlds of the "DC Multiverse."
13 One might compare here the television series *Pennyworth*, which premiered in late July of 2019 on the Epix cable network, just a month before the premiere of *Joker* at the Venice Film Festival. A sort of spy story that attempts to add interest through links to the Batman franchise, *Pennyworth* is essentially the origin story of the Wayne butler Alfred Pennyworth; this series follows a young Pennyworth as he becomes involved in an international intrigue that combines elements of the spy drama, the political thriller, and

the alternate history science fiction drama. It also features a young Thomas Wayne as an American agent battling against dark fascist forces. In this case, though, at least one critic, Sam Barsanti, complained that the series would actually be more effective without the distracting Batman connections.

14 In another interesting connection between *You Were Never Really Here* and *Joker*, the former film features Dante Pereira-Olson as a young version of Phoenix's character, who appears in flashback scenes that establish that the character had been abused by his father in childhood. The same actor plays the boy Bruce Wayne in *Joker*.

CHAPTER TWO

The Cultural Logic of Early Neoliberalism
Joker as Postmodern Art

Joker begins as Arthur Fleck puts on clown makeup while a radio news report (about the growing crisis in the city as a result of an ongoing garbage strike) sounds in the background. The film then suddenly cuts to a busy city street where Fleck, now in full clown garb, is working on the sidewalk as a sign twirler outside Kenny's Music Shop, advertising the fact that the shop is going out of business, bearing the ominous warning "Everything Must Go." Though Fleck smiles and dances as he twirls the sign, he is performing near a large pile of garbage bags that have collected on the sidewalk, while the very fact that he is announcing the demise of a local business serves as a clear sign that the city might be in a state of decline. It's a sort of snapshot allegory of neoliberalism, as garbage collects around the edges of spectacle and performance. We also see, a couple of doors down from the music shop, the marquee of a porn theater (showing a film called *Strip Search*, which does not seem to correspond to any real-world films), suggesting that the city might be in a state of moral, as well as physical, collapse.

Suddenly, some street kids (of color) come down the sidewalk, grab Fleck's sign and make off with it, with Fleck in hot pursuit. He chases them through the streets, past several piles of garbage bags, and into an alleyway, where they attack him, beat him senseless, and leave him lying on the ground in physical and spiritual agony, beside the now-broken sign. To this point, the film seems grittily realistic, a study in pathos. The city seems the quintessence of embattled urban decay, while Fleck seems the very embodiment of the sad clown. He is an object of pity, hardly a formidable figure. Yet, as I noted in the previous chapter, almost everything the film's theatrical audiences would have heard about it has led them to assume that Fleck, the Joker of the title, is also the Joker who has long been known in American popular culture as the most important of the various supervillains who serve as antagonists to the DC Comics superhero Batman, a figure eclipsed in importance as a comic book superhero only by Superman. And, of course, the audiences would also likely know that the city in which this opening action occurs is Gotham City, home of Batman, even as the ambience of the opening street scene is clearly that of the Times Square area of New York City in the late 1970s and early 1980s, including the fact that New York experienced multiple garbage strikes during this period.

This opening juxtaposition of graphic realism with graphic novels is an indication of the texture of this entire film, in which the line between fiction and reality is consistently blurred. This blurring, meanwhile, is only one aspect of *Joker* that identifies it as a work of postmodern art, one informed by continual interpretive uncertainties. The obvious framework within which to read the film is the one provided by the long legacy of Batman comics, films, and even one notable campy television series, as I discussed in the previous chapter. In that sense, *Joker* can be regarded as one two-hour-long postmodern simulacrum, in the Baudrillardian sense of a copy of which there is no existing original in reality, a film that is a representation, not of material from reality, but of pre-existing fictional material, material that is itself not particularly rooted in realism. At the same time, the visual and thematic texture of the film's opening minutes suggests a film that is firmly rooted in urban reality.

Granted, audiences familiar with the Batman franchise would have already been quite accustomed to dark, dystopian visions of Gotham City on screen, beginning with Tim Burton's original *Batman* from 1989. And they would have also likely known that Gotham City, from the very beginnings of the franchise, has been fairly transparently based on New York City, as has Superman's Metropolis, New York being very much the center of the early comics industry. But neither Burton's two Batman films nor Christopher Nolan's later "Dark Knight" trilogy, both of which show us a dark Gotham City, could have prepared audiences for the level of detailed realism with which *Joker* represents Gotham as a city in the grip of urban decay. Nor could they have prepared us for the extent to which *Joker* roots its action in the material and political realities of the time period in which this action is set.

That time period is specifically late 1981, although the film draws upon historical realities from several years on either side of that time— and, to an extent, even from 1969 to 1992, as I will explain later in this volume. This rootedness in historical reality does not, however, diminish the postmodern quality of the film. In fact, it makes the film *more* postmodern by creating continual interpretive hesitation about just what sort of film we are watching. Just when we think we are watching a superhero film, we are reminded that this film features no superheroes and no over-the-top superhero action. Just when we think we are watching a gritty urban crime drama, we are reminded that everything in this film is mediated, not only by the entire legacy of the Batman franchise, but also by an entire panoply of other films and film genres, with television making key contributions to the texture of the film as well. In the remainder of this chapter, I will outline my own understanding of what it means for a film to be postmodern, as well as indicating the ways in which *Joker* exemplifies this understanding.

Postmodernism as the Cultural Logic of Late Capitalism

In characterizing *Joker* as a postmodern film, I draw primarily upon the seminal theorization of postmodernism put forth by Fredric Jameson in his study *Postmodernism, or, The Cultural Logic of Late Capitalism* (1991). Jameson's work is particularly relevant here, partly because it remains the most authoritative theoretical account of the fundamental nature of postmodernism, even more than 30 years later. But Jameson's work is also especially valuable as a window through which to view *Joker* because his theorization of postmodernism was developed through the 1980s and is thus firmly based in the time period during which *Joker* is set. That Jameson's work was still so current when *Joker* was released in 2019 speaks to the basic accuracy of his insights into postmodernism as a product of late capitalism. But there are also changes in capitalism that have occurred between 1991 and 2019 that are important to take into account when applying Jameson's vision of postmodernism to *Joker*.

The most important of these is that, in the 30 years since Jameson was formulating his original theorization of postmodernism, it has become obvious that the phenomenon of neoliberalism is central to late capitalism. However, in his postmodernism book, Jameson barely mentions neoliberalism, even then treating it as a sort of extreme and marginal form of free market capitalism that he relates primarily to the work of right-wing economist Milton Friedman. After all, in its current form, neoliberalism arose primarily in the 1980s and was thus very new when Jameson was developing his theory of postmodernism. Since that time, the notion of neoliberalism has become much more mainstream in academic characterizations of late capitalism, as scholars have come better to recognize how central unfettered free market capitalism is to late capitalism in its current form. I will keep this development in mind in my discussion of

Joker and postmodernism, although it will become particularly relevant in the second half of this study, when I place *Joker* within the context of political history from the 1960s to the 2020s.

I will keep in mind all along, though, the work of Mark Fisher, whose *Capitalist Realism* (2009) is largely an update of Jameson's work. What Fisher calls "capitalist realism" is essentially the same thing as Jameson calls "postmodernism," with 20 more years of history behind it, years that have only extended what Jameson saw as the weak utopian imagination of postmodern culture. In particular, Fisher emphasizes the growing popular conviction in the years after Jameson's work that there is no alternative to free market capitalism, partly because of the collapse of the Soviet Union, which occurred just after the writing of Jameson's postmodernism book. This collapse contributed greatly to the increased prominence of neoliberalism, a phenomenon that itself has added to a growing sense of hopelessness that is perhaps reflected in the situation of Arthur Fleck, showing him to be a character of 2019 as much as of 1981. Indeed, drawing on the work of Oliver James, Fisher suggests that rising rates of "mental distress" are related to the growing power of neoliberalism, which again seems quite relevant to Fleck's predicament. As Fisher puts it, this trend shows that "instead of being the only social system that works, capitalism is inherently dysfunctional, and that the cost of it appearing to work is very high" (24). *Joker*, one might say, is a film made in Fisher's capitalist realist world that is set in Jameson's postmodern world.

Jameson's theorization of postmodernism includes two principal components. First, and most important, Jameson outlines the historical conditions under which postmodernism arises, concluding that postmodernism is specifically the cultural form that directly reflects the ideology of late capitalism. In this historical phase, capitalist modernization is essentially global and essentially complete, with cultural products (such as films) becoming just as thoroughly commodified as everything else. Second, Jameson details the ways in which the status of postmodernism as the "cultural logic of late capitalism" is reflected in the characteristics of specific individual works of postmodern art.

In arguing that the history of world culture has entered an important new historical phase that he labels as "postmodernism," Jameson declares, "What has happened is that aesthetic production today has become integrated into commodity production generally: the frantic economic urgency of producing fresh waves of ever more novel-seeming goods (from clothing to airplanes), at ever greater rates of turnover, now assigns an increasingly essential structural function and position to aesthetic innovation and experimentation" (4–5). That *Joker*, however innovative and impressive it might be as a work of cinematic art, is a commodity—that it was produced first and foremost for marketing to a general public in order to create profit for its corporate backers—seems beyond dispute. Such is the case for Hollywood films in general, of course, but the status of *Joker* as a thoroughly commodified product of a highly commercialized culture industry seems especially clear. Though the film's official production budget of roughly $60 million was far less than the typical superhero movie from the Marvel or DC universes, it was a substantial investment, nevertheless. And the film was well promoted and widely distributed around the world, backed by the full might of the Warner Bros. studio, a subsidiary (like DC Comics) of the multinational media conglomerate Warner Media, itself a subsidiary of the massive AT&T, a megacorporation with a market capitalization of over $200 billion. The result, of course, was a major commercial success that saw the film bring in more than $1 billion in worldwide box-office receipts, over two-thirds of which came from outside the United States and Canada.

Given that Warner's much-touted *Justice League* (2017), with a budget of $300 million, had brought in only $658 million, *Joker* was a major commercial success—and a somewhat surprising one. The film was dogged by pre-release controversy, centering on fears that its ultra-violence and its seemingly sympathetic portrayal of a character who is essentially a serial killer might deliver a dangerous message. Yet this controversy seemed to attract audiences to the film, rather than keeping them away. Meanwhile, the R-rating given the film would typically be expected to limit commercial potential, but *Joker* blew past expectations to become easily the top-grossing R-rated film of all time in terms of worldwide box-office receipts. Moreover, while superhero films have recently become the most commercially successful phenomenon in film history, *Joker* is now the most commercially successful big-budget superhero film of all time in terms of the crucial measure of the ratio of box-office receipts to production cost (Mendelson).

Jameson also argues that the sometimes extreme nature of postmodern works of art can be at least partly attributed to a revolt against the conscription and institutionalization of a once-shocking and scandalous modernism as the official high culture of modern capitalism. This attempt to overcome the canonization of modernization, however, is for Jameson entirely unsuccessful:

> As for the postmodern revolt against all that, however, it must equally be stressed that its own offensive features—from obscurity and sexually explicit material to psychological squalor and overt

expressions of social and political defiance, which transcend anything that might have been imagined at the most extreme moments of high modernism—no longer scandalize anyone and are not only received with the greatest complacency but have themselves become institutionalized and are at one with the official or public culture of Western society. (*Postmodernism* 4)

The remarkable mainstream success of *Joker*—box-office champ and winner of 11 Academy Award nominations, despite the seemingly shocking and often tawdry material that it contains—would seem to be the perfect illustration of what Jameson is talking about here. The film certainly contains a great deal of "psychological squalor," while its overt representation of political revolt is surely anything but threatening to the capitalist order. The movie, of course, provoked considerable controversy and critical disagreement. Thus, writing in the *New Yorker*, Richard Brody calls the film "a viewing experience of rare, numbing emptiness," complaining that it was informed by "a cynicism so vast and pervasive as to render the viewing experience even emptier than its slapdash aesthetic does." Reviewing the film for *Time* magazine, Stephanie Zacharek declares that "the movie lionizes and glamorizes Arthur even as it shakes its head, faux-sorrowfully, over his violent behavior." Ultimately, she decides that "*Joker* made me realize that my tolerance for shoddily thought-out visions of glamorized nihilism is lower than ever. Sometimes a movie makes you recoil—and no matter how many awards it wins, your instincts are the only golden thing that matters." And, finally, Bill Newcott of the *Saturday Evening Post* called *Joker* "a hollow Fabergé egg of a film, crafted with over-the-top artistry on the outside, empty of meaningful context beneath its brittle shell. […] It all reminds me of a Goth teenager: He dresses in black, circles his eyes with mascara and mopes around in his room, all the time with no idea what he's so depressed about."

Such high-profile critical denunciations obviously did little to curb the box-office appeal of the film or to prevent its numerous awards, beginning with its premiere at the Venice Film Festival, where it took home the Golden Lion, the festival's top honor. *Joker* then went on to garner all those Oscar nominations (more than any other film of 2019), although the negative criticisms might have contributed to the fact that the film won the Oscar only for Hildur Guðnadóttir's powerfully effective score and for Joaquin Phoenix's spectacular performance in the title role. Of course, so thorough was the critical rejection of *Joker* in some quarters, that even that performance had its detractors, as when Matthew Lickona suggested that Phoenix's attempts at "creepily contorting" shouldn't even be considered acting. All in all, though, no matter how many critics (or viewers) expressed dismay at *Joker*'s ultra-violence and failure to condemn that violence, it is clear that the film was widely accepted as a work that fits quite comfortably within the global culture of late capitalism.

The way in which the urban setting of *Joker* is presented is also crucial to the postmodernity of the film, and in at least two senses. For one thing, the film exists within an almost totally manmade world, with all vestiges of nature having been erased. Even when we do see swathes of green, as in the luscious grounds of Wayne Manor, the greenery is immaculately sculpted and carefully controlled. As Daraiseh and Booker note, "these grounds contain a highly controlled, highly *owned* version of nature. In this world, art and culture—and even nature—have joined everything else in the march toward total commodification."[1] As Daraiseh and Booker also note, this description corresponds quite well to Jameson's vision of the world in which postmodernism arises as one in which the process of capitalist modernization is essentially complete. Jameson thus characterizes the postmodern world (in contrast to the modern one) as one where

> Everything is now organized and planned; nature has been triumphantly blotted out, along with peasants, petit-bourgeois commerce, handicraft, feudal aristocracies and imperial bureaucracies. Ours is a more homogeneously modernized condition; we no longer are encumbered with the embarrassment of non-simultaneities and non-synchronicities. Everything has reached the same hour on the great clock of development or rationalization (at least from the perspective of the "West"). This is the sense in which we can affirm, either that modernism is characterized by a situation of incomplete modernization, or that postmodernism is more modern than modernism itself. (*Postmodernism* 309–310)

Gotham City in this sense is, not surprisingly, reminiscent of a number of other cinematic cities. The most obvious of such cities are the Gothams of Burton or Nolan, but another that quickly comes to mind is the darkly dystopian Los Angeles of *Blade Runner* (1982), a film that (oddly enough) is set in 2019 (the year of *Joker*'s release) but was released in 1982 (close to the date of the action of *Joker*). The Los Angeles of *Blade Runner* is not a gleaming metropolis of the kind that might have been imagined in earlier science fiction. Instead, it is every bit as dirty, crowded, and decaying as the Gotham City of *Joker*. And the world of *Blade Runner* is one in which nature has been so thoroughly effaced that even animals have been replaced by manmade replicas—echoing the apocalyptic hints that humans themselves might be on the verge of being supplanted by the manmade "replicants" that are so central to the film.

The Los Angeles of *Blade Runner* also resembles *Joker*'s Gotham in another way that recalls Jameson's characterization of postmodernism. As I have pointed out elsewhere, the geography of *Blade Runner*'s Los Angeles is extremely confusing and disorienting, making it impossible to map the city and to tell where any part of it might be located in relation to any other part. As I further note,

> This inability to map one's position within the overall system of the city is a perfect example of what the prominent cultural critic Fredric Jameson has identified as the typical disorientation of the individual subject within postmodern society. Indeed, drawing upon the work of urban theorist Kevin Lynch, Jameson specifically compares the difficulty of getting one's cognitive bearings within the world system of late capitalism to the difficulty of finding one's way about in the postmodern city—or within individual postmodern buildings, for that matter. (*Alternate Americas* 181–182)

Very much the same thing might be said about the Gotham City of *Joker*. Indeed, even those who try to map the city by simply assuming that its geography should roughly match that of New York City will find themselves thwarted. None of New York's well-known landmarks—such as the Statue of Liberty or the Empire State Building—can be seen in the film. Moreover, while many of the film's scenes were shot on location at real sites, those sites are often not located in New York. The now-famous steps on which Arthur Fleck does his iconic manic dance to the music of Gary Glitter are indeed located in the Bronx at West 167th Street, connecting Shakespeare Avenue and Anderson Avenue; on release of the film, they immediately became a favorite site for tourists, influencers, and locals to take photos, although traffic to the site would soon be curbed due to the Coronavirus pandemic. But the film's initial street scene, so reminiscent of the Times Square Area, was actually filmed in Newark, New Jersey, while the exterior of Wayne Hall, which features in a key scene, was shot at the Hudson County Courthouse in Jersey City, New Jersey. Shooting in such locations was no doubt partly influenced by a desire to find sites that still had a 1981 "feel," but it is also facilitated by the fragmented sense of the city that is presented in the film, which has no interest in providing a coherently mapped geography.

This kind of failure of mapping is, for Jameson, a natural effect of the global system of late capitalism, which is so vast and complex that individuals find it almost impossible to understand how the system works or what their place in it might be. This impossibility of effective cognitive mapping is, for Jameson, one of the reasons why postmodern individuals find it so difficult even to maintain a stable sense of self. Thus, for Jameson, the notion of alienation, so crucial to the modernist project, is no longer sufficient to encompass the severity of the individual's loss of a coherent sense of how they connect to the world around them. Jameson suggests instead the notion of "psychic fragmentation" as a better description of the individual's scattered sense of self and world (90). *Joker*'s Arthur Fleck again epitomizes this situation: while it might be tempting to describe him as radically alienated, it seems accurate to say that his "alienation" is *so* radical that it really constitutes something else altogether.

At several points throughout his postmodernism book, Jameson compares postmodern psychic fragmentation to the experience of someone suffering from schizophrenia, although it is in an earlier formulation that he makes this connection most overt. Drawing upon the work of Jacques Lacan, Jameson argues that, amid the increasing complexity and fragmentation of experience in the postmodern world, the individual subject experiences a loss of temporal continuity that causes him or her to experience the world somewhat in the manner of a schizophrenic patient. "The schizophrenic," Jameson says,

> is condemned to live a perpetual present with which the various moments of his or her past have little connection and for which there is no conceivable future on the horizon. In other words, schizophrenic experience is an experience of isolated, disconnected, discontinuous material signifiers which fail to link up into a coherent sequence. The schizophrenic does not know personal identity in our sense, since our feeling of identity depends on our sense of the persistence of the "I" and the "me" over time. ("Postmodernism and Consumer Society" 119)

Jameson, of course, is here speaking metaphorically and clearly does not intend to suggest that living in the harried and confusing world of late capitalism makes everyone medically schizophrenic. But his formulation does suggest that characters with certain psychological disorders might also function metaphorically as effective representations of the fragmented nature of life under late capitalism. Meanwhile, although the exact nature of Fleck's personal disorder in *Joker* is never made entirely clear, it is clearly the case that he suffers from a considerable degree of failure in cognitive mapping and that he has a very uncertain purchase on reality. He thus represents an extreme version of the kind of confusion that informs the relationship of the typical postmodern subject with the surrounding world.

Granted, *Joker* suggests (without providing a clear diagnosis) that Fleck is literally mentally ill, so that there is nothing in his condition that necessary deviates from realism. However, there is ample precedent for the use of characters with certain mental conditions to stand in for the kind of psychic fragmentation associated by Jameson with the postmodern. For example, I have noted elsewhere some of the ways in which the title character of Woody Allen's *Zelig* (1983) functions in this way (*Postmodern Hollywood* 34–35). An even better example (and one more relevant to *Joker*) is Christopher Nolan's *Memento* (2000), another violent crime drama built on the fragmented psychological condition of its protagonist. Here, Leonard Shelby (Guy Pearce) has suffered a brain injury that renders him unable to retain new memories for more than a few minutes. Thus, Shelby lacks any real sense of the connectedness of one moment to another, thus literalizing the fragmented and schizophrenic experience of time that Jameson associates with postmodernism. Meanwhile, the editing of *Memento* mimics Shelby's disjointed movement through time, leading to considerable interpretive confusion as audiences try, along with Shelby, to piece together the events of the film as they are presented to them. Among other things, the plot of *Memento* proceeds essentially in reverse chronological order. Thus, the events of this film are filtered through Shelby's distorted experience of reality, very much in the disorienting way that the events of *Joker* are filtered through the mind of Fleck.

Fleck's condition is crucial to the status of *Joker* as a postmodern film in that he serves as the film's only important point-of-view character, so we see essentially all of the film as a representation of his own experience. Because Fleck seems to have difficulty in separating his own fantasies from reality, viewers of the film can never quite trust that the events we see on the screen are actually happening within the world of the film. Indeed, although he does not literally narrate the film, Fleck does serve as a sort of filmic version of the unreliable narrator, made unreliable because he himself cannot trust his own perceptions. As a result, when discussing events that are shown on screen during this film, one must continually qualify any remarks by noting the possibility that the events being described might well be taking place only in Fleck's head.

As *Joker* begins, we have no awareness of this difficult interpretive situation. Through the first several scenes there is no reason to believe that what we see on screen is any less reliable than what we see in any other fictional film. The cut between the first scene of Fleck in front of a mirror and the second scene of Fleck on the street twirling his sign is certainly abrupt, but there is nothing in the cut to make us suspect that the whole street scene might be going on in Fleck's head. At the end of this scene, as Fleck lies in that alleyway, the film's title is superimposed in garish yellow, filling the screen, followed by another abrupt cut to a close-up of Fleck's pained face as he laughs mirthlessly (possibly due to a specific psychological disorder, although the film later calls that into question). This laughing (indistinguishable from crying, really) occurs in the shabby, cluttered office of a black woman identified by her name badge as a "Health Department Social Worker" (played by Sharon Washington).[2] Fleck then speaks his first words of real dialogue in the film: "Is it just me, or is it getting crazier out there?"

This question is one that many of us asked ourselves during the Trump years, so (among other things) it is the first indication of the film's remarkable ability to resonate with both the 1981 setting of its action and the 2019 time of its release, although it perhaps became even more familiar in 2020 and 2021, especially when the social worker essentially nods her agreement: "It's certainly tense. People are upset. They're struggling, looking for work. These are tough times."

The reference here would appear to be to the fact that, according to the U.S. Bureau of Labor Statistics, the U.S. unemployment rate at the end of 1981 (the first year of the Reagan administration) was at 8.5 percent, the highest since the American entry into World War II finally ended the Great Depression at the end of 1941. In any case, we learn from this scene that Fleck is now required to report to this social worker for counseling sessions and that he was earlier "locked up." A quick insert, presumably a flashback, briefly shows Fleck beating his head against the door of an "observation room," dressed in a manner that suggests he is an in-patient at a mental hospital. Back in the present, Fleck then asks for an increase in his medication, at which the social worker points out that he is on seven different medications already. We still have to do a bit of piecing together, but by this time it is fairly clear that Fleck is meant to be understood to be a mental patient, formerly incarcerated as an in-patient in a secure facility and now acting as a supervised out-patient. Again, though, we have yet to see anything to suggest that Fleck's mental condition particularly affects the reliability of what we see on the screen.

That Fleck perhaps suffers from multiple psychiatric conditions is further emphasized in a next scene, which cuts rapidly from the social worker's office to a city bus, on which Fleck has an encounter involving his laughing disorder. He then gets off the bus, fills his multiple prescriptions at a pharmacy, then trudges past more piled up garbage bags and up those now famous steps toward the apartment that he shares with his aging mother. Here we get our first idea of the squalid conditions under which the Flecks live. Then, as Arthur and Penny watch the television talk show *Live with Murray Franklin*, we get our first real idea of the power of Arthur's fantasies. As they watch the show, we suddenly see Fleck in the show's live audience, whereupon he is noticed by Franklin and called down to appear with him on stage. The film then cuts back to the Fleck apartment, where Arthur is actually still watching with his mother. There is no interpretive confusion here: he has obviously been in the apartment all along, simply fantasizing about joining Franklin, his comedy hero, on his show. But we have nevertheless been tipped off that what we see on the screen in the film might be the product of Fleck's fantasies, suggesting that he has a tendency to descend into fantasies so intense that they seem real to him.

This aspect of the film will be reinforced later, as the film clearly reveals that Fleck's budding romantic relationship with his neighbor Sophie, shown developing through much of the film, was all a fantasy on his part. Again, the fact that we have seen several episodes from his relationship with Sophie on the screen suggests that Fleck's fantasies about the young woman are so intense that they might seem real to him, just as they were initially presented as real to us. Then, about two-thirds of the way through the film, Fleck (apparently) lets himself into Sophie's apartment; when she sees him there, sitting on the couch, she is clearly terrified in a way that would seem inappropriate if they were indeed involved in a relationship. At this point, the film quickly replays all of the moments in which we have seen Fleck and Sophie together as a couple, showing these moments first with Sophie present and then again with her absent. The implication is clear: there has been no relationship, and all of the moments Fleck had shared with Sophie as an apparent couple were simply fantasies on his part. For me, this sequence suggests that Fleck had confused these fantasies with reality, although the film leaves open the possibility that he knew perfectly well that they were mere fantasies. However, Fleck's strong reaction to his encounter with Sophie in her apartment perhaps suggests that he only now realizes that he had merely imagined his relationship with her, which sends him spiraling into an even more severe psychological disturbance. Tellingly, it is only seconds later in the runtime of the film that we are shown the scene in which Fleck apparently murders his mother.

By now, however, once the sequence of moments shared with Sophie has been "erased," we have been alerted to not fully trust anything we see in this film, which means that it is almost impossible to come to any definitive interpretation of events we see on the screen. This kind of radical indeterminacy is, of course, often associated with postmodern narratives, which are typically designed to disrupt precisely the kind of logical and orderly decoding that realist narratives are designed to undermine. Allen Thiher, for example, has distinguished between modernism and postmodernism within the framework of modern philosophies of language. For Thiher, modernism sought the epiphanic revelation of an essential image; postmodernism calls into question the existence of any such essence. This fundamental dichotomy suggests a modernist view of language that is at heart still representational, while postmodernist language is thoroughly non-representational. Another way of putting this is that modernism still believes in a fundamental "truth," or "reality," even though this truth might lie beneath the easily observable surface and might be difficult to uncover without detailed and painstaking excavation. It can, however, eventually be revealed. For postmodernists, there is no ultimate stable truth, only interpretation, which means that no interpretation can be definitive. It is, of course, merely a step from this position of radical epistemological skepticism to one of total nihilism, something of which postmodernism has sometimes been accused—and which numerous commentators have attributed to the worldview of *Joker*. Indeed, Fleck himself, appearing on *Live with Murray Franklin*, openly declares that he doesn't believe in "anything," but of course we should be careful not to equate the point of view of the protagonist with the point of view of the film. In Fleck's case, it is not clear that we can even believe him when he says he doesn't believe in anything, given his clear belief that he has somehow been wronged by the world.

Joker, Pastiche, and Fragmentation

While Jameson's principal project in characterizing the phenomenon of postmodernism is to explore the relationship between postmodern culture and late capitalism, he also provides a number of descriptions of the characteristics that identify specific works as postmodern. Although he perhaps expresses the idea most clearly in the early essay "Postmodernism and Consumer Society," Jameson also makes clear in the postmodernism book his view that there are two principal formal characteristics of postmodern artworks: that they are typically constructed via techniques of pastiche and that they are typically highly fragmented in form.

By pastiche, Jameson means the tendency of postmodern artists to borrow liberally from both the style and content of earlier works, treating the entire cultural tradition as a sort of aesthetic cafeteria from whose menu they can nostalgically pick and choose without critical engagement with the works being borrowed from or concern for the historical context in which those styles originally arose. Referring to this practice as the "random cannibalization of all the styles of the past," Jameson, argues that this form of pastiche is,

> like parody, the imitation of a peculiar or unique, idiosyncratic style, the wearing of a linguistic mask, speech in a dead language. But it is a neutral practice of such mimicry, without any of parody's ulterior motives, amputated of the satiric impulse, devoid of laughter and of any conviction that alongside the abnormal tongue you have momentarily borrowed, some healthy linguistic normality still exists. (*Postmodernism* 17)

David Harvey observes a similar tendency in postmodern culture when he notes that

> postmodernists simply make gestures towards historical legitimacy by extensive and often eclectic quotation of past styles. Through films, television, books, and the like, history and past experience are turned into a seemingly vast archive "instantly retrievable and capable of being consumed over and over again at the push of a button" [Taylor 105]. [...] The postmodern penchant for jumbling together all manner of references to past styles is one of its more pervasive characteristics. (*Condition* 85)

Importantly, for both Jameson and Harvey, this practice is not a choice on the part of individual artists, but an imperative necessitated by the conditions of life under late capitalism. Jameson particularly emphasizes his view that, partly because they themselves suffer from the psychic fragmentation he associates with the postmodern condition, postmodern artists are simply unable to develop and maintain the kind of distinctive personal styles that Jameson attributes to modernist artists. In his view, "the producers of culture have nowhere to turn but to the past: the imitation of dead styles, speech through all the masks and voices stored up in the imaginary museum of a now global culture" (*Postmodernism* 17–18).

Without specific reference to Jameson, the term "pastiche" has been widely employed in early reviews of *Joker*, and *Joker* would indeed appear to epitomize what Jameson is referring to here. Most of these reviews have focused on the extensive way in which Phillips draws upon films from roughly the historical period in which the action of *Joker* is set, particularly early films of Martin Scorsese, such as *Taxi Driver* (1976) and *The King of Comedy* (1982). In general, critics of the film have referred to its use of pastiche as a way of criticizing its excessive reliance on Scorsese in particular and other predecessors in general. Thus, in a Christian-themed review that decries the moral emptiness of the film, Tara Isabella Burton describes *Joker* as "a Scorsese-style pastiche," while Ani Bundel argues that "the film references Scorsese so thoroughly, one wonders if the producers were giving the filmmaker residuals." In a similar vein, Glenn Kenny's very negative review of the film (filled with oddly personal attacks on what he sees as Todd Phillips's lack of social consciousness) suggests that Scorsese might have originally been enlisted as an executive producer on the film (although he dropped out before production) "as a way of heading off a plagiarism lawsuit."

I will discuss *Joker*'s engagement with such films in much more detail in the next chapter. For now, it is sufficient to point out that *Joker*'s borrowings from earlier films are obvious enough that the film would certainly seem to be an excellent example of the kind of pastiche construction that Jameson associates with postmodernism. Meanwhile, *Joker* is also an excellent example of the kind of formal fragmentation that Jameson associates with postmodernism, even beyond the fact that Arthur Fleck would seem to exemplify the psychic fragmentation that Jameson sees as crucial to the postmodern experience.

Of course, film is inherently fragmented in that it consists of a sequence of images, typically screened at 24 frames per second (although some recent films have been shot at a higher frame rate). However, this rate leads to an illusion of continuous movement, so that this sort of fragmentation is not really perceivable to audiences. The more important (and noticeable) formal fragmentation in film occurs at the level of the cut, in which what is seen on the screen undergoes a more or less sudden and sometimes radical shift, interrupting the illusion of smooth and continuous movement. The traditional Hollywood style of editing was designed to make these cuts seem so natural as to be almost unnoticeable to audiences, allowing them to follow the action, rather than the editing. There have, of course, always been films that employed cuts that call attention to themselves, as in the famed jump cuts of Jean-Luc Godard's *Breathless* (1960). More recent postmodern films have often employed more violent and more frequent cuts that create a sense of frenetic action, in a technique that is often attributed to the influence of music videos on film editing. *Joker*, however, employs intrusive cuts in a much more sophisticated way that helps to create a sense of confusion that mimics the unsteady psychic condition of its protagonist.

47

Such cuts in *Joker* are of two primary kinds. One is the sort I have already mentioned as the first cut in the film, in which the scene shift is unusually sudden or abrupt, often clearly involving both spatial and temporal dislocation. Cuts of this sort are sprinkled throughout *Joker*, creating a cumulative unsettling effect, even though no one cut is by itself particularly significant in that sense. The more significant cuts are ones in which the scene after the cut seems specifically designed to call into question the reliability of the scene before the cut, perhaps because Fleck has just returned to reality from his fantasies. The most obvious examples of this sort of cut are probably those that occur in the sequence of scenes, noted above, in which Fleck is first shown in the company of Sophie, then shown again in exactly the same scene after a cut, but now with Sophie absent.

There are, however, a number of other significant cuts of this sort, most of them involving a particular sort of match cut, in which Fleck is shown in one scene, then suddenly appears in a completely different setting, but in the same physical posture, creating the suggestion that he might have been in the second setting all along, while merely imagining himself to be in the first setting. We are prepared for these cuts in that early scene in which Arthur is shown watching *Live with Murray Franklin* while obviously fantasizing the inserted scene, but the more radical, and destabilizing, cuts are those that do not make it entirely clear what they are supposed to signify. One of the most interesting examples of this kind of match cut occurs at the end of a scene in which Fleck confronts Thomas Wayne in the posh restroom at Wayne Hall, during a charity screening of Charlies Chaplin's *Modern Times* (1936) for a formally dressed audience of Gotham's elites. It's very odd viewing for this particular crowd, the proletarian orientation of the film running directly contrary to the inclinations of the formally dressed, rich, and powerful audience. Indeed, the entire sequence that begins with Fleck's arrival at the hall is one of the moments in the film that smacks most strongly of having either occurred entirely in Fleck's imagination, or at least at having been greatly modified by that imagination.

In the scene, Fleck dons an usher's uniform and sneaks into the auditorium where *Modern Times* is apparently being screened. We are then treated to a view of the film's famous roller-skating scene, in which Chaplin (in what is basically a clown routine) veers dangerously (but obliviously) close to a drop-off while swooping about on his skates. Importantly, the scene is set in a fancy department store lavishly stuffed with expensive luxury goods and standing in stark contrast to the poverty that reigns on the streets outside the store. The scene thus suggests the huge gap between the haves and have-nots that was a central reality of the Depression years in which *Modern Times* was made and that is also central to the economic fabric of Gotham City in *Joker*. Fleck enjoys the scene in a way that suggests that he is familiar with the film, which would be no surprise given Fleck's desire to have a career in comedy and given Chaplin's lofty status in the annals of comedy. This scene then ends when Fleck follows Wayne into a restroom at Wayne Hall and essentially demands to be recognized as Wayne's son; Wayne responds by simply punching Fleck in the face. After Wayne exits, we see Fleck laugh-crying as he leans on the sink in the fancy restroom, whereupon a sudden visual match cut shows Fleck in the same position, but now leaning on a countertop in the kitchen in his shabby apartment. This cut tends to support the possibility that the encounter with Wayne (and, by extension, the entire scene at Wayne Hall) was a mere fantasy on Fleck's part, although it does not unequivocally *prove* that the scene was a fantasy. We are given few unequivocal interpretive clues in *Joker*. In any case, the strength of Fleck's emotional reaction to this experience/fantasy is clear: in a scene that was apparently improvised by Phoenix, he immediately empties out the contents of his refrigerator, then climbs inside, closing the door.[3] Tense music makes us wonder whether Fleck might suffocate inside (we've all heard those stories about people suffocating inside refrigerators), but then a ringing telephone is heard as the camera is still focused on the outside of the refrigerator. An audio match cut continues the ringing of the phone (it's a call from a booker for *Live with Murray Franklin*, inviting Fleck to appear on the show), although Fleck is now lying in bed, suggesting quite strongly the possibility that he might also have merely imagined climbing inside his refrigerator (in response to his imagined encounter with Thomas Wayne), his reverie now interrupted by the ringing phone. The film's intrusive cutting thus helps to establish the notion that there might be several different layers of "reality" in this film, but also that the layers are typically difficult to untangle.

Interestingly, these jarring cuts tend to occur soon after moments that are of special emotional intensity for Fleck, establishing the cuts as a sort of representation of Fleck's disjointed mental state. For example, especially abrupt and puzzling cuts occur soon after each of Fleck's depicted murders, beginning with that moment on a subway when three obnoxious Wall Street types who have been crudely hassling a young woman on the train turn their ire on Fleck when he begins, in full clown wig and makeup, to have one of his laughing fits. One of the men taunts Fleck by delivering a surprisingly adept rendition of Stephen Sondheim's "Send in the Clowns," written for a 1973 musical but first made widely famous by Frank Sinatra's

No Joke: Todd Phillips's *Joker* and American Culture

1973 recording, followed by Judy Collins's releases of the song in 1975 and 1977.[4] It is, in short, a song Fleck would probably know well, perhaps making more likely the notion that he might have fantasized this entire encounter after having heard about the shootings from the media. In any case, as shown on the screen, the men eventually assault Fleck, knocking him to the grimy floor and repeatedly kicking him in an almost exact replication of the assault on Fleck by those street kids at the beginning of the film. This time, though, Fleck promptly (and improbably) pulls out his revolver and shoots the three men dead (although he has to chase one of them outside the train before shooting him).

After this last shooting, Fleck runs up the steps of the subway station and through litter-strewn nighttime streets, eventually taking refuge in a grungy public restroom in a park, reminiscent of the public bathrooms that were central to the events leading up to the Tompkins Square Riots of 1988 in New York City. Seemingly overcome with emotion, Fleck suddenly starts to perform a strange oneiric dance, accompanied by Guðnadóttir's cello-heavy score, that contrasts dramatically with his sordid surroundings. It's a strange, non sequitur moment—and was apparently again ad libbed by Phoenix on the spot (Sharf, "Bathroom"). But the scene makes an important contribution to the atmosphere of the film and to its delineation of Fleck's behavior as not following logical norms. Then this scene suddenly ends, mid-dance, with a cut that finds Fleck exiting the elevator in his apartment building, although the somber (clearly non-diegetic) music that accompanies the dance continues across the cut, establishing a sort of unsettling continuity between these two settings. We then see Fleck stalk determinedly down the hall to Sophie's apartment, where he knocks on the door and then kisses her passionately as she answers the door, then responds warmly, closing the door behind them as they move inside, presumably toward a moment of sexual connection.

It isn't clear at this point in the film, but the later revelation that his entire relationship with Sophie has been fantasized makes it obvious that this doorway encounter with Sophie is happening only in Fleck's mind. By extension, we must then wonder whether the bathroom dance and the subway shootings might have been fantasized as well. After all, the skill shown by the bumbling Fleck with this weapon seems highly unlikely, while it is also the case that this whole scene has the texture of a fantasy, partly because it suddenly endows Fleck with unexpected abilities while allowing him to get revenge on precisely the sort of arrogant and privileged individuals who have made him feel inferior his whole life. For literalists, it might also be pointed out that Fleck is shown firing eight

JOKER AS POSTMODERN ART

Figure 1. Arthur Fleck suddenly becomes a formidable killer on the subway.

shots without reloading in this sequence, even though he appears to be using a Smith & Wesson Bodyguard .38 revolver (of the kind used by Bernhard Goetz in the famous New York subway shootings of December 1984), a model that can, in fact, hold only five bullets. Along these same lines, Fleck's "victory" over his assailants on the train could easily be seen as a fantasy re-enactment of his earlier encounter with the street kids who stole his sign, this time with a much more successful outcome for Fleck (enabled by the fact that it is only happening inside his mind).

It should be emphasized, though, that this vision of the subway scene as a fantasy re-enactment of the alleyway scene in no way precludes the possibility that the earlier scene was also a fantasy (Figure 1). Meanwhile, most of the people in Gotham seem to be aware of the subway killings, which are widely reported in the local media, so it appears certain that, within the world of the film, these killings did occur. However, the identity of the killer is never determined, and it is quite possible that Fleck generated the fantasy of being the killer only *after* learning of the killings in the Gotham media. (The only clue to the killer's identity is that he supposedly wore a clown mask—which Fleck never does, though this detail might have caused him to identify with the killer.) We do not really know enough about Fleck's specific psychological condition to be able to tell what sort of fantasies he might entertain, just as we cannot really tell when (or whether) he might confuse his fantasies with reality. What we do know is that there are, in fact, a number of doublings—such as the alleyway scene and the subway scene that revises it—that create dialogues between scenes that potentially revise our understanding of these scenes.

No Joke: Todd Phillips's *Joker* and American Culture

In another case of paired scenes, if the attack on Fleck in the subway mirrors the earlier attack on him in the alleyway, the scene in that grimy public restroom will be recalled by the later encounter between Fleck and Wayne in the posh bathroom at Wayne Hall. There is a fairly obvious way in which the comparison of these two bathrooms serves as a reminder of the stark divide in material experience that separates the haves and the have-nots in Gotham. Otherwise, though, the relationship between the two bathroom scenes is unclear. The later Wayne Hall scene seems more unlikely than the public bathroom scene, just as the later assault scene on the subway seems more unlikely than the one in the alleyway. Again, no ultimate conclusions are possible, but one could argue that, in these two cases at least, the later scene, by calling attention to the fact that it might be a fantasy, signals us to be on the alert for such fantasies and perhaps causes us to wonder whether the earlier parallel scene might have been a fantasy as well.

After the scene (during a nighttime rainstorm) in Sophie's apartment during which we learn that their relationship had been fantasized by Fleck, he goes back to his apartment and sits on the couch in his not-so-tidy whities, experiencing another of his laughing fits. Then another abrupt cut places him suddenly in the hospital room of his mother, who has apparently had a stroke. In a key sequence, Arthur sits (smoking, as usual) beside Penny's bed and reminds her that it was she who told him that his nervous laugh was a "condition. That there was something wrong with me." He tells her he has now concluded that he has no such condition, but that this very unhappy laugh just expresses who he is. He then calls her on her narrative about his perpetual state of childhood happiness. "I haven't been happy one minute of my entire fucking life," he tells her, clearly near tears. What really makes him laugh, he tells her as he rises and moves toward her bed, is that "I used to think that my life was a tragedy, but now I realize it's a fucking comedy." Then, in what might well be the film's most shocking moment, he calmly and methodically murders his mother by pressing a pillow over her face, suffocating her. She struggles briefly, then succumbs. Fleck turns away from the bed and stands by the window, bright sun streaming down on his face, as the theme from *Live with Murray Franklin* begins to play on the soundtrack.

Then, another sudden, destabilizing audio match cut shows him back in the apartment (dressed differently) watching television with that music still playing; he then interrupts the flow of the music by rewinding a videotape of the Franklin show on which the music is playing, just after a guest is shown coming on stage. That Fleck has taped the show indicates that he has not merely been watching it, but also studying it. Fleck then

JOKER AS POSTMODERN ART

goes into a pantomime routine, pretending that he himself is the guest on the show, indicating the way in which he uses these tapes for a sort of rehearsal. But was he there in the apartment all along, studying the show? Did he really kill Penny, or was it just a fantasy?

Immediately after this rehearsal for appearing as a guest for Murray Franklin, Fleck is shown dying his hair preparatory to putting on clown makeup, suddenly near-naked again, while Sinatra's classic 1966 rendition of "That's Life" (Murray Franklin's personal theme song) plays on the soundtrack. Then, accompanied by the song (which seems to be playing only in Fleck's head, but is later heard actually to be playing on a radio in the apartment), Fleck launches into another of his trance-like dances (something he seems to do soon after committing—or fantasizing—a murder). Then, with the song still playing across another audio match cut, Arthur is shown (cigarette again in hand) putting on the white base for his clown makeup, during which process he crumples up an old photo of a young and beautiful Penny, with the notation "Love your smile … T.W."[5] on the back, apparently a note of endearment from Thomas Wayne. Fleck is then interrupted by his doorbell, whereupon he slips a pair of scissors into his back pocket and goes to answer the door. The visitors are his former co-clowns at Ha-Has Talent Booking, the diminutive Gary (Leigh Gill) and the burly Randall (Glenn Fleshler), who have come by to console him in the wake of his mother's death, indicating that some time has passed since her death (and perhaps providing another clue that Fleck might not have killed her, given that he was just shown doing so only moments earlier). It is certainly quite possible that she merely dies as a result of her stroke and that her death triggered Fleck's fantasy of killing her. Fleck tells them that he feels good, having stopped taking his medication. Soon afterward Fleck is shown in the film's most graphically violent moment, as he plunges those scissors into Randall's throat and eye socket, before gratuitously banging the man's bloody head several times against the wall (Figure 2).

After some tense moments in which we worry about Gary's potential fate, Fleck lets the little man go (even giving him a kiss on his bald head); after all, Fleck's only grudge was with Randall, who had (apparently) given him the gun that started his downward spiral by causing him to lose his clown job. Indeed, by this time it is becoming clear that, however deranged he might be, Fleck does not kill (or fantasize killing) at random but in response to some perceived wrong that has been done to him. Then, with Fleck still in his apartment (and with Randall still lying on the floor), we begin to hear Gary Glitter's oh-so-familiar "Rock and Roll Part 2" on the soundtrack. This music then continues across a whole sequence

No Joke: Todd Phillips's *Joker* and American Culture

Figure 2. Fleck brutally stabs his co-worker Randall in the eye with scissors.

of audio match cuts showing Fleck, now in full Joker makeup and garb, strutting down the hallway of his building, going down in the elevator, then suddenly appearing on those treacherous-looking steps outside the building, where he performs (cigarette in mouth, of course) the most memorable of his several dances in the film.

Many have seen this scene as the crucial announcement that Fleck has now become the confident Joker, rather than a mere obscure mental patient. In any case, it's an impressive physical performance by Phoenix, especially given the fact that he was greatly weakened by the radical weight loss he underwent for the role. This high-kicking dance is also pure spectacle, made all the more so by the Joker costuming, by the striking stone steps down which Fleck dances, and by the music itself, which is now clearly not literally diegetic,[6] although it is easy to imagine that it might be sounding inside Fleck's head. A hit song in 1972, this purely instrumental piece (except for the shouts of "Hey!" that punctuate the song) became especially well known in the United States in the early 1980s when it came to be played more and more during live sports events as a means of revving up crowds (and athletes), as well as to punctuate scores or victories. It's a testosterone-drenched, chest-beating song, really, and it is fitting that Fleck thinks of it with his blood high in the wake of his latest killing (whether real or imagined) and in anticipation of his upcoming big moment as a guest on *Live with Murray Franklin*.[7]

One might compare the spectacular nature of this dance to a parallel scene that occurs in Agnès Varda's *Cléo from 5 to 7* (1962), in which the title character (played by Corinne Marchand) dances and sings down a flight of rustic steps in Paris's Parc Montsouris, singing a song that seems narcissistic. However, no one is watching as she performs, and (unlike the scene in *Joker*) it's a very quiet, low-key moment. She is simply performing (a cappella) for her own amusement—and perhaps to distract her from her anxieties about the expected results of some medical tests. She is not making any kind of statement and is not performing to be seen by anyone, male or otherwise, so that the words of the song she sings ("My precious and capricious body/The azure of my daring eyes/My alluring figure is the bait/That will never deceive/And everyone longs to taste"). become almost a parody of the typical moment of the male gaze, rather than an enactment of it, a reading that is reinforced by the fact that a major element of this film involves the way in which Cléo overcomes her initial status as a vain and willing object of the male gaze.

In the case of Cléo, this performance on the steps can be related to her status as a professional entertainer. In the case of Fleck, the dance down the steps (and his other dances in the film) might be better understood as a matter of fantasy, perhaps inspired by his own consumption of dancing in popular culture, including advertising, the central artistic form of neoliberalism. As Colleen Dunagan has argued, dancing has long been a key tool of visual advertising and has become especially important during the era of neoliberalism. For Donagan, "advertising's appropriation of dance-as-spectacle directs attention to the importance of the consumer body as the site of consumption and the *performance* of self. In other words, advertising produces bodies-as-spectacles whose performance signals agency" (8).

Fleck, of course, has an extremely tenuous grip on his own identity and is clearly desperate to assert some sort of agency. In addition, Fleck has complained during the film that he often feels invisible, so his overt attempt here to make a spectacle of himself in this scene can be taken as an effort to be seen and acknowledged at last. Ironically (but perfectly in keeping with Fleck's unstable mental state), no one is watching (except viewers of the film), although the triumphant dance is interrupted when the two detectives investigating the subway shootings appear at the top of the steps (while the music switches from Gary Glitter's rowdy glam-rock to Guðnadóttir's somber score), sending Fleck back to earth. He scurries off in fear, looking like anything but a formidable supervillain. The detectives chase Fleck through garbage-strewn streets, although he manages to elude them (even after a violent collision with a taxi) long enough to make it aboard a train whose passengers are mostly in clown masks and clown makeup, part of an emergent kill-the-rich

No Joke: Todd Phillips's *Joker* and American Culture

Figure 3. Fleck runs down a garbage-strewn sidewalk, pursued by police.

political movement partly inspired by the subway shootings (Figure 3). The detectives make it aboard the train as well, but Detective Burke (Shea Whigham) ends up being badly beaten by the "clowns" after he shoots one of them in a scuffle. The train stops and the passengers begin to spill out onto the platform. Fleck looks on and does a gleeful little dance as he watches Burke on the ground being kicked, now occupying the position in which Fleck had been shown twice in earlier moments of the film: Fleck's antagonist is now suffering the fate he himself had suffered in the alleyway and in the subway.

As if to emphasize that this (possibly fantasized) scene is comforting rather than traumatic for Fleck, he is now shown walking away from the scene, without the kind of jarring cut that typically follows a scene of violence in this film. Eventually, though, we cut to the site of *Live with Murray Franklin* and see Fleck chuckling to himself in the dressing room as he watches a news report noting that both of the detectives were in fact assaulted on the subway and have now both been hospitalized. Then follows Fleck's next murder, as he shockingly shoots the smug Franklin in the midst of his appearance on the show. He then puts a second bullet in Franklin's chest, does a quick little, almost perfunctory, dance, then starts to speak close up into the camera, when the station interrupts the feed and goes to a test pattern. For once there is a diegetic explanation for a sudden post-murder cut. The camera then slowly pulls back, revealing an entire wall of 24 TV monitors, most of them showing news reports about Fleck's escapades or even an actual scene from earlier in the film (Figure 4). Thus, in what is perhaps the most striking moment of fragmentation in the

JOKER AS POSTMODERN ART

Figure 4. The movie screen is suddenly overwhelmed by television screens.

entire film, we suddenly see the screen filled by these monitors, broken up into 24 different screens, the normal 24 frames per second of a film suddenly replaced by 24 frames of television all at once.

Some of these screens, incidentally, show material that is not obviously related to Fleck's career, including commercials for a Ford Thunderbird automobile, Kellogg's cereal, and for Energizer batteries, featuring the Energizer Bunny, one of the most famous icons in the history of American advertising. These auxiliary scenes presumably help to place Fleck's experience within the larger context of American society, making the point that this entire society is saturated with media images. The Thunderbird commercial, touting the new "automatic overdrive" feature, is clearly from 1980, which is roughly appropriate to the setting of the film.[8]

It should be noted, however, that the Energizer Bunny did not appear in an ad on American television until October 30, 1988, making that commercial another example of the kind of blurring of the historical setting that we often see in *Joker*, a blurring that will be discussed in more detail in the next chapter.

Particularly relevant as a gloss on this moment in the film is Jim Collins's argument that what makes television truly postmodern is not so much the content of any particular program as the inherent fragmentation that occurs due to the fact that multiple programs are simultaneously available via the same multichannel medium. For Collins, television is thus the central example of the simultaneous presence of multiple styles that for him is characteristic of the "postmodern context." However, what characterizes postmodern culture is not the dominance of any particular style, but the "recognition that culture has become a multiplicity of competing signs" (114–115).

At this point, all hell essentially breaks loose in the editing of the film, mirroring the chaos that has erupted in the streets of Gotham. What follows is a frantic series of violent scenes, including the murders of Thomas and Martha Wayne—by a gunman whose final words to Thomas Wayne mirror Fleck's final words to Murray Franklin, suggesting that he might have been inspired by watching Fleck's appearance on Franklin's show. These killings, as I noted earlier, are shown occurring while Fleck is unconscious and thus represent one of the few events in the film that is apparently not related from Fleck's point of view—unless, of course, he is dreaming it while unconscious. Fleck, meanwhile, regains consciousness and is hailed as a hero by the clown-faced crowd of rioters while he once again dances, this time on the hood of a crashed police car. Then, one of the film's most sudden cuts occurs as the screen goes to black, then comes back with Fleck laughing, now being interviewed by a psychiatrist in Arkham State Hospital, in a scene that doubles the earlier scenes in which he consulted with his social worker, especially as both of the interviewers are black women. Further sudden cuts then punctuate this confusing final sequence, the meaning of which has been widely debated. For example, this sequence might or might not involve the murder of the psychiatrist, followed by Fleck's attempted escape from the hospital; it also might or might not imply that he's been in the hospital all along and that basically *everything* we've seen was his fantasy. And so on.

For my purposes here, though, what is important about the final sequence from the apparent shooting of Franklin to the end of the film is that it *is* confusing (because it continually cuts from one moment to the next, leaving out crucial information), adding a final exclamation point to the fragmented nature of the entire film. In any case, the abruptness of the cuts during all of the sequences I have described has an overall destabilizing effect, illustrating Jameson's point about the way in which formal fragmentation in postmodern art tends to reflect the psychically disturbing texture of life under late capitalism.

This formal fragmentation is also related to a breakdown in narrative coherence that, for Jameson, is closely related to a loss of genuine "historical sense" that he sees as a crucial consequence of the postmodern condition. Jameson here means much more by "historical sense" than the ability to comprehend specific phenomena (or cultural works) within the historical context in which they occurred or were produced. In particular, historical sense involves "a perception of the present as history" (*Postmodernism* 284). That is, it involves the ability to think of the present as participating in the historical process, through which it is connected both to the past and to the future—to think of the present as the future of the past and as the past of the future. But it is just this ability to think of history as a continuous narrative process that Jameson believes to have been largely lost in the era of late capitalism, where the frenetic pace of innovation and change creates a disorienting sense of time as a fleeting series of present moments that are difficult to understand as part of a process leading logically from the past to the present and then to the future.

Robert Crary has described this process of rapid change in a way that makes clear the relationship between this process and the fragmentation of personal identities that Jameson associated with postmodernism. For one thing, Crary argues that human identities have come, in the twenty-first century, to be defined more and more in relation to our consumption and use of specific technologies and devices that themselves are continually replaced by newer models and thus quickly rendered obsolete. This rapid pace of innovation and replacement means that our identities must themselves be revised and updated at an increasingly dizzying pace, while those identities are rendered more unstable in the first place by the knowledge that the devices we so cherish are temporary and provisional:

> Now the brevity of the interlude before a high-tech product literally becomes garbage requires two contradictory attitudes to coexist: on one hand, the initial need and/or desire for the product, but, on the other, an affirmative identification with the process of inexorable cancellation and replacement. (*24/7* 45)

Thus, eventually, the consumerist desire that drives subjects under late capitalism becomes a desire not for the commodity itself but simply for the newness that the latest version of the commodity represents and for the sense of being up-to-date on all the innovations being produced by the consumerist system. But, of course, this displacement of desire from an actual physical object onto a fleeting and largely symbolic process contributes to the growing insubstantiality of experience in the postmodern world, helping to make it harder and harder to maintain a sense that anything is "real." Arthur Fleck's disengagement from reality would appear to allegorize this phenomenon, just as the inability to distinguish reality from Fleck's fantasies that is so central to the experience of watching this film would appear to place the viewer of this film in somewhat the same uncertain position as Fleck himself.

Joker itself also has a very complex and highly uncertain relationship with history. On the one hand, as I will discuss in more detail in the following chapter, the film engages in an extensive dialogue with the historical time in which the events of the film take place, even if it does blur the context of the film beyond its nominal setting in 1981 to include the years preceding and following that setting. At the same time, as I discussed in the previous chapter, *Joker* also has a strong connection to the world of Batman comics, and there is a very real way in which the film is not set in *any* time period in our world, because it is not set in our world at all. Gotham City may be a relatively transparent fictionalization of New York City (and "Gotham" has been used as a nickname for New York at least since 1807, when Washington Irving used it that way), but it is a fictionalization, nevertheless. In a sense, of course, all fictional events occur in what are essentially alternate universes, but these universes (especially in the realist tradition) are typically mappable onto the real world in a fairly direct way, but that is not really the case with *Joker*, which draws so extensively on the overtly unrealistic source of Batman comics that the film's relationship with the real, historical world becomes difficult to determine.

In addition, even when *Joker* draws upon the "real" world of 1981 and thereabouts, it often does so through the mediation of fictional cultural products from that period. For example, the film's Gotham might be obviously derived from New York circa 1981, but it is derived less from the real historical New York than it is from the New York of that period as represented in fictional works from that period, especially the early films of Martin Scorsese. This tendency is fairly typical of postmodern culture, in which reality, as Harvey puts it, is often "shaped to mimic media images" (85). In point of fact, though, *Joker*'s relationship with history is highly complex, partly because of the way it engages both with real material history and with history as reflected in cultural works, and partly because it is very much a work of 2019, as well as a work declaredly located circa 1981. This complex engagement with history ultimately illustrates quite well Jameson's concerns about the loss of historical sense in works of postmodern culture, constituting still another way in which *Joker* functions as an exemplary work of postmodernism. That engagement will be examined in more detail in the following chapters.

Notes

1   The Wayne Manor scenes were shot on the campus of the Webb Institute, an undergraduate engineering college in Glen Cove, New York. This same college stood in for Wayne Manor and its grounds in the *Gotham* television

series and in the films *Batman Forever* (1995) and *Batman & Robin* (1997). This setting thus provides one of the many links between *Joker* and the Batman universe.

2   A closer look at the name badge shows that this social worker is named "Debra Kane," in an apparent nod to Batman (and Joker) co-creator Bob Kane. It should also be noted that Bruce Wayne meets a social worker named "Debra Kane," who works with child abuse cases in the 1995 novel *Batman: The Ultimate Evil*, by Andrew Vachss.

3   On Phoenix's various improvisations, see Burwick.

4   Sinatra's rendition of the song also appears on the soundtrack of the film. See Chapter 5.

5   The handwriting on the back of this photo looks extremely similar to that in Penny's letter to Wayne that we saw earlier in the film, although the "T.W." appears to have been stylized differently than the body of the note. There is certainly at least a chance that Penny forged this note, supporting the notion that she had either imagined or fabricated her entire romantic relationship with Wayne. Realizing this might be one reason why Fleck crumples the photo, although we can only speculate about his feelings here.

6   As has been made clear by a widely posted video shot by a bystander as the filming of the scene was underway, no music was played on set during the dance, perhaps making Phoenix's performance all the more impressive.

7   It might also be noted that this scene both resembles and differs from an earlier scene in which Fleck dances down the grimy stairway from which he exits after having been fired from his clown job at Ha-Has. The contrast between these two scenes presumably suggests Fleck's ascent from defeat to victory.

8   Capturing even more of the flavor of the early 1980s, this commercial features spokesmodel Erin Gray, who, by 1981, had become one of the darlings of American television, thanks to her role as Col. Wilma Deering in the series *Buck Rogers in the 25th Century* (1979–1981).

CHAPTER THREE

"You Talkin' to Me?"
Joker and the Films of the 1970s and 1980s

Joker alludes to the world of 1970s and early 1980s film even before the film itself begins, displaying at the opening of the film the Warner Bros. logo that was used during that period (1972–1984, actually) rather than the updated one that would normally have been employed in 2019. Meanwhile, most contemporary reviews of *Joker* noted the influence of specific films from that same period, with a special emphasis on Scorsese's *Taxi Driver* (1976) and *The King of Comedy* (1982). That influence is pervasive, and a consideration of these films enriches *Joker* immensely. Meanwhile, *Joker* also directly alludes to other films of the period, mostly through a shot of a movie theater that is currently screening or advertising a number of films, all of which were released in 1981, providing the clearest identification of that year as the year of the film's action. By so doing, *Joker* not only evokes the entire world of film during the period in which its action is set, but also uses that cinematic world to establish a connection with the historical world as well.

Late in *Joker*, just before the film's re-enactment of the crucial scene of the killing of Bruce Wayne's parents, we see the Waynes (who seem to have chosen an odd evening to go to the movies, given that the streets of Gotham have erupted in widespread violence) as they leave a movie theater where the marquee announces the showing of two films that were released in 1981: Brian De Palma's *Blow Out* (a postmodern neo-noir thriller featuring a psychotic killer and containing suggestions that our perceptions of reality can be deceiving) and *Zorro, the Gay Blade* (an adventure comedy featuring a black-masked hero who is widely acknowledged to have been one of the inspirations for the Batman character).[1] *Blow Out* was released on July 24, 1981, while *Zorro, the Gay Blade* was released on July 17, 1981, so it makes sense that they might be showing at the same time, although it seems, at first glance, an odd mix of films.

NO JOKE: TODD PHILLIPS'S *JOKER* AND AMERICAN CULTURE

But perhaps, as Daraiseh and Booker suggest, that is the point, because "this combination suggests the mashup of disparate elements that runs throughout *Joker*—and throughout postmodern art as a whole."

Three other films are also referenced in this theater scene (all of which, by the way, were distributed by Warner Bros., even though *Blow Out* and *Zorro, the Gay Blade* were not). On one side of its front door, the theater displays a poster for the Dudley Moore comedy *Arthur*, released on July 17, 1981. This film does not appear to have all that much in common with *Joker*, except for the name of its title character. That name also seems to be the main link to the film whose poster appears on the other side of the front door, John Boorman's *Excalibur*, a film based on the legend of King Arthur that was released on April 10, 1981.

After the Waynes turn the corner and head down the alleyway that will lead them to their deaths, they pass one additional poster displayed outside the theater, this one for the werewolf movie *Wolfen* (released on July 24, 1981). It is not entirely clear why this film is relevant to *Joker*, other than the fact that the presence of a reference to this horror movie suggests points of contact between *Joker* and horror in general, as I will explore in the next chapter. In addition, werewolves are often depicted as ordinary, even downtrodden individuals who transform into dangerous killers, which makes that subgenre of horror especially relevant to *Joker*. Meanwhile, the reference to *Excalibur* seems slightly anachronistic, given that it was released three months before all of these other films, although a commercial success such as *Excalibur* could well still have been running in July, while the references to all of these other films that were released in July potentially suggest a late-July date for the setting of the film.

Of course, I have already noted that the opening scene of *Joker* clearly indicates that its action begins on Thursday, October 15. If we assume from all these film references that the year must be 1981, then that information matches this opening, because October 15 did indeed fall on a Thursday in 1981. Meanwhile, what internal visual evidence we have in the film suggests that this October date is much more likely than a July date for the action of *Joker*, because all of the people in the streets of Gotham seem to be wearing coats or jackets, which would certainly not be the case in July, especially if one associates Gotham with New York, which is typically quite hot in July.[2] All of this likely suggests that Phillips chose to refer to films that were released in 1981 in order to verify that this year corresponds to the historical setting of *Joker*, but didn't worry much about details such as release dates, choosing instead to refer to films that, for one reason or another, have some sort of connection to his own film. This somewhat contradictory attitude (taking so much trouble to include details that locate the action in a specific year but not worrying much about the month) resembles the film's overall attitude toward its historical setting (sometimes being very precise about the action taking place in 1981, sometimes content to suggest a more generalized setting somewhere in the 1970s or 1980s).

The reference to *Excalibur* also provides one of the many connections between *Joker* and the Batman universe, because the film *Batman v Superman: Dawn of Justice* (2016) also shows the Waynes being murdered outside a movie theater that is displaying a poster for *Excalibur*.[3] This connection suggests that the timeline of *Batman v Superman* is roughly the same as that in *Joker*, given that the Waynes are killed during the run of *Excalibur* in both films. Otherwise, there does not seem to be much of a connection between *Joker* and *Batman v Superman*, especially as the Joker does not appear in the latter at all.

That Phillips would indicate the year in which the action of *Joker* is set primarily through references to other films also suggests the postmodern nature of *Joker*'s dialogue with history, which involves both an extensive (and often playful) intertextual conversation with past films (and, of course, the entire tradition of Batman comics) and a serious, but somewhat vague, engagement with material history, which itself is treated as a sort of text. As I noted earlier, *Joker* essentially treats material history and cultural history in the same way, as a sort of library of texts from which to draw style and content. I have identified this tendency as postmodern, although it might also be identified under the parallel labels of poststructuralism and post-Marxism. Discussing the tendency of the latter two to treat material history as if it were a text, Jameson argues that history consists of the concrete lived experience of real people and that "history is not a text, not a narrative, master or otherwise, but that, as an absent cause, it is inaccessible to us except in textual form, and that our approach to it [...] necessarily passes through its prior textualization, its narrativization in the political unconscious" (*Political Unconscious* 35).

Joker, I think, illustrates very well what Jameson is talking about here. The films to which *Joker* refers through the inclusion of this marquee and these posters are not in themselves particularly important in terms of adding content to the film. In fact, they have a sort of playful (one might say "jokey") quality that seems out of step with the darkness of much of the film. This quality is, however, very much in step with the way in which allusions to earlier works frequently function in postmodern texts. In addition, these film references do participate in an important way in *Joker*'s dialogue with the historical past, first by indicating that the film's action is set in 1981 and second by announcing a belief that films

65

constitute such a crucial part of the texture of any given time in American history that it is difficult to evoke past times without at least some consideration of the films that were being produced in those times. Of course, the most important way in which *Joker* does this is not so much through the films that are mentioned on marquees and posters as through the films from which it unapologetically borrows. The most important of these are the early films of Martin Scorsese, especially *Taxi Driver* and *The King of Comedy*, although I would argue that *Mean Streets* (1973) is an important predecessor as well.

Before discussing these Scorsese films in relation to *Joker*, I should also note that *Joker* appears to have taken inspiration from a number of other films of this very special period in American film history. Among other things, the fact that Phillips chose to draw so heavily on films of the 1970s points to the fact that this period was such a rich one for American film. As Phillips himself put it in an interview, "*Taxi Driver*, obviously, is one of my favorite movies, but it's not directly that. I think it's more a time period of movies" (Dominguez). Central here, of course, is the New Hollywood movement, in which Scorsese was only one of a number of innovative young directors who redefined both the aesthetics and the business of American film. This movement was marked, as much as anything, by its diversity, with central works ranging from all-time classics such as Francis Ford Coppola's *The Godfather* (1972) to box-office smashes such as Steven Spielberg's *Jaws* (1975), the film that made the summer blockbuster a major emphasis of Hollywood marketing. Moreover, this phenomenon extended beyond such mainstream films to virtually every genre of American film, as when Roman Polanski's *Chinatown* (1974) built upon immediate predecessors such as Boorman's *Point Blank* (1967) to resurrect the legacy of film noir or when the huge commercial success of George Lucas's *Star Wars* (1977) helped to usher in a decade-long Golden Age in American science fiction film. Horror film—from blockbusters such as William Friedkin's *The Exorcist* (1973) to rough-hewn low-budget works such as Tobe Hooper's *The Texas Chainsaw Massacre* (1973) or John Carpenter's *Halloween* (1978)—also experienced a renaissance during this period, about which I will have more to say in the next chapter.

Dramatic character studies driven by bravura acting performances—of the kind provided by Robert De Niro in Scorsese's early films—were a particularly prominent component of the New Hollywood movement. At least two such films—Sidney Lumet's *Serpico* (1973), featuring Al Pacino, and Miloš Forman's *One Flew Over the Cuckoo's Nest* (1975), featuring Jack Nicholson—have been prominently mentioned by Phillips as influences. The relevance of *Cuckoo's Nest*, with its emphasis on mental illness, is fairly obvious. The relevance of *Serpico* might be less obvious, although Phillips's own comments on that film as a character study would seem to identify that relevance as residing in the film's focus on its title character. Indeed, Pacino delivers a riveting performance as Serpico, a man whose job as a righteous policeman might seem to set him apart from *Joker*'s Arthur Fleck. However, Serpico's very righteousness sets him at odds with most of his fellow police and ultimately makes him a lonely outcast. Thus, it is easy to see how *Serpico*'s basic strategy of building its narrative on the central character's rejection by those around him could have provided an important model for *Joker*.

Nevertheless, it is clearly the early films of Scorsese that are most productively read as predecessors to *Joker*. One Scorsese film, the much admired *Raging Bull* (1980), I would place very much in the same category as *Serpico* in the sense that its main relevance would be its focus on its central character, this time with the extra element that it stars Robert De Niro, who plays an important role in *Joker*. It is also worth noting that De Niro gained approximately 60 pounds in order to portray the overweight state of the aging central character, Jake LaMotta, just as Joaquin Phoenix famously lost over 50 pounds in order to play the emaciated Fleck. It is also important to note that both Frank Serpico and LaMotta were real people, so that their portrayal in these films had a strong basis in reality, as opposed to *Joker*, which has its basis in comic books, films, and other fictional works, as befits its postmodern character.

Joker and *Mean Streets*

Mean Streets resembles *Joker* in both its content and certain stylistic and narrative strategies, as when it ends in uncertainty, with many questions unanswered. The film takes place on the streets of a dark and dangerous New York City, while De Niro's "Johnny Boy" Civello is a borderline psychopath who becomes a danger to everyone around him, thus making him a forerunner to Arthur Fleck. Perhaps the most interesting choice made by Scorsese in this film involves the use of references to other films to help set its sociohistorical context, as does *Joker*. However, *Mean Streets* employs these references in a somewhat different way that reflects its status as a fundamentally modernist work as opposed to *Joker*'s postmodernism. In particular, Scorsese uses references to other films in a very concrete and integral way, as part of the lived environment of his characters, who in fact often speak in movie quotes. These films are not treated as representations of reality; they are a *part* of the reality in which the film takes place.

No Joke: Todd Phillips's *Joker* and American Culture

The references to films begin early in *Mean Streets*, when several of the characters (young men on the fringes of the criminal underworld of New York's Little Italy, where the Corelone family operated at a much higher level in *The Godfather*) decide to attend a film to spend the $20 in loot they just scored by scamming some teenagers. As they arrive at the theater, we see a shot of a whole series of brightly lit marquees advertising a number of films that together indicate the richness of film fare that would have been available in New York at the time. These marquees announce such "respectable" films as Elia Kazan's *The Arrangement* (1969, starring Kirk Douglas) and *Rage* (1972, starring and directed by George C. Scott, who had won a Best Actor Oscar for *Patton* the year before). These marquees also mention such European imports as the French–Italian crime drama *Borsalino* (1970, starring Jean-Paul Belmondo) and *The Eighteen Carat Virgin* (1971), an X-rated Swedish import, suggesting the cosmopolitan variety of the films involved. The movie the characters actually see, however, is John Ford's classic Western *The Searchers* (1956), and *Mean Streets* even includes a brief look at a serio-comic fight scene from this classic Western as the characters watch.

The inclusion of *The Searchers* within *Mean Streets* suggests that this film was an important formative influence on Scorsese even before *Taxi Driver*, to which it has so often been noted as a predecessor, including by Richard Slotkin. Slotkin concludes that the American national identity was shaped in violence, that the Western film helped to create an agonistic vision of the United States as a nation built through triumph over "savage" enemies. For him, the Western, with its visions of victories over wild-eyed Native Americans, embodies this sense of national identity perhaps more than any other cultural phenomenon. He notes, however, that, by the 1970s, the Western was being displaced in its role as a cultural expression of the American national identity, even though this identity itself remained largely unchanged. In particular, for Slotkin, the displacement of the Western from its place on the genre map did not imply the dissolution of the underlying structures of myth and ideology that had given the genre its defining cultural force. Rather, those structures were abstracted from the elaborately historicized context of the Western and parceled out among genres that used their relationship to the Western to define both the disillusioning losses and the extravagant potential of the new era (633).

Slotkin identifies the science fiction adventure (especially *Star Wars* and *Star Trek*), the urban crime film, and the slasher film as among the most important genres that took the place formerly occupied by the Western as a structure for conveying mythic energies. The first of these would seem to have relatively little to do with *Joker*, but the latter two are extremely relevant. For example, Slotkin singles out *Taxi Driver* (1976), one of *Joker*'s most important predecessors, as the "most artful version" of a new kind of crime film that featured "urban gunslingers." Slotkin goes on to argue that *Taxi Driver* intersects with what was perhaps Wayne's greatest Western in the sense that it "uses the captivity/rescue narrative plan of *The Searchers* to give a perversely mythic resonance to its portrait of the violent urban loner, suggesting that he may be as distinctly American a 'type' in our day as Ethan Edwards was in his" (634).[4]

Importantly, though, Slotkin notes that

> both the urban vigilante and the horror/slasher genres *invert* the Myth of the Frontier that had informed the Western. The borders their heroes confront are impermeable to the forces of progress and civilized enlightenment; if anything, the flow of aggressive power runs in the opposite direction, with the civilized world threatened with subjugation to or colonization by the forces of darkness. (*Gunfighter Nation* 635)

This reversal, of course, was very much in line with the dark American national mood of the 1970s and 1980s, a mood in which the widespread publicity granted to serial killers, beginning especially with the media frenzy over the Manson murders, participated in a central way.

Meanwhile, Slotkin's vision of the Western as epitomizing the way in which the American national identity was shaped in violence also points to a reason why this film might be featured in *Mean Streets*. The Western, *Mean Streets* suggests via its inclusion of *The Searchers*, also went into the shaping of the violent characters who feature in Scorsese's film. At the same time, this connection also potentially provides a commentary on the violence in American film as a whole, suggesting that violent films might potentially contribute to the violent tendencies in American society. Moreover, by providing this commentary via a reference to a film released almost two decades before its own release, *Mean Streets* provides a reminder that, while the New Hollywood films might have reached new heights in the representation of violence thanks to the collapse of the Production Code, violence had been an important component of American films from the very beginning—and even during the reign of the Code.

It makes sense that the would-be gangsters of *Mean Streets* might have taken their inspiration from the Western, rather than from gangster films. After all, Westerns were ubiquitous in American culture when the young men of *Mean Streets* were growing up, while there were few truly notable gangster films between the rash of films that invented the genre in the early 1930s and the release of *The Godfather* only a year before *Mean Streets*. Subsequently, of course, gangster films became a major element of American popular culture, with Scorsese himself making a major contribution to that development with films such as *Goodfellas* (1990). Thus, by the time the now-classic gangster-oriented television series *The Sopranos* debuted on HBO, it was able to feature gangster characters who were deeply immersed in the legacy, not of Westerns, but of gangster films, especially the *Godfather* sequence, while that sequence seems also to have inspired Tony Soprano to look back to the gangster films of the 1930s as well.

Later in *Mean Streets*, the two main characters (played by De Niro and Harvey Keitel) attend another film, making it clear that movie-going is a frequent activity in their circle. In this case, the film they see (and of which we again see a snippet) is *The Tomb of Ligeia* (1964), part of Roger Corman's series of Edgar Allan Poe adaptations that was one of the highlights of 1960s horror film. This film does not seem to be especially related to *Mean Streets*, although it does again contain a considerable amount of violence. It is also worth noting that Corman (who had produced and distributed Scorsese's 1972 film *Boxcar Bertha*) was initially involved in negotiations both to finance and distribute *Mean Streets*, although other backing was eventually found to produce the film, while Warner Bros. eventually agreed to distribute it. It is possible that the inclusion of *The Tomb of Ligeia* in this way is partly a simple indication of Scorsese's connection with Corman and partly a way of establishing a certain atmosphere for Scorsese's film, which is both quite dark in tone and haunted by certain supernatural resonances supplied by the devoted (perhaps even fanatical) Catholicism of Keitel's character, whose status as an aspiring gangster conflicts strongly with his religiosity, causing him to attempt to atone for his sins by sacrificially devoting himself to trying to save De Niro's Johnny Boy from his own dark inclinations.

This theater in *Mean Streets* also displays an array of movie posters, for a wide variety of films, including the science-fiction/horror hybrid *X: The Man with the X-Ray Eyes* (1963), produced and directed by Corman, John Boorman's *Point Blank* (1967), and John Cassavetes' *Husbands* (1970). Presumably this scene was shot on a set in Los Angeles, along with the film's other interiors, so that Scorsese apparently chose these posters intentionally. As a result, it is relatively easy to find connections between *Mean Streets* and the films featured in these posters. I have already noted Scorsese's connection with Corman, while Cassavetes played a key role in encouraging Scorsese to make *Mean Streets* according to his own vision, rather than to continue directing films for hire for producers such as Corman (Biskind 239). And *Point Blank* is a film that has frequently been cited as an important predecessor to the kind of gritty and violent (but stylish) early films made by Scorsese. This film, of course, also provides a link to *Joker*, whose movie posters also include a Boorman film in *Excalibur*.

Mean Streets is sprinkled with other movie references as well, as when see a shot from the street of the Waverly, a historic Greenwich Village arthouse cinema (now the IFC Center),[5] whose marquee announces that they are currently showing the Andy Warhol produced *Heat* (1972). The characters also sometimes quote films in their dialogue, again emphasizing that movies play an important role in their lives. Ultimately, while one might tease out some special significance in many of the specific film references in *Mean Streets*, I think that the central effect of these references is simply to enrich the film's representation of the cultural milieu in which its characters live—and in which Scorsese himself grew up. Whether or not Phillips chose to include film references via marquees and posters in his film as a nod to *Mean Streets* is immaterial; the important fact is that both films indicate that a representation of life in New York in the 1970s and 1980s must acknowledge the importance of film and of the city's many movie theaters to the texture of daily life there.

What is also important, and what makes it quite valuable to compare the film references in *Mean Streets* and *Joker* is the fact that, while both films refer to other films in similar ways and for some of the same reasons, they do so in very different spirits. For one thing, Scorsese is unconcerned with using his film references to indicate the temporal setting of his film, because it is clear that the action of his film is to be understood to be taking place essentially in the present time of the film's release in 1973. His inclusion of films that were released from 1956 to 1972 is in no danger of causing confusion about the film's historical setting; instead, this range of films merely indicates the variety of offerings that might be on show in New York at any given time, in terms not only of release dates but also of genres—from Westerns, to crime dramas, to science fiction, to horror, to art films, to adult films.

In *Joker*, however, the marquees and posters all represent films that were chosen especially to be included in *Joker* itself and thus all have some relevance to *Joker*, even if a superficial one. Meanwhile, all of these films were released in 1981, thus emphasizing the 1981 setting of *Joker* itself, 38 years before the time of the film's release. The inclusion of references to these 1981 films in *Joker* does very little to flesh out the film's depiction of the cultural milieu in which Arthur Fleck lives, however, which makes the mention of the films relatively unimportant, especially as Fleck is shown watching none of the films mentioned on the marquee and posters in *Joker*. I think the difference between *Mean Streets* and *Joker* can again be encompassed largely within a recognition that *Joker* makes such allusions in a playful postmodern spirit that regards cultural products of the past as items on an à la carte cultural-historical cafeteria menu. The marquees and posters in *Mean Streets*, on the other hand, are included in an essentially modernist spirit. The New York City of 1973 in Scorsese's film does not function as a text. It functions as a very tangible material reality. At the same time, cultural products (especially films) are very much a part of reality and must be considered before that reality can be understood.

Joker and *Taxi Driver*

Almost all of the early reviews of *Joker* noted the numerous similarities between *Taxi Driver* and *Joker*, including the obvious parallels in the atmospheres of decay that the two films associate with New York and Gotham City, which are so crucial to the textures of these two films. Another obvious parallel is the fact that both *Taxi Driver* and *Joker* feature unbalanced and embittered protagonists who jot down their random thoughts in journals and ultimately turn to multiple murder. But the similarities go far beyond the most obvious ones, as in the fact that both films involve political campaigns and candidates who are or nearly are assassinated, thus reflecting the prominence of assassination in American life in the years leading up to the time in which these films are set.

Movie marquees also figure in *Taxi Driver*, and in much the same way as in *Mean Streets*. In *Taxi Driver*, one of his best-known and most admired films, Scorsese presents us with an even more detailed look at the streets of New York, focusing primarily on the city's dark underbelly. *Mean Streets* features De Niro as a borderline psychopath (and thus something of a predecessor to Fleck), but even this character is a member of a specific subcultural community. *Taxi Driver*, on the other hand, features De Niro as a lone protagonist who is entirely without community (and thus is even more of a predecessor to Fleck). In one of his most iconic roles, De Niro plays Travis Bickle, one of American cinema's most memorable and strikingly realized characters. A disaffected and radically alienated Vietnam vet, Bickle bitterly cruises the dark streets of nighttime New York, despising his passengers and the entire culture from which they emerge, driving his taxi through the night because his insomnia will not allow him to sleep. All the while, Bickle dreams of an apocalyptic cleansing rain that might clear the city's streets and sidewalks of the garbage and filth (both literal and moral) that he perceives all around him.

Taxi Driver again provides us with glimpses of a number of theater marquees (as Bickle drives by them), announcing films such as Clint Eastwood's *The Eiger Sanction* (1975) and the Charles Bronson vehicle *Mr. Majestyk* (1974). Both are no doubt again found art, although Scorsese had many New York marquees from which to choose and these were no doubt chosen for specific reasons, such as the fact that both Eastwood's and Bronson's characters are Vietnam war veterans who find themselves in violent post-service conflicts.[6] It is also clear that Scorsese carefully chose a marquee that we see displayed especially prominently near the beginning of the film, advertising the showing of *The Texas Chain Saw Massacre* (1974). The significance of this particularly violent early slasher film in terms of setting the atmosphere for *Taxi Driver* is quite clear. On the other hand, the vast majority of the marquees that we see are for pornographic films, adding substantially to *Taxi Driver*'s project of depicting New York, at least as seen by Bickle, as a cesspool of moral decay (although Bickle also seems to be a fan of such films, which he regularly visits).

Such films even play an important role in the plot of the film, a key part of which involves Bickle's fascination with Betsy (Cybill Shepherd), a volunteer who works in the New York office of the presidential campaign of Senator Charles Palatine (Leonard Harris). Bickle clearly sees the luminous Betsy as a sort of beacon of purity and light amid the contamination and squalor that he otherwise perceives around him in the city, so he goes to the campaign office and strikes up an acquaintance with her. Apparently intrigued by Bickle's odd demeanor, Betsy agrees to go for coffee and later to go to a movie. But their relationship is quickly cut short when Bickle, who apparently has no sense of social propriety, takes Betsy to an adult theater (although a slightly upscale one, by the standards of the theaters Bickle typically patronizes). This theater is showing two adult films (perhaps as a double feature, although that isn't entirely clear), consisting of the 1975 porn "classic" *Sometime Sweet Susan* and something called *Swedish Marriage Manual*, which doesn't seem to correspond to any actual film at all but was apparently invented just for use in *Taxi Driver*. It is, in any case, in the course of watching this second film that Betsy becomes embarrassed and bolts from the theater, after which she spurns Bickle's subsequent invitations, sending him spiraling into a plan to assassinate Palatine. This impulse will be thwarted, but the same energies that drove it culminate in Bickle's quest to free the young prostitute Iris (Jodie Foster) from sexual servitude in the film's violent climactic sequence.

No Joke: Todd Phillips's *Joker* and American Culture

Bickle's plan to assassinate Palatine seems pretty misguided as a way of teaching Betsy a lesson, which certainly indicates that Bickle's thinking is a bit muddled. This plan, though, has a real-world precedent that inspired Schrader to include it in his screenplay. In particular, Schrader drew upon Arthur Bremer's accounts in *An Assassin's Diary* (1974) of the experiences that led him to stalk both Richard Nixon and George Wallace and then finally, in 1972, to shoot and wound Wallace and three others at a campaign rally (very much like the rally at which Bickle attempts to shoot Palatine). It was, of course, Bickle's attempt to assassinate Palatine that provided important inspiration for John Hinckley Jr.'s attack on Ronald Reagan in 1981, while the chain of inspiration goes back further to the fact that Bremer himself had been at least partly inspired by a film, in this case Stanley Kubrick's *A Clockwork Orange* (1971).

One way in which Arthur Fleck differs from predecessors such as Bremer, Bickle, and Hinckley (as well as *A Clockwork Orange*'s Alex DeLarge) is in the strongly psycho-sexual character of the impulses that drive the other four to kill. Fleck, despite his fascination with Sophie, seems virtually asexual. His killings are not undertaken (or imagined) for overtly sexual reasons, although one could certainly see a psycho-sexual motivation behind the killing of his mother. And one could also argue that Fleck seems to be trying to reassert his shattered manhood in his string of killings (whether they are imagined or literal). In *Taxi Driver*, though, Bickle's sexual motivations are much more overt, including the fact that he so obviously embodies the Freudian cliché of employing guns as phallic surrogates.

This motif, incidentally, is reinforced in *Taxi Driver* in one key scene that it would be almost impossible to imagine happening in *Joker*. In this scene, a cuckolded husband (played by Scorsese himself) hires Bickle's cab to take him to an apartment building inside which his wife (at least according to him) is in the process of cheating on him with a "nigger." In addition to this racist animus, Scorsese's character also delivers a shockingly direct description of his intention to employ his massive gun (a .44 magnum) to wreak horrific revenge on his wife. "Did you ever see what a .44 magnum pistol would do to a woman's face? It'll fucking destroy it, just blow it right apart. That's what it can do to her face. Now, did you ever see what it can do to a woman's pussy? That you should see." Bickle listens intently, but does not comment. However, given that this scene occurs only a few minutes of runtime after Bickle has been spurned by Betsy, it seems reasonable to assume that the speech by Scorsese's character provided a good deal of inspiration for Bickle to try to assassinate Palatine as a way of getting back at Betsy.

Despite the relative squeamishness of *Joker* with regard to sex, one crucial motif that is foregrounded in both films is the embattled state of American masculinity. Taubin, looking back to the portrayal of Ethan Edwards in *The Searchers*, notes that the typical image of American masculinity was already being challenged in that film, which makes it a forerunner of *Taxi Driver*, even though the later films goes much farther.

> But by the mid-1970s, the ideal image of white masculinity was not merely fissured as in *The Searchers*; it had broken to bits under the pressure of the feminist and civil rights movements. In this context, Travis's paranoia can be read as a hyperbolic version of the doubts and defensiveness the average guy was feeling—continues to feel—about being a man. (*Taxi Driver* 27)

Many reviewers of *Joker* also focused on its portrayal of Arthur Fleck as a man whose masculinity is seriously under threat. Lacking a father, assaulted and humiliated by a gang of children, henpecked by his mother, confronted by female counselors, unable to strike up a real relationship with Sophie, and unable to hold a job even as a rent-a-clown, Fleck seems to fail in almost every way in which American masculinity has traditionally been measured. Indeed, some critics felt that the film was far too sympathetic to Fleck's embattled masculinity, seeing the film as a sort of ode to "incel" culture and thus providing one more reason to be appalled by it.[7] Bundel sums up the controversy, arguing that the film seeks sympathy for Fleck

> as an "incel" like white male, even if it provides very little context for why we should (or why we should not). So it's not surprising the film has been interpreted as taking these men who murder friends, family members, classmates and strangers, and saying "but you understand we should feel sorry for them right?"

The contexts are very different, of course, but one might say very much the same thing about Bickle and *Taxi Driver*, although I would argue that any sympathy that these films show for their murderous protagonists resonates crucially with certain developments late in the two films, in which both protagonists are depicted as having become public heroes.

Indeed, perhaps the most important way in which reading *Joker* against *Taxi Driver* can illuminate the former film is through a comparative consideration of the outcomes of the murderous projects undertaken by Travis Bickle and Arthur Fleck. After his bloody assault on the seamy establishment in which Iris works as an underage hooker, Bickle almost commits suicide as the police arrive, but finds that his gun is out of bullets. He then sits resignedly on a couch and pantomimes shooting himself in the head by placing his bloody index finger at his temple and mimicking the motion of firing a pistol. The gesture is a significant one, suggesting as it does that Bickle believes his project is over and that he has nowhere to go from here. Having killed all of Iris's captors, he has done all that he can do and can only hope that she will now somehow be restored to her parents. Meanwhile, he apparently assumes that he is going to be arrested and perhaps charged with murder.

This pantomimed pistol shot to the temple, by the way, provides what is possibly a very direct link to *Joker*, where a similar gesture plays an important role. When we first see Sophie in *Joker*, she is riding in a rickety elevator with her daughter and Fleck in the crumbling building where they all live. She signals to Fleck her frustration with this building by making that gesture of shooting herself in the head, surprisingly establishing a sort of personal connection with her strange neighbor. It's an odd gesture, especially as it is not entirely clear whether Sophie is actually expressing frustration with the building or annoyance that her daughter has tried to insert herself in her conversation with Fleck. Given that the film eventually indicates that Fleck fantasizes an entire personal relationship with Sophie, it also seems reasonable that her use of this gesture in the elevator also occurred only in Fleck's mind as a fantasy that she would want to make contact with him, which might explain Sophie's apparent puzzlement when Fleck makes the gesture back to her in the hall after they exit the elevator. Meanwhile, if Fleck merely ginned up this gesture in his own imagination, one could conjecture that the idea might have originally occurred to the impressionable Fleck because he remembered it from the well-known moment near the end of *Taxi Driver*. That might also explain the moment later in the film in which Fleck sits on Sophie's couch and once again makes that same finger pistol to the head gesture.

After all, *Taxi Driver* was released five years before the events of *Joker*, so that it seems reasonable that Fleck might have seen *Taxi Driver* at some point—if it exists in the world of Gotham. The movie marquees and posters on display within *Joker* clearly indicate that many of the films that were released in the real world of 1981 were also released in the world of *Joker*, suggesting that, at least as far as films are concerned, these two worlds intersect significantly. And, if Fleck has indeed seen *Taxi Driver*, then it is likely that he might have been influenced by it in ways that go well beyond this one gesture. For example, in one scene of *Taxi Driver*, we see Bickle watching television while fondling a firearm, which is something we also see Fleck doing in *Joker*. But, more than such specific actions, any influence of *Taxi Driver* would likely be more general, with Bickle's turn to violence perhaps providing inspiration for Fleck's.

After Bickle's "surrender" near the end of *Taxi Driver*, we suddenly cut to a moment in the future, where we see him, surprisingly, not only alive and well, but thriving. He still lives in his shabby apartment, but now we are treated to views of newspaper clippings he has taped to the walls. The headline in one of these clippings reads "Taxi Driver Battles Gangsters," while another (which includes a subheading reading "Taxi Driver Hero") announces "Reputed New York Mafioso Killed in Bizarre Shooting," and still another proclaims, "Taxi Driver Hero to Recover." A fourth clipping's headline reads "Parents Express Shock, Gratitude." It soon becomes clear that these parents are the Steensmas, the parents of Iris, because Mr. Steensma's voice is then heard reading a letter that has been received by Bickle, which informs us that they have retrieved Iris from New York and restored her to their home in Pittsburgh. Mr. Steensma enthusiastically thanks Bickle for making Iris's return possible.

It seems likely that Bickle will not see Iris again, as Mr. Steensma notes that they cannot afford another trip to New York. To this extent, this moment resembles the ending of *The Searchers*, in which John Wayne's Ethan Edwards has restored the stolen Debbie Edwards (Natalie Wood) to her home but does not join the joyous family reunion, instead turning away and heading off into the distance, becoming a classic Western lone hero. Indeed, Taubin notes that it was Edwards' loneliness that made Scorsese think of him as an appropriate model for Bickle (whereas screenwriter Schrader was more interested in Edwards as a character whose psychosexual problems drive him to violence).

Bickle might certainly remain lonely at the end of *Taxi Driver*, but those clippings indicate that he has essentially become a hero, even if he is still a somewhat anonymous one. The headlines, after all, like the title of the film, refer to him as "taxi driver" rather than by name. It is, in fact, clear that the emphasis on labeling him via his job suggests a certain lack of true individual identity, just as Arthur Fleck's taking on of the persona of "Joker" suggests something similar (although perhaps more radical). In *Taxi Driver*, meanwhile, we are then treated to one final sequence that makes the ending even more of a triumph for Bickle. Chatting with some other cabbies who are all parked in front of a hotel, Bickle finds that Betsy has gotten into the back of his cab. She looks especially dreamy in the back seat of his darkened cab. Palatine has won the presidential nomination, and it is now, Betsy mentions, 17 days until the election.[8] She also mentions that she has read about Bickle's exploits in the paper, and it is clear that she is intrigued by his newfound hero status. He drops her off, refuses her payment, and drives away with a terse "so long," accompanied by a slight smirk that suggests his sense that he has now gained the upper hand in their relationship, now being the one who is doing the rejecting.

This ending seems so unlikely that many observers have felt that it surely cannot be meant to be taken literally. Some observers have postulated that Bickle was actually killed in the shootout and that the rest of the film consists of his dying fantasies. Alternatively, the film certainly leaves open the possibility that Bickle did survive, but that this personally triumphant ending is still just his fantasy. To the extent that we question whether what we see on the screen in *Taxi Driver* in this ending or anywhere else is actually occurring within the world of the film or is only occurring within Bickle's mind, then *Taxi Driver* becomes a direct predecessor to *Joker* in terms of its interpretive uncertainty. At the same time, it is certainly the case that this sort of uncertainty plays a much smaller role in *Taxi Driver* than it does in *Joker*, which I take to be a marker of the extent to which *Taxi Driver* employs a fundamentally modernist aesthetic and epistemology (based on a belief in an existing reality that can be represented), while *Joker* employs postmodernist ones (based on a view of reality as having always already been constructed).

In this sense, it might be valuable to note that both Scorsese and Schrader have said that they do not regard the ending of *Taxi Driver* as Bickle's fantasy, dying or otherwise. If that is the case, then the ending of the film certainly portrays the New York media as showing sympathy for Bickle. However, this fact certainly does not mean that the film itself heroizes Bickle or presents him as a character with whom we are supposed to sympathize. Indeed, this reading of the film is surely best taken as a critique of the way in which the media have glorified Bickle's violent exploits—and (by extension) the way in which the media (and perhaps the general population) glorify and heroize violent acts in general.

This reading also, of course, could be extended to suggest that *Taxi Driver* might be read as a critique of the glorification of violence in *film*, much like the reference to *The Searchers* in *Mean Streets*. Of course, such criticisms are always walking a fine line in that an effective critique of the excessive representation of violence in film almost certainly requires that excessive violence be represented in the film that is performing the critique. And, once that excessive violence is shown in the film, there is always the possibility that someone will see the film as glorifying that violence. Indeed, *Taxi Driver* drew some of the same criticisms as *Joker* in terms of its treatment of violence, largely based on its failure entirely and unequivocally to repudiate the actions of its protagonist; it was also criticized by the eminent leftist critic Robin Wood for a political incoherence that Wood attributes to a fundamental conflict between the points of view of Scorsese (which Wood characterizes as "liberal humanist") and of Schrader (which Wood characterizes as "quasi-Fascist") (45). This incoherence, according to Wood, can also be partly attributed to a generic clash within the movie that produces a muddled view of the protagonist: *Taxi Driver*'s roots in the Western suggest Bickle as a version of the "gunfighter hero whose traditional function has always been to clean up the town"; at the same time, its overlap with the horror genre suggests Bickle as "the psychopath monster produced by an indefensible society" (47).

I think that Wood is absolutely on target to the extent that *Taxi Driver* can be faulted for attempting to represent genuine social problems of its era via the personal problems of its troubled protagonist. Its mix of genres might also lead to a certain political incoherence. I will discuss the political implications of *Joker* in much more detail in Chapters 8 through 10, but I will note for now that *Joker*'s mix of genres also includes the Western and the horror film, but then adds in extra dimensions because of its dialogue with the superhero film and because it is a historical period film. As a result, even though *Joker* includes much more overtly political material than does *Taxi Driver* (mostly in the form of the rebellion that builds throughout the film, erupting all-out near the end), it might be expected to be even more politically incoherent.

That this rebellion adopts Fleck as its iconic hero suggests an important parallel with the heroization of Bickle in *Taxi Driver*. Moreover, while we don't see anything quite as explicit in this sense in *Joker* as those newspaper clippings at the end of *Taxi Driver*, it is clear that reports of the subway shootings in the Gotham media (especially on television, clearly the dominant medium in Gotham, but also in the newspapers) have propelled Fleck to his unlikely hero status. The commuters aboard the train that Fleck rides on his way to Wayne Manor appear to be reading editions of two different local newspapers, both of which feature the growing rebellion as their front-page headline. One paper bears a huge headline reading "Vigilante Clown Still At Large," while the other paper's headline reads "Kill the Rich: A New Movement." Fleck, meanwhile, is viewing the interior of the "Vigilante Clown" paper, looking at a two-page layout on Wayne's announcement of his candidacy for mayor, including coverage of a planned protest at an upcoming gala at Wayne Hall. (The story on Wayne's candidacy, incidentally, also contains an ad for "TV Emporium," in another sign of the centrality of television to the society of Gotham.)

No Joke: Todd Phillips's *Joker* and American Culture

We can only speculate about whether this newspaper story and his disastrous visit to Wayne Manor soon afterward together triggered Fleck to fantasize the entire later sequence at Wayne Hall. In terms of the relevance of *Taxi Driver* here, what is important is that the "vigilante clown" seems to be receiving some of the same kind of press coverage that had been given to the "taxi driver hero." The fact that these stories help to inspire mass civil unrest, however, does take the critique in *Joker* beyond the media to the general population, suggesting a populace so filled with anger and resentment that they are willing to embrace a murderer. Of course, we have even more reason to suspect that virtually anything depicted in *Joker* is a fantasy than we do with *Taxi Driver*, but the fact that the rebellion in *Joker* is so public and seems to be so widely acknowledged tends to suggest that this rebellion really does occur within the world of the film (and that it really was at least partly triggered by the subway shootings). Of course, it is not entirely clear that Fleck actually is the vigilante clown so admired by the protestors in the streets of Gotham, but certainly seems to be the case that he imagines himself to be that figure and thus to have finally been noticed and acknowledged as a figure of value. In this sense, the outcome of *Joker* closely parallels that of *Taxi Driver*, except that the former essentially ends with a coda that calls Fleck's triumphant conclusion into question by showing him back in Arkham State Hospital (where he might, in fact, have been all along).

Joker and *The King of Comedy*

The King of Comedy has a conclusion that resembles that of *Taxi Driver*, as well as the provisional ending of *Joker*, about which I will have more to say below. Most obviously, though, *The King of Comedy* serves as a predecessor to *Joker* in that it features a lonely and troubled protagonist who longs to be a successful comedian and whose main comedic role model is both a comedian and a talk show host. In this case, the talk show host is one Jerry Langford (played by comedy legend Jerry Lewis), while the aspiring comedian is one Rupert Pupkin, played by De Niro again, which adds a twist of irony to the relationship between *The King of Comedy* and *Joker*, given De Niro's casting as the talk show host in the latter.

In many ways, the actual plot of *The King of Comedy* resembles *Joker*'s plot more closely than does the plot of *Taxi Driver*, although *The King of Comedy* was released a year after the events of *Joker*, so that in this case there would be no chance that Arthur Fleck might have seen the film and been inspired by it. However, *The King of Comedy* was filmed, (largely in

New York City) from June to October of 1981, so that the filming ended almost exactly at the same time the action of *Joker* begins, making the events of the two films very close to contemporaneous, given that there is no indication that the action of *The King of Comedy* is to be considered as anything but roughly contemporaneous with the making and distribution of the film.

That action begins with a sequence, interrupted by the opening credits, in which Langford tapes a show and then exits the studio through a crowd of adoring fans (including Pupkin), who are waiting outside hoping to score autographs. Pupkin claims not to be as devoted to autograph hunting as some of the others, but when Langford appears, we realize that Pupkin is dressed exactly like his hero (except for his decidedly unstylish white belt and shoes, which perhaps mark him as a poor copy of his model). For his part, Langford pushes his way through the crowd (granting no autographs) and into the waiting limo, only to find that a crazed female fan (Masha, played by Sandra Bernhard) is already waiting for him there. Pupkin rescues Langford by pulling him back out of the car until Masha can be extracted, after which Pupkin himself follows Langford as he gets back into the car. Pupkin explains that he is an aspiring comedian who has long studied Langford's work and is now ready to take advantage of any opportunity Langford might be able to offer him. This encounter starts a long string of contacts in which Pupkin essentially stalks and eventually kidnaps his hero (with the help of Masha and a toy gun). He then leverages his hostage into an appearance on *The Jerry Langford Show*. That appearance (which involves an unfunny monologue about how neglected and abused Pupkin was in his childhood) then propels Pupkin to fame, boosted even more by his abduction of Langford and subsequent arrest and imprisonment. By the end of the film, Pupkin has been released on parole, the memoirs he wrote in prison have become a best-seller (soon to be a major motion picture), and Pupkin himself returns triumphantly to the airwaves.

Beyond the obvious overall plot parallels, the local correspondences between *The King of Comedy* and *Joker* are numerous and often striking. Pupkin, for example, likes to practice for his hoped-for appearance on the Langford show by rehearsing in his apartment, where he has, in fact, gone one better than Fleck by setting up a full replica studio, including cardboard cutouts of Langford and guest Liza Minnelli (who had starred with De Niro in Scorsese's *New York, New York* in 1977). Pupkin also apparently shares that apartment with his mother—or at least the voice of his mother (supplied by Scorsese's own mother, Catherine Scorsese)— which can occasionally be heard hectoring him in the film. However, given that we never actually see her (and given that, during his monologue on the Langford show, Pupkin claims that his mother has been dead for nine years), it seems quite possible that Pupkin simply imagines occasionally hearing his mother's voice.

Pupkin, in fact, often shows an uncertain grasp on reality. Immediately after his encounter with Langford in the beginning of the film (in which it is already clear that Langford does not particularly welcome Pupkin's overtures), we immediately cut to a restaurant where Pupkin and Langford are having lunch. Suddenly, it appears that they are close friends. Now, however, Langford is playing the supplicant, virtually pleading with Pupkin (now apparently a star) to take over his show for six weeks as a personal favor. This conversation, however, is punctuated by cuts back to Pupkin in his home basement studio, acting out this pretend conversation, with his mother's voice yelling at him to quieten down. As with the early scene in *Joker*, in which Fleck watches Murray Franklin with his mother then imagines himself actually on the show, there is no ambiguity about the fact that this scene is a mere fantasy.

In general, the line between fantasy and reality is much clearer in *The King of Comedy* than it is in *Joker*, although it is, in fact, sometimes difficult to tell what is really happening in the world of the film and what is only happening in Pupkin's mind. Immediately after the imaginary luncheon conversation with Langford, Pupkin goes to a bar where a beautiful young black woman is working at the bartender. This woman, Rita (played by Diahnne Abbott, then De Niro's real-world wife), will turn out to play much the same role in *The King of Comedy* that Sophie plays in *Joker*. Pupkin has apparently had something of a crush on Rita since they were together in high school 15 or 20 years earlier, although it is clear that she barely remembers him. They begin to talk, and he asks her out to dinner. She says it might be a bit late for that, at which he laughs heartily (but inauthentically). But then, while the same laugh continues, they suddenly *are* at dinner. He attempts to wow her with his autograph collection and with stories of his own impending fame, which he hopes to share with her, perhaps beginning with a weekend with Langford at Langford's "summer house."

Nothing that happens in this scene seems absolutely impossible, but the editing of the scene, with that sudden cut from bar to dinner, calls the entire scene into question, especially as another sudden cut at the end of Pupkin's date with Rita finds him once again back in his basement studio. In any case, whatever one makes of this particular scene, it is clear that Pupkin envisions his relationship with Rita as being much more significant than it really is, even if it is not as entirely imaginary as

Fleck's relationship with Sophie. For example, in one later scene, Pupkin does apparently take Rita out to Langford's palatial summer house. Langford, however, sternly rejects the visit, leading to the end of Pupkin's relationship with Rita and propelling Pupkin into the plot to kidnap Langford with Masha.

The imaginary nature of most of Pupkin's relationship with Rita had already been made very clear in a key scene in which he envisions himself as a guest on an episode of *The Jerry Langford Show*, even as he is, in fact, sitting in the reception area at the offices of Langford's show, unable to get in to see Langford.[9] In this episode, as a surprise to Pupkin, Langford has arranged for Pupkin and Rita to be married on the show, with ceremonies presided over by none other than their old high school principal, George Kapp,[10] who is now a justice of the peace. Meanwhile, musical accompaniment is provided by Victor Borge at the piano, adding showbiz flair to the event.[11] Kapp begins the ceremony with an apology to Pupkin on behalf of all those who doubted or abused him, making the moment even more of a triumph for Pupkin. Then, however, before the actual vows, Kapp throws it to a commercial, after which the film cuts back to reality.

This obviously imaginary episode of the Langford show illustrates the fact that, in most cases, *The King of Comedy* differs from *Joker* in that the film supplies at least some internal evidence that makes it possible for viewers to distinguish fantasy from reality, even if Pupkin cannot. To an extent, this fact can again be taken as a sign that Scorsese's film employs a fundamentally modernist aesthetic, while Phillips's film employs a postmodernist one that is much less respectful of the boundary between fantasy and reality. The one major exception is the film's ending, in which Pupkin receives such an unlikely level of success that it is tempting to wonder whether this ending (which so closely resembles that of *Taxi Driver*, but with a lighter tone) might simply be Pupkin's fantasy—perhaps entertained from behind bars. Nothing in the film, however, overtly indicates that this is the case, even though it seems unlikely that Pupkin's success and fame could ever be so extreme, his picture, for example, appearing simultaneously on the covers all major magazines on the newsstands.[12]

Ultimately, *The King of Comedy* was clearly a major influence on *Joker*, as Todd Phillips has openly admitted. And this influence goes beyond the basic scenario, to specific scenes and motifs, to the style of editing. The same can also be said for *Mean Streets* and *Taxi Driver*, so it is clear that *Joker* almost goes out of its way to identify Scorsese as an especially important predecessor, however much it might also be the case that *Joker* evokes the entire period of 1970s and 1980s American film. Surely these connections can be taken largely as an homage to Scorsese's early films and to the ways in which they took American film in some innovative new directions, some of which ultimately helped to make films like *Joker* possible. To an extent, then, Phillips seems to have selected Scorsese as a model out of admiration, although it is also the case that one might consider Scorsese here to be a specific exemplification of the larger phenomenon of New Hollywood film, chosen because it is much easier to make connections to specific individual films than to broad phenomena. At the same time, the numerous similarities between *Joker* and films such as *Mean Streets*, *Taxi Driver*, and *The King of Comedy* is also a key marker of the difference between these films. Like the modernist artists lauded by Jameson for their ability to develop distinctive individual styles, Scorsese was exploring genuinely new cinematic territory in his early films.[13] He did not, in short, have himself as a predecessor. Phillips, on the other hand, *did* have Scorsese as a predecessor from whom he could borrow in a postmodern fashion.

Notes

1 Standard DC Comics continuity holds that Bruce Wayne's parents had been killed just after they and eight-year-old Bruce had attended a screening of the 1940 film *The Mark of Zorro*, although in some versions the film involved is the 1920 silent film of the same title. *Zorro, the Gay Blade* is presumably the film the Waynes were attending, as all of the other films referenced in the scene would seem to be inappropriate viewing for young Bruce. Meanwhile, Zorro himself is generally understood to have been an inspiration for the creation of the character of Batman (as well as for Bruce's decision to *become* Batman).

2 According to the Internet Movie Database (IMDb.com), the film was shot in New York and New Jersey from September 10 to December 3, 2018, which explains why the people in the film seem to be dressed for autumn and matches the date of October 15 as the beginning of the action.

3 See Curran for a discussion of this apparent "Easter-egg" connection.

4 This comment is not mere conjecture. It is well known that Paul Schrader, the screenwriter of *Taxi Driver*, employed *The Searchers* as a narrative model. Indeed, Amy Taubin describes *The Searchers* as the "ur-text for Taxi Driver," although she also notes that Schrader's vision of *The Searchers* was somewhat darker than Scorsese's (25).

5 Among other things, the Waverly was the original home (beginning in 1976) of midnight showings of *The Rocky Horror Picture Show* (1975), spawning a long-running pop cultural phenomenon.

6 It is also worth noting that both Eastwood—in *Dirty Harry* (1971)—and Bronson—in *Death Wish* (1974)—were probably best known during this period for films in which they played characters with vigilante tendencies that link them to Travis Bickle.

7 There is, as Žižek notes, even a subgroup of incels known as "clowncels," though he does not see Fleck as operating in the spirit of this group ("More on *Joker*").

8 This information, incidentally, would mean that *Taxi Driver* ends on October 15, 1976—the exact day and date on which *Joker* begins five years later.

9 This episode features another guest who is a woman psychologist/sex therapist (in this case, Dr. Joyce Brothers, in a cameo role) as one of Langford's guests. Brothers, of course, was ever-present as a guest on talk shows of the 1980s, as was Ruth Westheimer, so this appearance is not a big surprise. My guess is that the sex therapist we see on *Live with Murray Franklin* is more a nod to Brothers and *The King of Comedy* than to Westheimer and *The Dark Knight Returns*, although it could, of course, be both.

10 Kapp, played by himself, was actually a high school chemistry teacher in Brooklyn.

11 Known for his combination of comedy and music, the Copenhagen-born Borge had been a prominent presence on American television since the 1950s. He was often referred to as the "Clown Prince of Denmark."

12 In addition, New York's "Son of Sam" law, passed in 1977 in the wake of the arrest of serial killer David Berkowitz, would have made the publication of Pupkin's book problematic.

13 This is not to say that some new Hollywood directors were not already openly postmodernist. The central example here would appear to be Brian De Palma, whose early borrowings from Hitchcock would seem to epitomize the phenomenon of postmodern pastiche, as described by Jameson. Thus, John Belton calls De Palma the "most postmodern" of the filmmakers of the "film-school generation," where "film-school generation" is essentially a synonym for "New Hollywood" (307). Similarly, I have elsewhere argued that "De Palma's own recycling of images and motifs from Hitchcock demonstrates, perhaps more than any other single phenomenon, the way in which the object of representation in the artifacts of postmodern culture is often not reality but other cultural artifacts" (*Postmodern Hollywood* 124).

CHAPTER FOUR

Arthur, Portrait of a Serial Killer
Joker and Horror Film

If *Joker* resonates in special ways with the early films of Scorsese, it also has a special relation with a number of types of horror films from a time roughly contemporary with the historical setting of its action and to a time roughly contemporaneous with its production and release. For example, the subject matter of *Joker* has a great deal in common with that of the slasher films that were so prominent in the 1980s. Meanwhile, as a high-budget, well-made studio product, *Joker* also has much in common with the wave of "prestige" horror films produced in the 2010s. And, of course, both of these intersections correspond to the ability of *Joker* to engage in broader dialogues with the dual historical contexts of the times of its action and of its production. *Joker*, of course, is able to maintain this dual focus partly because there are real parallels between the 1980s and the late 2010s and partly because the 1980s and the 2010s participate in the same historical process involving the growth of neoliberalism. Of course, if the 1980s and 2010s are in many ways very similar, the recent nostalgia for the 1980s might seem to be mostly displaced, but the nostalgic tone of the Reagan years themselves clearly provides a key source for the recent nostalgia for those years.

From this point of view, I will begin this chapter with a discussion of two recent films that follow *Joker* in looking back to the 1980s in a mode of horror, rather than nostalgia. The first of these, Sean Durkin's *The Nest* (2020), overlaps considerably with the horror genre, even if it does not, at first glance, appear to be an all-out horror film. It contains no murders and no conventional monsters, although this story of a family that unravels in the face of 1980s-style striving and greed essentially treats the socio-economic climate of the 1980s as a monster. The film stars Jude Law as Rory O'Hara, a working-class Englishman who has worked his way up the economic ladder, eventually achieving success as a stock broker after moving to New York. His attempts to continue his upward climb include a return to England, where he moves his American family into a capacious country manor that has all the hallmarks of a haunted house, though it is haunted, not by spirits, but by the historical legacy of class inequality and exploitation that made such houses possible in the first place. Conditions go from bad to worse, and the whole family is cracking beneath the strain by the end of this understated, but powerful, narrative. Meanwhile, the film also suggests that the economic inequality that has haunted Western history reaches a particularly dangerous point amid the scramble for wealth that marked the 1980s, among other things reminding us that many conditions in Thatcherite Britain were quite similar to those in Reaganite America, both of which would eventually morph into today's global neoliberalism, in a historical narrative that provides important background to *Joker*.

Also of interest among recent horror films is Jon Stevenson's *Rent-A-Pal* (2020), which shows some evidence of being influenced by *Joker* in its focus on David Brower (Brian Landis Folkins), a lonely guy who lives with his mother, whom he eventually murders, although in this case he himself is killed (by being stabbed with a pair of scissors, the weapon used by Arthur Fleck to kill his former co-worker Randall) before he can claim a second victim. In addition to certain basic plot similarities, *Rent-A-Pal* seems to be set in the 1980s, given Brower's attempts to find love via a videocassette-based video dating service, a service that eventually supplies him with an apparently haunted videotape on which one Andy (Wil Wheaton) offers to befriend Brower, but ultimately drives him to murder. As with Fleck and *Joker*, how much of this plot actually takes place in the world of the film and how much arises from Brower's hallucinations is left open to viewer interpretation. But the fact that Brower's emotionally impoverished existence takes place in the 1980s delivers still another telling indictment of the Reagan decade.

Specific horror films have not figured prominently in discussions of films that directly influenced the making of *Joker*, although there has been some discussion about whether *Joker* qualifies as a horror film. After all, it was released at a time when sophisticated "prestige" or "elevated" horror movies were becoming a major phenomenon in American film. Films such as Jordan Peele's *Get Out* (2017) and Ari Aster's *Hereditary* (2018) were among the most important films released in the years leading up to *Joker*. Perhaps, then, it is no surprise that one of the most enthusiastic early reviewers of *Joker*, Phil de Semlyen, declared *Joker* to be "a truly nightmarish vision of late-era capitalism—arguably the best social horror film since *Get Out*." In another early review, Chris Evangelista called *Joker* "a violent, nihilistic horror film masquerading as both a character drama and a comic book movie." Other reviewers have been more equivocal about the status of *Joker* as a horror film, as when Will Ashton concludes that *Joker* gives us "a chance to see inside the mind of a madman and explore the inner recesses of turmoil, grief, anger and, yes, terror that floats around inside his conscious. There's reason to believe that this description alone makes it qualified to be categorized as a horror movie." After careful consideration, Drew Dietsch, writing for the horror film website *Bloody Disgusting*, concludes that *Joker* is not only a horror film, but "one of 2019's biggest horror films" ("Horrors"). Dietsch even suggests two specific horror films that he sees as being "like cousins" to *Joker*: *Maniac* (1980) and *Henry: Portrait of a Serial Killer* (1986). Elsewhere on the same site, Dietsch proposes a list of seven horror films that should be watched as preparation for watching *Joker*, including these two, as well as *Man Bites Dog* (1992), *American Psycho* (2000), *The Last Circus* (2010), the 2012 remake of *Maniac*, and *The Voices* (2014) ("7 Horror Films").

Dietsch's list is a good one, even though it might be a bit heavy on relatively obscure European horror comedies. Indeed, the fact that films such as *Man Bites Dog*, *The Last Circus*, and *The Voices* (which I am fairly certain were not important influences on Phillips) can illuminate *Joker* in some interesting ways can be taken as a testament to the intertextual richness of Phillips's film, which sends out so many feelers toward other texts that connections can be found even when they were not intentionally established by the filmmakers. *Man Bites Dog*, for example, is an oddly comic Belgian mockumentary in which a film crew follows a serial killer as he goes about his "business," eventually becoming implicated in his killings. In so doing, it addresses some of the same issues with regard to the modern media that are also important in *Joker*. To me, though, the charming and eloquent serial killer of *Man Bites Dog* has very little in common with Arthur Fleck, just as its mockumentary style has little to do with the sophisticated cinematic style of *Joker*. The other films mentioned by Dietsch seem more relevant, however, as I will describe below, in conjunction with a discussion of many others, all of which can be roughly sorted into three categories: killer clown movies, films about killers with an uncertain grip on reality, and films about psychotic killers, including the important horror category of the slasher film. After briefly discussing some of the horror films in each of these categories that I think can contribute to our understanding of *Joker*, I will conclude this chapter with a summation of the various things that *Joker* has in common with the horror genre as a whole and of the various ways on which reading the film within the context of horror film can enrich our understanding of it.

No Joke: Todd Phillips's *Joker* and American Culture

Killer Clown Movies

Given that Arthur Fleck begins *Joker* as a clown before becoming a serial killer, one subgenre of horror films that seems particularly pertinent to *Joker* is the killer clown film. It is also relevant to the political significance of *Joker* that multiple commentators have suggested killer clowns as a fitting emblem for the Trump era. Perhaps, then, it was no surprise that *American Horror Story: Cult*, the seventh season of that long-running television horror series (the first season produced and released during the Trump presidency), turned to killer clowns as a central expression of its vision of an America gone frighteningly mad.[1] It also features a central villain who is first seen as a murderous MAGA lunatic in the person of Kai Anderson (Evan Peters), though Kai ultimately begins to pursue an agenda of his own. He is, in fact, principally an agent of chaos, although he does have high ambitions, becoming first the leader of a gang of killer clowns and later the leader of a dangerous cult (and a senatorial candidate). Indeed, as the title indicates, *Cult* points to a whole series of cult phenomena in American history, with cult leaders such as Charles Manson, Jim Jones, and David Koresh figuring as predecessors to Kai (and even played by Peters in flashback segments). Trump and the atmosphere surrounding him are meanwhile suggested as the culmination of this cult legacy. As Kai puts it, "politics now is all a cult of personality."

Reviewing *American Horror Story: Cult* for *Rolling Stone* magazine, Jenna Scherer notes the timeliness of its motifs, although she sees it as a bit too broad and unrealistic to be effective as satire. For my purposes, it is also significant that she calls Kai "a classic genre villain in the vein of the Joker," thus suggesting the comic book villain as an appropriate embodiment of certain energies of the Trump era, two years before the release of *Joker*. And the analogy has continued. In response to the January 6, 2021, Capitol insurrection, actor Jim Carrey tweeted out a GIF of Trump as a killer clown (with a golf ball nose). And James Poniewozik, reporting on that same insurrection, referred back to *American Horror Story: Cult* in noting that we now "live in the era of weaponized irony and killer clowns." *Joker*, it would seem, really does capture something fundamental about the American political climate in the time it was produced—and in the time it is set.

It is no secret, of course, that clowns can be scary. There is even a medical term, "coulrophobia," that describes an unreasoning fear of clowns. There have even been occasional popular outbreaks of anti-clown hysteria, a recent example of which was the social-media-fueled great clown scare of 2016, in which sightings of sinister clowns were reported in a variety of locations in the United States and then Britain in the weeks leading up to Halloween (and to the U.S. presidential election).[2] Given the long legacy of scary clowns, it is not surprising that there is no shortage of horror films that have taken advantage of the frightening potential of clowns, although some of them have also utilized the supposedly comic purpose of clowns to produce horror comedies. Perhaps the best-known of these is the preposterous cult classic *Killer Klowns from Outer Space* (1988), a film about deadly alien invaders who happen to look exactly like circus clowns and who come to earth in search of humans to harvest for food. This film, other than the fact that it was made in 1980s and thus reflects some of the sensibilities of that time, has very little in common with *Joker*, however. More serious horror films involving clowns do a bit more to illuminate *Joker*, at least in the sense of placing Arthur Fleck within a tradition of representing clowns as individuals who might have a tendency to turn to murder. In addition, it is worth noting that the original comic book version of the Joker character can be seen as an important forerunner of all the modern evil clowns in horror movies.

In addition, it should be noted that the 1980s were, in general, a particularly rich period in the production of fictional images of evil clowns, possibly influenced by the Pogo the Clown persona of serial killer John Wayne Gacy.[3] The important 1982 horror film *Poltergeist* (directed by Tobe Hooper and produced by Spielberg) was perhaps the first major film to take advantage of this inspiration with its use of a possessed clown doll as a key horror image.[4] Then, the late 1980s saw a spate of killer clown movies, none of which was a particularly great work of cinematic art, but which cumulatively suggested a growing interest in the motif at the time. Perhaps, though, what films such as *Funland* (1987), *Blood Harvest* (1987), and *Out of the Dark* (1989) have most in common (other than the presence of killer clowns) is a kind of gleefully inappropriate subversion of the stodgy capitalist conformism of the Reagan era. It might be sufficient to note that the killer clown of *Blood Harvest*, for example, is played by none other than Tiny Tim to give an idea of the tenor of these films.

One of reasons for the sudden uptick in the production of killer clown films in the late 1980s might have been the success of Stephen King's 1986 novel *It*. Here, the "It" of the title is a supernatural, dimension-hopping, shape-shifting entity that can take on a variety of forms, showing a special proclivity for taking on the form of whatever frightens a specific victim the most. It is thus an ideal, all-purpose horror film monster, although the principal form it takes in the novel is that of Pennywise the Dancing Clown, a choice that is itself potentially a testament to the scariness of clowns. In any case, this clown is particularly deadly, returning every

27 years (thus, essentially, once every generation) to the town of Derry, Maine, for a rampage of killing, especially of children.

King's novel was adapted in television mini-series form in 1990, with Tim Curry turning in a bravura performance as Pennywise. Meanwhile, like Pennywise himself, the story would return again 27 years later, in the form of Andy Muschietti's *It* (2017), which grossed over $700 million worldwide and thus became the top-grossing horror film of all time, maintaining that title until it was supplanted by *Joker* two years later (if one considers *Joker* a horror film). In the film, which begins with a prologue set in the fall of 1988 but is mostly set in the summer of 1989, Pennywise attacks Derry, but is defeated by a combined effort of a marginalized group of young teen outsider "types." All of the members of this group are in one way or another hampered by their family situations, while they are also seriously oppressed by a gang of local bullies, so that Pennywise is definitely only one of their problems.

Indeed, *It* is as much an exploration of what it is like to come of age in a small town in the late 1980s as it is a horror film. Its focus on the 1980s, including heavy use of period music in the soundtrack, has a nostalgic air, as the kids tool about town on their bikes in what appears to be a simpler age. In this, *It* participates in a wave of recent films that have been dominated by 1980s nostalgia, including such entries as Steven Spielberg's *Ready Player One* (2018). At times, *It* seems almost Spielbergian itself, except that it refuses to paint the 1980s in entirely rosy hues: most of the characters, in fact, have pretty terrible lives. Probably the most interesting thing about the film's treatment of 1980s nostalgia, meanwhile, is the fact that King's novel, written just over 30 years before the release of the film, is filled with 1950s nostalgia, which is then moved forward to the 1980s in the film, a phenomenon that makes clear that the current wave of 1980s nostalgia in American popular culture is largely a simple transplantation of the wave of 1950s nostalgia that was so prominent in American culture in the 1970s and 1980s.[5]

That the film version of *It* appeared 27 years after the television adaptation, just as Pennywise appears in Derry every 27 years, points to the fact that there is a gap of essentially one generation between the 1980s and the 2010s, just as there was a gap of a generation between the 1950s and the 1980s. This fact also illuminates the phenomenon of cultural nostalgia that has been so prominent in recent American popular culture. In short, filmmakers and other creators of the 1980s were perhaps remembering their own childhood experiences when producing works that were nostalgic for the 1980s, just as creators of the 2010s were nostalgically looking back on their own childhood memories of the 1980s. From this point of view, of course, it is also worth noting that *Joker* was produced roughly one generation after the time of its action, but that it clearly opposes these sorts of nostalgic representations.

Of course, killer clowns have remained continuously prominent in horror film beyond the 1980s, as in the rather dark *Carnival of Souls* (1998), which overtly alludes to the 1962 horror classic of the same title, but otherwise has relatively little to do with the original, shifting its emphasis from ontological confusion to a clown figure who also happens to be a dangerous stalker. Other recent examples have involved the work of well-known horror film directors, indicating the growing prominence of killer clowns in American horror. Such films include Rob Zombie's *House of 1000 Corpses* (2003), *The Devil's Rejects* (2005), and *31* (2016), all of which feature sinister clown figures. The decidedly dark comedy *Clown* (2014), meanwhile, was co-produced by Eli Roth and directed by Jon Watts, a rising star who would eventually become the director of the big-budget superhero films *Spider-Man: Homecoming* (2017) and *Spider-Man: Far from Home* (2019). *Clown* mixes a sort of demonic possession story with gross-out body horror, as a cursed clown suit turns its wearer into a demonic, child-eating monster. And, of course, there is the figure of Art the Clown, a slasher figure who is central to *All Hallow's Eve* (2013), *Terrifier* (2016), and *Terrifier 2* (2021), all directed by Damien Leone.

Art the Clown is not fully developed in *All Hallow's Eve*, but he emerges as a truly gruesome and horrifying figure in *Terrifier*, only a year before the film adaptation of *It*. *Terrifier* is a film that loops back to the slasher film Golden Age of the 1980s, sometimes trying to beat that decade at its own bloody game. *Terrifier* is little more than a sequence of gruesome and bloody killings, with no apparent allegorical (or other) subtext. Here, Art the Clown (played by David Howard Thornton) undertakes a series of particularly violent and bloody killings that are reminiscent of those in 1980s slasher films but that sometimes veer into splatter film territory.[6] In one scene, for example, Art hangs a young naked woman upside down and then saws her in half lengthwise with a hacksaw, starting at the genitals. If that famous scene in which Freddy Kruger's claws approach Nancy Thompson's crotch in the bathtub was horrifying, this one is much more so—although it also teeters on the brink of ridiculousness and self-parody, making the purported misogyny of the slasher film all too explicit. Art also occasionally employs a gun for his killings, which is unusual in a slasher film, but which makes him even more of a predecessor to Arthur Fleck (who is essentially his namesake, "Art" being a common diminutive for "Arthur"). This film has a twist ending of sorts, but cleverness is not its forte: it's more of an in-your-face, bash-on-the-head assault. And Art (who never even speaks in the film) is a humorless killing machine (who also has some of the seeming invulnerability and ability to come back from the dead displayed by slashers such as Michael Myers and Jason Voorhees).

Meanwhile, if the original novel of *It* might have inspired the production of more killer clown movies in the late 1980s, the huge commercial success of the 2017 theatrical film of *It* no doubt contributed to the virtual explosion in the production of such movies since 2017. The wave of clownsploitation films to have appeared since 2017 includes such titles as *Circus Kane* (2017), *Clowntergeist* (2017), *Crispy's Curse* (2017), *Crepitus* (2018), *Clown Motel Massacre* (2018), *Don't Look* (2018), *Gags the Clown* (2018), *Clown Motel: Spirits Arise* (2019), *Clownado* (2019), *Haunt* (2019), *Wrinkles the Clown* (2019), *The Jack in the Box* (2019), *Drown the Clown* (2020), and *On Halloween* (2020). One might, of course, add *Joker* to this list, even though it obviously stands far apart from the other films in this list in a number of ways, including the fact that the clowns in these films tend to have virtually no psychological depth. Nevertheless, the very existence of this phenomenon points to one more way in which *Joker* was in tune with the pop culture ecology of its time, just as its subject matter is very much in tune with the historical reality of the 1980s.

Finally, perhaps the most interesting European film on Deitsch's list of horror films relevant to *Joker* is the Spanish horror comedy *Last Circus*, which features a murderous clown whose killing spree is triggered by his own tragic history. *Last Circus* is also one of a number of Spanish horror films (and films with horror connections that are not strictly horror films themselves) that look back to the Spanish Civil War or to the subsequent period of fascist rule in Spain—times that were, in historical reality, invested with considerable horror in their own right.[7] Among other things, these films as a group resemble *Joker* in that they employ horrific fictional events set in a past time in order to comment upon the political climate of that time, with potential implications for the present, as well. In addition to featuring a killer clown, *The Last Circus* is relevant to *Joker* in that it is also a brilliantly shot and touching work of art (itself nominated for the Golden Lion in 2010); it presents a truly compelling portrait of a central character who is not only a clown, but has been abused and humiliated all his life, ultimately becoming a murderous avenger. Set mostly in 1973, the film combines absurd humor with abject violence to present a portrait of a Spain that is still under Franco's rule but is riven with conflict and contradiction.

Movie Killers with an Uncertain Grip on Reality

Joker also taps into an extensive tradition of films about serial killers with an uncertain grip on reality, going back at least to Alfred Hitchcock's *Psycho* (1960), in which Norman Bates suffers from a serious mental illness that warps his perceptions of reality. Furthermore, this illness has been furthered by his problematic relationship with his mother, whom he ultimately killed. Bates is thus an extremely important forerunner of Arthur Fleck, even though *Psycho* lacks the radical interpretive uncertainty that runs through *Joker*, largely because Bates is not the point-of-view character in most of *Psycho*. At the same time, *Psycho* is a complex work of art that violates (often playfully) a number of audience expectations. According to Linda Williams, who sees *Psycho* as a marker of the beginning of postmodernism in film, the film is Hitchcock's most popular not because audiences are awed by its artistry but because they enjoy watching it, playing with their own identities as they do so. For her, *Psycho*

> needs to be seen not as an exceptional and transgressive experience working against the classical norms of visual pleasure, but rather as an important turning point in the pleasurable destabilizing of sexual identity in American film history: it is the moment when the experience of going to the movies began to be constituted as providing a certain generally transgressive sexualized thrill of promiscuous abandonment to indeterminate, "other" identities. (*Psycho*, 103)

Williams here touches on an aspect of *Psycho* that is highly relevant to *Joker*, which can also be quite formally playful (as in its use of innovative cuts), despite its dark subject matter. She also, however, identifies an element of *Psycho* that has influenced any number of films that came after it but that is largely missing in *Joker*: the primarily sexual energies that drive Bates's pathology.

Two of the most interesting films about killers with an uncertain grip on reality that are especially relevant to *Joker* both star Christian Bale (the actor who is perhaps most closely associated with Batman films) as their murderous protagonists. In particular, both Brad Anderson's *The Machinist* (2004) and Mary Harron's *American Psycho* (2000) feature Bale in lead roles as psychologically disturbed (apparent) killers who confuse fantasy with reality, making it finally unclear whether they actually committed their murders or not. *The Machinist* also resembles *Joker* in

No Joke: Todd Phillips's *Joker* and American Culture

that its lead actor lost large amounts of weight in order to take on an emaciated appearance appropriate to the character, an appearance that is particularly striking in comparison with Bale's impressive, sleekly muscled physique in *American Psycho*. These two films contrast in other ways as well, including the fact that Bale's Trevor Reznik in *The Machinist* is a downtrodden working-class character who shares much of Arthur Fleck's situation as an outcast from the American dream, while Patrick Bateman in *American Psycho* seems to be a highly successful investment banker, although this film rivals even *Joker* in the extent to which we can never be quite sure what is actually going on.

Bateman is ostensibly living the American dream, though, in his case, this dream turns out to be a nightmare (with significant satirical implications). One interesting aspect of *American Psycho* that links it to *Joker* is the fact that it takes place in 1987, just as the 1991 Bret Easton Ellis novel on which it is based is set in the late 1980s. And Bateman, of course, is the very embodiment of the self-serving capitalist greed that characterized the Reagan era, his mental instability serving as a demonstration of just how psychologically damaging the ethos of that era could be. Late in the film, Bateman (if he even *is* Bateman) is sitting at a table with several acquaintances who, as a group, represent very much the same kind of "Wall Street guys" that are killed on the subway in *Joker*. Then, Reagan himself comes on a television in the restaurant speaking calmly about the "Iran–Contra mess." One of the men at the table, Timothy Bryce (played by Justin Theroux, who also has a cameo role in *Joker* as a guest on Murray Franklin's show), reacts angrily to Reagan's cool and glib response to this scandal: "How can he lie like that? How can he pull that shit? How can he be so, I don't know, cool about it?" Bateman's response is a spate of inauthentic laughing, almost like one of Fleck's laughing fits, and the film hints that he probably sympathizes with Reagan, although he ultimately declines to engage with Bryce on the matter. Instead (still reeling from recent evidence that he might have imagined some of the killings he thought he committed), he retreats into his own mind and into an interior monologue that ends the film with a Joker-like embrace of chaos and nihilism.

If *American Psycho* demonstrates the subtle comic potential of violent serial killer films, *The Voices* (2014), directed by Marjane Satrapi (of *Persepolis* fame), is a black comedy that stays in a broadly comic mode almost throughout. It is, however, quite grisly, and there are a few moments when things get deadly serious. They certainly get deadly. Ryan Reynolds stars as protagonist Jerry Hickfang, a troubled and lonely young man who has apparently been psychotic since childhood and who (as long as he stays off his medication) has a tendency to hear voices, especially the voices of his dog and cat (also supplied by Reynolds), which urge him to act in opposite directions, much like those old cartoons in which a character is given conflicting advice from an angel and a devil, who stand on his shoulders and duel for control. The cat, of course, always comes down on the devilish side. In addition to hearing these voices, Hickfang has a great deal of difficulty distinguishing between reality and fantasy in general, another symptom of the serious mental illness that he apparently inherited from his mother and which became particularly acute when he killed her during his childhood.[8] In the course of the film, he also kills most of the other women he encounters, including his two love interests (played by Gemma Arterton and Anna Kendrick). He then butchers their bodies into small pieces and stashes their heads in his refrigerator, à la Jeffrey Dahmer. Subsequently, he perceives the heads as being alive and speaking to him. By the end, though, Hickfang and his pets have also been killed. Then, in a final weird twist, Hickfang posthumously joins the four women he murdered in the course of the film, happily dancing and singing with Jesus, presumably in heaven. This film has enough in common with *Joker* that it almost cries out for comparison, even though its tone is so very different from that of *Joker*. *Joker*'s intense engagement with cultural and political history is missing as well, so that, as a whole, this film, among other things, demonstrates just how unusually rich *Joker* really is, just as the greatness of Joaquin Phoenix's performance is highlighted by comparison with Reynolds, who does a perfectly credible job, but one that falls far short of Phoenix's in conveying the intense anguish undergone by his character.

There are, of course, any number of other films about psychotic killers, while such killers, by definition, tend to have difficulty getting a grasp on reality. There is, however, one particular phenomenon in American film that involves a special type of serial killer. This phenomenon is the so-called slasher film, which features especially violent, over-the-top serial killers who commit a series of graphic and gruesome murders. Such films can count *Psycho* as an important forerunner, while films such as *Black Christmas* (1974) and *The Texas Chain Saw Massacre* (1974) can be considered early slasher films. But the real heyday of the American slasher film began with John Carpenter's *Halloween* (1978) and ran through most of the 1980s, with a sort of coda in *The Silence of the Lambs* (1991), though it has been resurrected several times since then. In short, the slasher film was the most important phenomenon in American horror film during roughly the same period that serves as the historical setting for *Joker*, a fact that is surely not entirely coincidental.

No Joke: Todd Phillips's *Joker* and American Culture

Psycho Killers and Slashers

Joker differs substantially from the slasher films of the 1980s in that *Joker* is a state-of-the-art piece of filmmaking that employs all the resources of cinematic art and technology to produce a slickly crafted, well-made product, despite its dark subject matter. With a production budget of $60 million, *Joker* was extremely expensive for a slasher film, although such films had already begun to move in the direction of bigger budgets and higher production values, with such films as *The Silence of the Lambs* (1991), only the second film to win all of the "Big Five" most prestigious Academy Awards, leading the way. In addition, the films of the 2010s were marked by a dramatic rise in the profitability of horror films, leading to an overall increase in the resources the Hollywood film industry was willing to devote to such scripts. At the same time, the horror films of the 2010s were crucially informed by a rise in the prominence of "prestige" horror films, complex and sophisticated works of cinematic art with extremely high production values that brought new respect to the genre. Thus, *Joker* was actually very much in line with current trends within the horror film genre at the time of its production and has much in common with its contemporaries in the genre, even as it connects in so many ways with the slasher films of the 1980s.

The slashers at the center of the great franchises that were so prominent in American horror film in the 1980s are all powerful, larger-than-life figures who would seem to be far more forbidding than the largely abject Arthur Fleck—though Fleck does seem to be moving toward becoming a more formidable figure by the end of *Joker*. Indeed, Michael Myers himself begins *Halloween* as a rather frail-looking child who commits his first shocking murder while clad in a clown costume. Still, Myers ultimately becomes an unstoppable killing machine, a sort of allegorical embodiment of the dangers (real or imagined) that loom over all of us as we negotiate our lives. The hulking Jason Voorhees, of the *Friday the 13th* franchise, is not only physically powerful, but supernaturally durable. And Freddie Krueger, of the *Nightmare on Elm Street* franchise, is essentially an evil spirit who can enter the dreams of his victims, causing them physical harm. Like the clowns of most killer clown movies, these slashers generally have little psychological depth (although some of the many sequels that pad out these franchises add a bit more back story); mostly, they seem motivated by sheer malice and the desire to destroy. Some slasher films, though, feature killers who are much more human, driven by psychological disturbances with roots in their own personal histories.

Norman Bates of *Psycho* is, of course, the prototype of all of the slashers of this sort, which might partly explain why John Carpenter sought to work so many allusions to *Psycho* into *Halloween*—up to and including the "allusive" casting of Jamie Lee Curtis as the "final girl" in that film, Curtis being the daughter of Janet Leigh, the central female character in *Psycho*.[9] *Halloween*, meanwhile, was such a success that it helped to inspire the production of a spate of slasher films in the following years, many of which were so heavily influenced by *Halloween* that many of the traits of *Halloween* grew to become common conventions of the genre.

Other early slasher films also attempted to provide explanations for why their slashers have become slashers, thus resembling *Psycho* more than *Halloween*. Among these, *Don't Go in the House* (1979) seems linked to *Psycho* in a particularly direct way—although there is a possible direct link to *Halloween* implied in the film's ending. Here, Donny Kohler (Dan Grimaldi) is a man who has lived all his life alone with his mother in their rambling house, since his father left when Donny was five. Once his father left, Donny found himself at the mercy of his abusive (and mentally ill) mother, who periodically burned him on the gas stove to try to drive the "evil" out of him. Once his mother dies, Donny spirals into all-out insanity. Driven by voices in his head, he keeps his mother's mummified corpse in the house (à la Norman Bates), then lures a series of young women back to the house and burns them to death with a flamethrower to try to remove the evil from them. Then he dresses their charred corpses in his mother's clothes and arranges them in chairs around the parlor. Finally, Donny loses complete touch with reality and ends up burning down the house with himself in it.

Don't Go in the House then ends with an interesting coda in which a mother is shown abusing her young son, who is named Michael. After a beating, Michael begins to hear the same voices that had driven Donny to murder and looks ominously at the camera. We are left to interpret this last scene as we will, but it is at least possible to see it as a suggestion that some supernatural force had driven Donny, rather than simple mental illness; this same force might now be possessing Michael. We can also imagine, if we choose, that this boy is none other than Michael Myers, who had stepped into the American popular consciousness only a year earlier.

One of the most striking slasher films of the early 1980s was *Maniac* (1980), directed by William Lustig, whose prior experience had been primarily in porn. Indeed, some critics viewed *Maniac* itself as essentially pornographic, its excessively graphic depiction of bloody, sexually inspired violence being a bit too much even for a genre that is inherently excessive. *Maniac* does give us an unusually detailed look inside the mind of its central character, serial killer Frank Zito (Joe Spinell), a victim of childhood abuse at the hands of his now-deceased mother who subsequently kills a series of attractive young women. The film, however, is far from sympathizing with Zito, even if he is depicted as emotionally crippled and pathetic. There is a certain creepiness to its depiction of the killer that makes the film seriously disturbing. In particular, the truly insane Zito tends to scalp his victims and then nail their scalps onto the heads of mannequins in an attempt, in his confused mind, to somehow resurrect his dead mother.

This kind of "mother problem" is quite common among slashers of the early 1980s. One particularly colorful (if clumsily made) film in this vein is the obscure slasher *Pieces* (1982), which combines the project of resurrecting a murdered mother with the well-known Frankenstein motif. In particular, the slasher in this film murders and dismembers his mother when he is still a small child. Then, 40 years later, he combines his passion for assembling jigsaw puzzles of naked women with the ongoing trauma from his mother's murder to undertake a project of murdering (in gruesome fashion) a series of young co-eds and then attempting to re-assemble their severed body parts into a simulacrum of his dead mother.

Such motifs are not limited to films of the 1980s, however. *Maniac*, like so many other classic horror films, was remade in the twenty-first century, in this case by French director Franck Khalfoun in 2012. In terms of basic plot, the remake is quite similar to the original, although it shifts the action from New York to Los Angeles, perhaps weakening its potential relevance to *Joker*. The aesthetics of the later film are quite different also, primarily because it is shot almost entirely from the perspective of Zito (now played by Elijah Wood), extending a common slasher trope that began with *Halloween* and that makes the film even creepier by putting viewers in Zito's position throughout the film, the camera essentially positioned to allow us to see through Zito's eyes. The film thus literalizes the strategy used so effectively in *Joker* of centering the point of view of the protagonist. Of course, this strategy is particularly unsettling because Zito is such an unappealing character, an effect that is increased by the fact that Wood is a well-known actor who typically plays sympathetic characters, which makes his role as Zito even more unsettling.[10] In addition, the overall look of the film, as shot by cinematographer Maxime Alexandre, is somewhat unreal (one reviewer, Andrew Kay, complained that it looks and feels like a video game), further indicating that Zito simply sees reality differently than do other people. The 2012 *Maniac* also works in extended references to *The Cabinet of Dr. Caligari* (1920), apparently attempting to suggest that this film, however shocking, is part of a long and venerable cinematic tradition. Still, if anything, the violent scenes of murder and scalping are even more vividly graphic than in the original, so that, as a whole, the remake is both aesthetically superior to the original and more unpleasant to watch.

If nothing else, the 2012 remake of *Maniac* demonstrates the remarkable ability of the slasher genre to keep going even after it had been assumed dead—much like many slashers themselves. Indeed, *Joker* was made in the midst of one of the slasher genre's periodic comebacks, a fact that is worth noting, even though the slasher films of the 1980s are probably the most helpful for capturing the zeitgeist that Phillips is going for in his film. Still, beginning with Adam Wingard's *You're Next* in 2011 and extending through such films as Wingard's *The Guest* (2014), Mike Flanagan's *Hush* (2016), the aforementioned *Terrifier*, and the serio-comic *Happy Death Day* (2017), the years leading up to the production of *Joker* were particularly rich for the slasher film and related subgenres (such as the home invasion narrative and the rape-revenge film).

One key phenomenon of the 2010s was the extension of these subgenres on an international level, as in the case of many films of the so-called New French Extremity movement.[11] In this vein, one of the most interesting immediate predecessors to *Joker* as a film about a psychotic killer is Lars von Trier's *The House That Jack Built* (2018), a co-production of several European countries. Somewhat like *Joker*, *The House That Jack Built* is one of the most perplexing films of recent years: a carefully crafted work of art with many self-conscious aesthetic flourishes, such as the fact that the film uses Dante's *Inferno* as a major structural device. The film is essentially narrated by Jack himself, a deranged serial killer (very effectively played by Matt Dillon). In particular, Matt tells his story to one "Verge" (Bruno Ganz), who is guiding Jack into the depths of hell, just as the poet Virgil guides Dante in *The Inferno*. This narrative is completely episodic, consisting of tales of a series of "incidents" in Jack's career as a serial killer, which might (we are led to believe) have involved more than 60 victims. There is little indication that Jack confuses fantasy and reality, but he is certainly ill (Virgil, who regularly guides the damned through hell, suggests that Jack is the most depraved individual he has ever met). He is a much more methodical killer than is Arthur Fleck, approaching his killings with an absolute coldness that is quite chilling and frequently involves an almost heartbreaking cruelty and lack of feeling toward his victims. *The House That Jack Built* features grotesque and horrifying violence (especially against women, but also against men—not to mention children and small animals), yet it often veers into (very black) comedy at unexpected moments. In any case, this complex film demands careful unpacking while defeating interpretive closure, which makes it an important work for comparison with *Joker*.

John McNaughton's *Henry: Portrait of a Serial Killer* (1986) is probably the slasher film has the most in common with *Joker*. Actually, *Henry* bounced around the festival circuit for four years before finally being distributed to theaters in 1990, the delay occurring because both its shocking content and its way of delivering this content caused considerable controversy with the MPAA ratings system. Nevertheless, the film does a great deal to capture the prominence of serial killing as a phenomenon in American culture in the 1980s, a fact that makes it immediately relevant to *Joker*. Eventually released without a rating, *Henry* was thus assured of doing poorly at the box office, although it still took in six times its tiny production budget and has since become something of a cult classic, both much maligned and much admired by critics. Though essentially a slasher film, *Henry* violates virtually all of the conventions of that subgenre—which, among other things, suggests just how flexible the slasher film can be. Moreover, *Henry* (like *Psycho*) also demonstrates just how permeable the boundary between slasher films and more straightforward serial-killer films can be. After all, Henry himself (played with chilling effect by Michael Rooker) is not an imposing figure like Michael Myers or Jason Voorhees. Indeed, like Norman Bates and Arthur Fleck, he is simply a dysfunctional human. Much of the time, in fact, Henry seems relatively normal, almost likeable—until he suddenly, randomly, and without provocation decides to kill someone (usually, but not always, a young woman). *Henry* also differs from most slasher films in that Henry's killings mostly occur off-screen and are evidenced only by the on-screen appearance of mutilated bodies shown after-the fact. In fact, in what might be his most shocking killing, we see neither the act of murder nor the body, but simply get hints that he might have killed a young woman named Becky (Tracy Arnold), with whom he has established something of a romantic relationship after saving her from being raped (and possibly murdered) by her own brother, Otis (Tom Towles), who had earlier joined Henry in some of his killings.

One of the reasons why *Henry* is so disturbing is that its gritty, *cinéma-vérité* style (it was shot on 16 mm film) reinforces its hint that crimes such as those depicted in the film really do occur. Noting the film's air of almost documentary realism, Roger Ebert (typically no fan of the slasher subgenre) declared in his review of the film upon its 1990 release that *Henry* "is a very good film, a low-budget tour de force that provides an unforgettable portrait of the pathology of a man for whom killing is not a crime but simply a way of passing time and relieving boredom." Much of the seemingly realistic texture of *Henry* is its cinematic style, of course, but it is also the case that Henry himself is loosely based on real-life serial killer Henry Lee Lucas, adding a further note of realism.

The truly disturbing thing about Henry is that he is not literally an inhuman monster in the sense that many slashers are. He is, in fact, perfectly human and is even given a sympathetic back story: we learn that he suffered from childhood abuse at the hands of his mother, whom he eventually murdered, just as Lucas murdered his mother. This instance of matricide is one of the most obvious aspects of *Henry* that identifies Henry as a particularly important predecessor to *Joker*'s Fleck. Perhaps more importantly, though, *Henry* as a film also resembles *Joker* in the extent to which its basic nature, while grittily realistic on the surface, is declaredly postmodern.

For one thing, Lucas was, in many ways, the most postmodern of serial killers, because most of his "killings" were apparently fictional. While he was convicted of 11 murders and almost surely committed some murders, there is some question of the exact extent of his career as a murderer. There is strong evidence that he did not commit most of the murders for which he was convicted and could not have committed the one 1979 murder for which he was sentenced to death in 1984, a fact that caused then Texas Governor George W. Bush to commute Lucas's sentence to life in prison in 1998. While Lucas did confess (in 1982) to this killing, it turns out that he also confessed to hundreds, or even thousands, of other murders (most of which he surely did not commit), earning him the nickname the "Confession Killer."

Lucas's confession spree blurred the boundary between fiction and reality in much the same way that works of postmodern art often do. Brian McHale, for example, has argued that a central strategy used by postmodern writers involves the blurring of "ontological" boundaries, or boundaries between different levels of reality, as when fictional characters enter the worlds of their authors, or vice versa. Further, McHale (himself writing in the middle of the 1980s) sees this strategy as emanating from a general decline in faith that there is a real distinction between fiction and reality or that there is such a thing as a stable and concrete reality apart from human construction. As noted in the introduction to this volume, *Joker* participates extensively in this blurring of the boundary between fiction and reality.

Henry is also postmodern in the way it plays with audiences and their sympathies, in this sense operating very much in the spirit of *Psycho*. In a rare case of serial-killer teamwork, Lucas was also sometimes joined in his crimes by one Ottis Toole, who also confessed to far more murders than he actually committed. Toole is clearly the principal model for the character of Otis in *Henry*, although he also seems to have been carefully constructed as a character who is even more despicable than Henry, thus contributing to the film's strategy of luring viewers into sympathizing with Henry to some extent (although he always does something especially awful soon after these moments of sympathetic depiction, snapping viewers back to reality with a shock that they could have been tempted to sympathize with a man who is clearly a psychopathic monster).[12]

In one particularly chilling sequence, *Henry* even dramatizes its strategy of aligning its audience with its killers. Here, in one of the film's most disturbing crimes, we witness a home invasion in which Henry and Otis attack and murder a couple and their adolescent son. In particular, they are shown approaching the home, then the film suddenly cuts to the actual killings, which are being shown on a television set via videotape. We then witness the killings in this mediated fashion and learn only afterward that Henry and Otis have taped the murders and are now sitting together on Otis's shabby couch, watching the recording in very much the same way we have just been watching it. This sequence thus blurs the boundaries between different ontological levels in a very postmodern fashion; it also makes Otis and Henry members of their own audience, reminding us that we have been watching their killings in much the same way. As Isabel Pinedo puts it, "The audience is gulled and unwittingly implicated in a compromising manner in voyeurism" (103).

Pinedo was among the first critics to identify *Henry* as a work of postmodern cinema. For her, the film is a paradigmatic work of postmodern horror, informed by what she calls the "central force driving" such horror: "the constant threat of inexplicable violence aimed at the body. The film's striking sense of malevolence is rooted in the real-life manner in which the film constructs this threat" (99). For her, "*Henry* demonstrates the central lesson of the postmodern horror genre: that cloaked in a mantle of normalcy, chaos lies just beneath the surface ready to erupt at any moment" (105).

Henry's fragmented psyche, the randomness of his killings, and the lack of any real coherent plot all identify *Henry* as a postmodern work—and as a predecessor to *Joker*. In addition to the aesthetic similarities between *Joker* and *Henry* as works of postmodern cinema, the most obvious similarity between these two films has to do with the violent subject matter and with the way both films feature serial killer protagonists who are also the point-of-view characters and who are never explicitly disavowed by the films. Kimber notes that director McNaughton and co-screenwriter Richard Fire "sought simultaneously to redefine and push at the boundaries of horror film through the merging of what in cinematic terms we might call art and exploitation cinema" and that they humanized Henry by "taking spectators into the everyday life of a serial killer and encouraging them to identify and sympathize with him; refusing to offer a moral compass by means of which to judge Henry or the film; presenting a human monster who exists next to us in the real world; and breaking the illusion that the world is a safe place by having Henry elude the police" (7).

This description applies equally well to *Joker*, and *Joker* received some of the same complaints about its seemingly sympathetic treatment of its murderous protagonist. Commercially, however, the receptions received by these two films could not have been more different. Unable to secure an R rating, *Henry* remained on the margins of the film industry and grossed less than $1 million at the U.S. box office. *Joker* received an R rating relatively easily, went into wide distribution with the backing of a major studio, and grossed more than $1 billion worldwide, becoming one of the most commercially successful films of 2019. Partly because of this commercial success, *Joker* also received widespread critical attention (and a significant amount of acclaim), something that *Henry* has only accumulated slowly over the years.

Some of the reasons why *Joker* was received so much more successfully than *Henry* are obvious. For one thing, ultra-violent films were simply less shocking and controversial in 2019 than they were in 1990. Even more obviously, *Joker* is a film with extremely high production values, supported by its production budget in the tens of millions of dollars and furthered by the world-class performance by Joaquin Phoenix. Rooker's performance in *Henry*, meanwhile, is impressive, but it is surely neither as appealing nor as accomplished as the Oscar-winning performance of Phoenix. And the overall rough-hewn aesthetic of *Henry*, however appropriate it might be to the grisly subject matter, was surely never going to appeal to a wide mainstream audience.

In addition, *Joker* and *Henry*, regardless of how many things they might have in common, were surely not perceived by their contemporary audiences in the same way. *Henry* was made in the midst of the slasher film boom of that was such a powerful force in American horror film. That boom was certainly on the wane by 1990, but it is still the case that such films surely provided one of the principal contexts within which *Henry* would have been received by the film's original audiences. *Joker*, on the other hand, appeared at a time when films based on superhero comics had become the most powerful commercial force in the history of global cinema, and audiences doubtless flocked to see the film because they perceived it within the context of such films, which are themselves the leading example of the impact of neoliberalism on the global film industry, placing *Joker* very central to film marketing in 2019.

Meanwhile, if *Joker* is, in this sense, very much a film of its time, its content is much like that of many horror films of the 1980s, a time that Robin Wood has seen as particularly impoverished because the especially repressive nature of the Reagan decade deprived horror film of its most important energies. These energies, for Wood, arise from a return of the repressed, from the re-emergence of "the Other," which "represents that which bourgeois ideology cannot recognize or accept but must deal with" (65). Thus, for Wood, "the true subject of the horror genre is the struggle for recognition of all that our civilization represses or oppresses, its re-emergence dramatized, as in our nightmares, as an object of horror, a matter for terror, and the happy ending (when it exists) typically signifying the restoration of repression" (68).

Joker, I would argue, is a story of Arthur Fleck's struggle for recognition, a struggle that is made particularly difficult because, as Wood notes, repression was particularly effective in the 1980s. On the most obvious (and perhaps most problematic) level, *Joker* presents Fleck as an Other, as a mentally ill member of the economic underclass who erupts into murderous violence in response to his mental and economic disadvantages. Seen negatively, the film might be taken as identifying the poor and the mentally ill as Others who represent dangers to the mainstream population. Seen more positively, on the other hand, the film might be seen as locating the danger in a dysfunctional mental health care system and in an inequitable economic system. This potential systemic critique identifies the Other in the film as a social, political, and economic system that creates the sort of injustices that might drive individuals such as Fleck to murder. In this sense, *Joker* could be located in the tradition of political horror films that has included such entries as Brian Yuzna's *Society* (1989), Wes Craven's *The People Under the Stairs* (1991), and Jim Mickle's *Mulberry Street* (2006), leading to the recent films of Jordan Peele—including *Get Out* (2017) and *Us* (2019)—and to recent feminist horror films such as Coralie Fargeat's *Revenge* (2017), which are roughly contemporaneous with *Joker*.

However, the films in this list are quite clear in their identification of class inequality, racism, and sexism as the evils that are being criticized, rather than specific individual "monsters." *Joker*, on the other hand, is much more politically nebulous, as I explore in the final chapters of this volume. In particular, while *Joker* does seemingly make clear that Fleck's turn to murder is driven by inadequate health care and economic privation, it also provides for a sort of pseudo-Freudian interpretation that would locate Fleck's problems primarily in the poor parenting that he received in his early childhood and that has been exacerbated by the mental instabilities of his mother throughout his life. Moreover, any attempt to read *Joker* as a political allegory is also clearly weakened by the fact that the film fails to identify any specific alternatives to the systems that it potentially criticizes. Reading *Joker* within the context of the horror film thus does not provide final answers to the many questions surrounding the political implications of the film, but it does highlight these questions, which I explore in much more detail in Part II of this study.

Notes

1   One killer clown referred to as a fictional character within *Cult*, Twisty the Clown (John Carroll Lynch), is actually a holdover from an earlier season, *American Horror Story: Freak Show* (2014–2015), suggesting the overall prominence of killer clowns in American horror, even if *Cult* implies that killer clowns are a particularly appropriate metaphor for the Trump era. Lynch, incidentally, played the main suspect in *Zodiac*, although *Cult* hints (not entirely seriously) that the Zodiac killings were committed by a radical feminist cult.
2   See, for example, Poole on this topic.
3   Pogo features prominently in the 2003 film *Gacy*, based on the career of the serial killer.
4   The 2015 remake of *Poltergeist* makes even more use of this motif by introducing multiple clown dolls. A sinister killer clown was also featured in promotional posters for that film.
5   *It* deals only with the earlier segment of King's novel. The later segment is dealt with in a sequel, *It Chapter Two*, which was released in early September of 2019, just a few days after the premiere of *Joker* at the Venice Film Festival.
6   Splatter films and slasher films overlap significantly, of course, with the main difference being that splatter films tend to rely more on graphic, gross-out images of bodily destruction. As such, splatter films are often regarded as pure exploitation, whereas slasher films often have significance that goes beyond their own representation of violence. But see Mark Steven for an extended argument that the violence enacted in splatter films has much in common with the violence that is inherent to the capitalist system.
7   The greatest of these is probably Víctor Erice's *The Spirit of the Beehive* (1973), widely considered to be one of the greatest of all Spanish films. Among other things, this film is remarkable because it somehow manages to conduct a subversive critique of fascism even while fascist leader Francisco Franco was

still in power in Spain. Set in Spain, "around 1940," the plot centers on a young girl named Ana (Ana Torrent), who views the 1931 *Frankenstein* via a traveling cinema that comes to her village. The film, apparently, is meant to convey a fascist message of obedience and conformity, serving as a cautionary tale to warn against challenging the status quo. For Ana, though, it has the opposite effect, spurring her imagination and causing her to strongly identify with the outcast and misunderstood monster.

8   The film implies that the killing of Mrs. Hickfang might have essentially been an assisted suicide, although it is not clear whether Hickfang himself remembers the event accurately.

9   First identified by Carol Clover in the late 1980s as a common element of the slasher film, the "final girl" is a female character who typically survives the film, but only after being terrorized and having witnessed the deaths of several of her friends or others. This element of the slasher film is lacking in *Joker*, though the character of Sophie does come close in some ways.

10   It should be pointed out, though, that Wood also played a depraved killer in the 2005 film *Sin City*, so that his casting in *Maniac* was not entirely unprecedented.

11   On this movement, see Alexandra West.

12   The character of Becky is based on Becky Powell, Ottis's 13-year-old niece, with whom Lucas had a relationship and whom Lucas eventually murdered when she tried to leave him.

CHAPTER FIVE

"That's Life"
The Music of *Joker*

In addition to its extensive dialogue with American film, *Joker* also makes extensive use of music as a resource. Hildur Guðnadóttir's Oscar-winning score for *Joker* has received considerable critical praise, and rightfully so. That score does an impressive job of doing just what film scores are supposed to do by making a substantial contribution to setting the mood and atmosphere for many scenes of the film. But that score itself is only one component of the important role played by music throughout the film, the soundtrack of which includes a remarkably diversion selection of popular music (compiled by music supervisors George Drakoulias and Randall Poster). This soundtrack employs an extensive selection of (mostly) well-known songs that not only contribute to building atmosphere but also participate in the film's extensive dialogue with American (and Western) cultural history. In this way, these songs contribute to the tone and emotional impact of the film and also have a significant impact on the film's meaning.[1]

Guðnadóttir's Oscar win for *Joker* came on the heels of a Golden Globe win for the score and a Primetime Emmy for her music for the 2019 HBO mini-series *Chernobyl*. This flurry of awards helped to establish her as a force to be reckoned with in the world of film scores, though she was relatively little known when she was first chosen to write (and help perform) the score for *Joker*. Importantly, Guðnadóttir composed (and recorded) much of her score using the film's script, before it was filmed, so that a great deal of the music was available to be played during filming in order to provide atmospheric inspiration. This score has been almost universally praised, but it perhaps comes most strongly into play at a key moment in the film when Arthur Fleck, having recently committed (or fantasized about committing) murders that are particularly crucial to the plot of the film, performs improvisational dances to Guðnadóttir's music. In this scene, Fleck has just come from apparently killing the three Wall Street guys in the subway. Entering a grimy public

109

restroom and seemingly at wit's end, he suddenly begins to dance, as if trying to find expression for emotions that exceed his limited verbal powers. This oneiric dance, performed as if in a trance, is accompanied by Guðnadóttir's solemn and unsettling music, which thus seems like a sort of aural embodiment of those feelings. Of course, this music is not literally playing in the restroom, although we can imagine that Fleck might be hearing it in his fevered mind. As Mike Smaczylo notes, though, the music was, in fact, played on the set when this scene was being filmed, providing Phoenix with inspiration and allowing him literally to dance to the music. Guðnadóttir, according to Smaczylo, was highly impressed with the match between Phoenix's movements and her music, later saying that it was "completely unreal to see the physical embodiment of that music. His hand gestures were the same types of movements I felt when I wrote the music. It was one of the strongest collaborative moments I've ever experienced."

In a later scene, Fleck performs a similar dance in his apartment in his underwear, less than three minutes of run-time after killing (or apparently killing) his mother in her hospital bed. This time, however, the music that plays is perhaps the most important popular song from the entire soundtrack, Frank Sinatra's recording of "That's Life," which appeared in his 1966 album of the same title. This song, written by Dean Kay and Kelly Gordon and first recorded in 1963, was a major hit for Sinatra (reaching No. 4 on the *Billboard* Hot 100) at a time when the music charts were almost completely dominated by rock music. By 1981, the song had been so widely played that it was part of the soundtrack of American life; it was also a key part of the soundtrack of Fleck's life, given that it was the personal theme song of Murray Franklin, used prominently on his talk show.

Lucia Senesi reads *Joker* as a work of "pseudo-neorealism," noting that it has much in common with European neo-realist predecessors in terms of its emphasis on class inequality and on the suffering of the have-nots in capitalist society. The most important examples that she chooses for comparison are Jean-Luc Godard's *My Life to Live* (*Vivre sa vie*, 1962) and Antonio Pietrangeli's *I Knew Her Well* (*Io la conoscevo bene*, 1965) both of which feature downtrodden (in this case, female) protagonists who turn to dancing in times of particular stress—in a way that "confirms their individuality and their being." For Senesi, the message conveyed by these dancing scenes is clear: "even in a world where all is lost, even when your abusers control your body and your life, there is still a space for your innermost self and who you are will never be stolen from you" (9).

Of course, dance has often been featured prominently in film, a legacy that is acknowledged by the inclusion of that scene from *Shall We Dance* within *Joker*. Quite often, in the musicals of the 1930s, when the genre was at its peak, dance functions as an expression of joy and individual achievement that provides a few moments of respite from the difficulties of the Depression. But films such as *Joker*, as well as the films cited by Senesi, represent a more urgent attempt to maintain a sense of individual identity in the face of large, impersonal forces that might threaten that identity. I might also note, though, that dance in film has often also been an expression of connections between individuals, whether it be couples moving in tandem, as in any number of romantic musicals, or large troupes of dancers moving collectively, as in the case of all of the meticulously choreographed and finely synchronized dance numbers of American directors such as Busby Berkeley. And, of course, there are moments when this kind of dancing can be more overtly political, as in the recent case of Steve McQueen's brilliant *Lovers Rock* (2020), in which black Londoners dance so joyfully to Caribbean rhythms in a group declaration of their shared subcultural identities, identities that are endangered by the resentment that so often surrounds them in mainstream white London society.

That dance can so effectively function as a means of expressing joyful mutuality makes the lone, joyless dancing of Arthur Fleck in *Joker* all the more poignant, reminding us that, even if he were to succeed at holding his identity together, he will still stand apart from everyone else. Of course, the two dancing scenes that I have just discussed stand in stark contrast to a third key example of Fleck dancing, the moment in which, decked out in full Joker garb, he does that jaunty, defiant, high-kicking dance down the stone steps near his apartment building. Presumably, the stark contrast between the tone of this almost celebratory dance and the earlier, sadder, more introspective dances can be taken as a sign of the change in Fleck's mood and of his possible transformation from downtrodden underdog to budding supervillain. He is still, however, very much alone as he bounces down those steps (Figure 5). Of course, the music that accompanies this scene is also quite key to its effect. Gary Glitter's "Rock and Roll Part 2" was a top-ten hit in the United States and several other countries back in 1972, when it was first released. By the early 1980s, the song was being used more and more widely at American sporting events, where it was used to charge up fans and players with its high-energy rhythms. It was, in short, a prominent part of American popular culture in the early 1980s, with a particular association with violent sports such as ice hockey and NFL football. Its

No Joke: Todd Phillips's *Joker* and American Culture

Figure 5. Fleck, in full Joker costume, dances down the stone steps near his apartment, accompanied by Gary Glitter's "Rock and Roll Part 2."

ability to rouse crowds is thus very much in keeping with the themes of *Joker*, in which Fleck's antics appear to inspire crowds of protestors in the streets of Gotham.

Of course, the cultural history of "Rock and Roll Part 2" would subsequently be complicated by the fact that Glitter (real name Paul Francis Gadd) was arrested for downloading child pornography in 1997, an offense for which he was convicted and imprisoned in 1999. He later undertook a bizarre international career that involved additional charges of sexual misconduct with minors, charges that sent him to a Vietnamese prison in 2006 and that saw him sentenced to 16 years in prison back in the United Kingdom in 2015. Glitter's music has subsequently been removed from most venues, so that the choice to include it in *Joker* could not have been an innocent one. The suggestion, I think, is that Western popular culture is often part of a shiny veneer that covers dark and violent tendencies in late capitalist culture as a whole.

If "Rock and Roll Part 2" cannot be read apart from the problematic career of Glitter, it is also the case that other examples of music in *Joker* carry additional implications because of the artists with which they are associated. For example, Sinatra was one of the greatest stars in the history of American popular culture, becoming an important film actor as well as one of the leading singers of his generation. Thus, choosing his music for a key role in *Joker* is not without significance. Indeed, it should be pointed out that Sinatra also recorded a well-known (although perhaps not the *best*-known) version of "Send in the Clowns," the song that one of the Wall Street guys sings to taunt Fleck as he and his companions move toward attacking the hapless clown on the subway. This song, written for the 1973 Stephen Sondheim musical *A Little Night Music*, was a hit for Sinatra in 1973 and an even bigger hit for Judy Collins, charting for her in both 1975 and 1977. It is Sinatra's version, however, to which *Joker* points most directly, given that this version actually plays during the film's end credits.

This song certainly seems appropriate for a film about a literal clown, even though the song is not literally *about* clowns. It's a sad and bitter song of regret, sung by a spurned lover who has come to realize the folly of his love, having miscalculated the inclinations and desires of his loved one so spectacularly that he feels clown-like. The actual lyrics are not that directly relevant to the story of Arthur Fleck, except to the extent that his fantasized love for Sophie is so thoroughly divorced from reality. It is instead the melancholy tone of the song that seems so appropriate to Fleck and his failed life, a life that has now taken a sudden new turn due to his emergent status as a symbol of revolt, protestors who see him as a role model having occupied the streets of Gotham wearing clown masks that symbolize their own rejection of the respectable status quo.

Indeed, the tone of this song is very much in keeping with the tone of most of Guðnadóttir's score. Again, however, the fact that this song is associated with Sinatra adds an extra dimension to its contribution to the overall fabric of *Joker*. The megastar Sinatra is in some ways very much an establishment figure, with numerous connections in high places, an image of the kind of success that Fleck could never hope to achieve. At the same time, Sinatra's image was a complex one. His connections included several U.S. presidents, but rumors of his extensive connections with organized crime figures were widespread. In popular culture, Sinatra is believed to have been an important inspiration for the character of Johnny Fontane, the singer turned actor whose career gets a boost from the unrefusable offer made by Vito Corleone on his behalf in *The Godfather* (1972).

By identifying Sinatra's career as part of the cultural background of Arthur Fleck, *Joker* suggests that Fleck is not merely a one-of-a-kind psychopath but is instead the product of complex forces that are very much a part of mainstream American culture. Given the importance of "That's Life" to the film, though, it is also worth taking a more careful look at the lyrics of that song, which (at first glance) appears to be a come-what-may, shoulder-shrugging acceptance of life's ups and downs. And most of the song is just that, as the singer suggests that he has been through many setbacks and yet has always come back strong. Then, however, comes the crucial final stanza, which puts a much darker spin on the song:

> That's life (That's life), that's life and I can't deny it.
> Many times I thought of cutting out, but my heart won't buy it.
> But if there's nothing shaking come this here July
> I'm gonna roll myself up in a big ball and die.
> My, my.

Thus, the song ends by declaring that one more setback will be the last straw and that the singer is ready to give up and simply die if things don't get better very soon. Thus, all the expressions of resilience are erased by announcing that the singer's toughness is at an end. It's essentially a moment of despair—and one that is actually rather in keeping with Sinatra's performance of the song, which has a somewhat bitter edge throughout.

The turn to despair at the end of this song is also quite in keeping with the overall mood of pathos that underlies the scene in *Joker* in which Fleck dances to the song in his underwear, seemingly attempting to exude confidence and defiance, but not quite succeeding. It is also, of course, very much consistent with the overall arc of Fleck's entire life, which consists of one disappointment and defeat after another. As he tells his social worker, "All I have are negative thoughts." His experience in life, in fact, has been one of almost unmitigated anguish, until he is finally driven, either to murder or fantasies of murder.[2]

The other biggest star whose music is featured in *Joker* is Charlie Chaplin. I have already discussed the importance of Chaplin's 1936 film *Modern Times* to *Joker*, but it should also be noted that Chaplin was a gifted composer who wrote a sizeable body of music for his films. Strains of music from *Modern Times* sound several times in *Joker*, the most important example of which is that film's instrumental love theme, which was originally credited to Chaplin, even though it was actually composed in collaboration with noted film-music writer David Raksin and inspired by music from Puccini's opera *Tosca*.[3] John Turner and Geoffrey Parsons tweaked the song and added lyrics in 1954, also giving it the title of "Smile," which became a hit for Nat "King" Cole in 1955. This title certainly seems relevant to *Joker*, given the famed perpetual smile of its title character, and so it is entirely appropriate that the song is used in the film. The version used most prominently in the film, though, is the one recorded by Jimmy Durante in 1959, a choice that was again appropriate, given that Durante was more of a stand-up comedian than a singer, although he often incorporated singing into his act. Durante was also a prominent presence on American television throughout the years of Fleck's life (including many appearances on talk shows)—and so Fleck would no doubt be very familiar with the large-nosed comic.

Durante's "Smile" begins playing (non-diegetically) as Fleck concludes his disastrous open-mic performance at Pogo's comedy club, a performance that elicits few smiles except from an imaginary Sophie, who attends the performance in Fleck's fantasy. The song then continues playing on the soundtrack as Fleck is shown subsequently walking (with the imaginary Sophie) through Gotham's crowded streets, noticing a newsstand displaying newspapers with headlines such as "Clown Vigilante?" and "Killer Clown on the Loose." Reading the headlines, Sophie opines (in Fleck's mind), "I think the guy that did it is a hero." The song then continues through a moment in which Fleck and the imaginary Sophie share a laugh in a diner.

There is, of course, something seemingly poignant and ironic about the fact that this song plays during a sequence in which Fleck imagines himself making triumphant steps forward in his career as a comedian and in his relationship with Sophie, when he is, in fact, doing neither. In point of fact, the tune of the song is quite melancholy, matching the bittersweet experiences of Chaplin's Little Tramp character in *Modern Times* (and elsewhere). Moreover, the lyrics that were added to the song reflect this tune. They are not about how pleasant it is to smile in happy times; instead, they tout the value of smiling in the face of sadness and defeat. "Smile, though your heart is aching/Smile, though your heart is breaking" begin the lyrics, and the remainder of the song goes on in much the same way. As with "That's Life," then, "Smile" is actually a rather sad song masquerading as an uplifting one.[4]

Such music creates an almost Brechtian estrangement effect in the introduction of seemingly upbeat songs into this mostly tragic film, although the effect is given an extra twist by the fact that the songs themselves contain internal ironies. Similar effects are, in fact, achieved throughout *Joker*. For example, after the opening pre-title sequence that shows Fleck putting on clown makeup while the news plays on the radio, *Joker* cuts to its first real scene, accompanied by the film's first piece of music, "Temptation Rag," a lively, up-tempo number that seems perfectly well-suited to accompany Fleck's performance as a sign-spinning clown. We even see the sidewalk pianist playing the music, adding to the carnival-like atmosphere and making the music diegetic, a literal part of Fleck's performance.[5] The problem, of course, is that this scene ends so badly for Fleck, making this cheerful music ultimately inappropriate, signaled by the way in which it fades into the background as Fleck chases after the street kids who steal his sign, leaving the pianist behind.

This opening music would surely seem to be a simple example of the use of music to help establish an atmosphere, which is then rudely interrupted. The particular choice of ragtime music might, however, be more significant than is immediately obvious. I am thinking here of E. L. Doctorow's important 1975 novel *Ragtime*, whose title indicates the importance of ragtime music to the pre-World War I cultural milieu in which most of the novel is set. This optimistic music captures the high hopes that informed the opening years of the new American century, while also signaling the emerging prominence of African American creators and performers. Doctorow's novel, though, presents this optimism as a false one. As much as anything, Doctorow's novel is about the rising hopes of the American Left in the early years of the twentieth century, hopes that would ultimately be dashed by the coming of the World War I and the subsequent triumph of the new consumer capitalism that arose in America at about the same time as ragtime music. Doctorow's novel is, in short, about happy times that come crashing to earth—and thus has very much the same narrative arc as that early sign-twirling scene in *Joker*.

There are, in fact, other reasons that ragtime music is relevant to *Joker*, given that ragtime underwent a resurgence in popularity in the 1970s after the soundtrack of the 1973 hit film *The Sting* featured the ragtime piano music of Scott Joplin—via Marvin Hamlisch. Indeed, it is likely that this resurgence exerted an influence on Doctorow's *Ragtime*, published only two years after the release of *The Sting*. Moreover, *Ragtime* itself was adapted to a film (under the direction on Miloš Forman) that was released in November of 1981, corresponding almost exactly to the presumed historical setting of the events in *Joker*. Granted, *Joker* includes allusions to a number of films from 1981, as I have noted, and *Ragtime* is not one of those. Still, the references in *Joker* to films released in 1981 are numerous enough to constitute a signal that we should be looking for films from 1981 that might help to illuminate *Joker*.

The incorporation of "Temptation Rag" almost inevitably evokes the ragtime resurgence of the 1970s, a resurgence of which Doctorow and his historical narrative of the defeat of the American Left were key parts. In any case, the use of ragtime music in this early *Joker* scene does supplement Fleck's attempt to make the most of this potentially demeaning job and to feel good about it, only to be brutally humiliated. And I am also suggesting that recognizing the historical importance of ragtime music, especially as read through Doctorow, endows this humiliating scene with a sort of allegorical–historical dimension that makes it emblematic of the experience of the American working class as a whole.

As Fleck lies suffering in the alleyway at the end of this scene, the first brief snippet of Guðnadóttir's score kicks in, with electronically enhanced string music that is quickly accompanied by the display of the giant yellow title, which at this point is made to seem all the more ironic by the tone of the music, suggesting that Fleck's situation is no joke. We then cut immediately to the scene of Fleck mirthlessly laughing in front of his counselor, completing the initial announcement that Fleck's experiences are definitely no joke. The score, which Guðnadóttir composed largely on her halldorophone (a synthesizer-enhanced cello), will continually re-emphasize this point throughout the film, perhaps most effectively in the bathroom scene, discussed above, in which Fleck begins to dance, almost as a form of meditation—and almost as if he can hear the music, which thus becomes a sort of aural representation of his anguished mental state.

One of the most striking aspects of the soundtrack of *Joker* is its diversity. Songs such as Sinatra's rendition of "That's Life" and Durante's performance of "Smile" represent strong links to mainstream American culture, featuring well-known performers and very familiar songs. Yet both of these songs run somewhat against the rock-dominated grain of American popular music in the years between 1959 and 1966, when the two songs were recorded. Those are also, of course, formative years during which Arthur Fleck would have become a teenager, and we can imagine that, under the influence of his mother, he might have had more exposure to this sort of music than to 1960s music, already moving in countercultural directions that would have been familiar to his fellow teens. This music thus subtly suggests the extent to which Fleck's young life was dominated by his mother, leaving him lonely and disconnected from children of his own age. From this perspective, it might be significant that Fleck's high-kicking dance down those stone steps is performed to a more contemporary and more rock-oriented song, perhaps announcing that he has emerged from the shadows of his childhood (and his mother) to become his own person at last, even if a warped and broken one.

Other popular contemporary songs heard in *Joker* also seem to have been carefully chosen. For example, in one early scene in which Fleck changes in the dressing room with other employees of Ha-Has, we can dimly hear the radio playing a song in the background. That song, appropriately enough for this group of literal clowns, is "Everybody Plays the Fool," in the version that was a major hit for the R&B group The Main Ingredient back in 1972. This song is typical of the popular songs used in *Joker* in that, while it appears to have an upbeat message that seeks to reassure the person to whom the song is addressed that he need not feel embarrassed to have been foolish and unsuccessful in love, it actually conveys a rather dark message of what love is like, suggesting that love affairs are quite typically disappointing and that lovers are almost universally abused and discarded, having been rendered vulnerable by the blindness of love.

It is also perhaps significant that this song plays at Ha-Has, because it is only one of several examples of material that is heard there on the radio, which seems constantly to be on. At another point, for example, Fleck hears Jackson C. Frank's 1965 song "My Name Is Carnival" on the radio at Ha-Has, something he finds quite remarkable because "Carnival" is his "clown name at work," as he tells his social worker when he reports hearing the song. His reaction suggests that he might not previously have been familiar with this song, although that is not entirely clear. In any case, the songs that appear in *Joker* are always well chosen, and this one is no exception. Not only does the name "Carnival" match Fleck's clown name, but Frank's story somewhat parallels Fleck's. The somewhat disjointed lyrics of this song depict the world as a sort of surreal carnival where chaos reigns, with the possible suggestion that the singer is unraveling as well. Indeed, after the release of the one album that contains this song, Frank was diagnosed with schizophrenia and depression, battling mental illness for the remainder of his life, which ended when he died of pneumonia at the age of 56 in 1999. By 1984, Frank was in New York, homeless, destitute, and living on the street, although he was also in and out of psychiatric institutions, where the treatment he received was clearly insufficient, which comes as no surprise given the state of America's mental health care system after its near dismantling by the Reagan administration.

The final popular song that is introduced in *Joker* is a much more prominent one: "White Room," a hit for the British supergroup Cream in 1968 and a song that has become a rock standard, covered since by many other groups. It is thus another song from Fleck's teen years and one that was prominent enough that Fleck would likely know it. The success of this song no doubt owes a great deal to its driving, energetic music, featuring rock legends Eric Clapton on guitar and Ginger Baker on drums. And this is also doubtless much of the reason why this song was chosen for the film. The song's intro begins to play as we are still seeing those 24 television screens in the wake of the apparent shooting of Murray Franklin, with media babble announcing such things as "Gotham is burning" also sounding. Then we cut to the streets of the city and to a speeding police car with Fleck as a prisoner in the back seat, lights flashing and siren sounding. The first verse of the song also sounds at this point:

"In a white room with black curtains near the station/Black roof country, no gold pavements, tired starlings."

As this music is heard on the soundtrack, Fleck slowly breaks into a smile as he observes the chaos in the streets around him, apparently thinking to himself that he might have had a hand in creating this situation. The upbeat-sounding music seems to mirror Fleck's lifting mood, and it is not at all farfetched to imagine that this music is, once again, sounding in his head. In addition (like so much music of the 1960s), the music, especially Clapton's guitar (played through a wah-wah pedal), is rather psychedelic, which seems in keeping with Fleck's generally unbalanced state of mind but is also very much in tune with the almost surreal situation in the city at large. Meanwhile, the music is once again at odds with the lyrics, which appear to echo the confusion that reigns in the streets of Gotham at this point. The lyrics seem to express a certain sense of crisis and strain, even mental anguish, making them much less upbeat than the music. They are also extremely enigmatic and ambiguous. These lyrics, in fact, are very much like *Joker* itself, defying any final and conclusive interpretation. For example, coming as they do at this late point in the film, the lyrics potentially suggest that Fleck has actually been locked up in Arkham all this time, perhaps imprisoned within a "white room." Indeed, a line shortly into the song strongly supports such an interpretation: "I'll wait in this place where the sun never shines;/Wait in this place where the shadows run from themselves."

These are the last lyrics that can be heard on the soundtrack shortly before the police car is smashed into, first by an ambulance that is being driven by a clown-masked protestor, and then by a speeding cab, rendering all of the inhabitants of the cop car unconscious. The ambulance driver and another clown-masked protestor pull Fleck from the car and toward freedom. This unlikely, almost miraculous, escape adds support to the notion that this whole escape sequence is really just Fleck's fantasy and that he is in fact either transported to Arkham without this intervention or was actually in Arkham all along. In any case, Fleck is soon shown regaining consciousness as crowds of protestors, now seeming more like revelers, cheer him on. In response, he once again begins briefly to dance to Guðnadóttir's music, although his moves now are decidedly more an expression of triumph, topped off by a gesture in which he uses the blood still flowing from his mouth to paint the signature Joker grin on his face. He stands atop that cop car, arms outstretched and adoring crowds at his feet, when suddenly the screen cuts to black.

We once again hear his pained laugh and suddenly find that a handcuffed Fleck is now in some sort of therapy session—in a white room, as it turns out. One wonders if he is laughing at this point at the fantasy he has just had of himself dancing atop that car, cheered on by his followers. Then Sinatra's "That's Life" once again kicks in on the soundtrack, while Fleck mouths the lyrics in accompaniment, suggesting that this time the music is in his head for sure. A quick cut then shows Fleck walking down a white hallway, leaving tracks of blood behind, presumably suggesting that he has brutally murdered the woman who was interviewing him and that he is now attempting an escape. Of course, this murder (and this escape) might also simply be occurring in Fleck's mind. In any case, at the end of the hall, he does one last jaunty dance (still to Sinatra's rendition of "That's Life"). Then, as Fleck is apparently being chased (almost comically) by someone, the film closes with the end of the song, with the dark turn toward an imagined death that I discussed above. Then the credits begin to roll, to the accompaniment of Sinatra's version of "Send in the Clowns."

As opposed to all the 1981 films referenced in *Joker*, the popular songs used in the film—from "Smile" (1959) and "That's Life (1966), to "White Room" (1968), "Rock and Roll Part 2" (1972), and "Send in the Clowns" (1973)—were not released at a time that is contemporary with the action of the film. Instead, they are all somewhat earlier, having been released in Fleck's formative years. One implication of this fact might be that Fleck is more attuned to the music of his adolescent and young adult years than to his older years, something that is probably true of most people. At the same time, the use mostly of music from the 1960s and early 1970s might provide another link to the early films of Scorsese, which put well-known popular songs at the very center of their soundtracks.

In this, Scorsese's early films were not unique; an unprecedented use of popular music in soundtracks was, in fact, a common characteristic of New Hollywood films. Nevertheless, the music of *Joker* and that of Scorsese's early films share several things that are worthy of note. For example, Bernard Herrmann's brooding score for *Taxi Driver* has much in common with Guðnadóttir's score for *Joker* in terms of setting a mood that seems in tune with the protagonist's troubled state of mind. But *Mean Streets* and *The King of Comedy* are perhaps even more reminiscent of *Joker* in the way they use well-known popular songs in their soundtracks. *The King of Comedy*, for example, includes tracks by an eclectic range of popular artists that include Ray Charles, Chrissie Hind, Talking Heads, Tom Waits, Robbie Robertson, Ric Ocasek, Tom Petty, and Van Morrison, although most of the songs are not among the best-known hits of those artists. Charles's 1959 recording of "Come Rain or Come Shine," which plays during the opening credits, probably comes closest to the kind of well-known songs that are so important to *Joker*.

It is, however, *Mean Streets* that resembles *Joker* most in this regard. Just as Scorsese uses references to film to help establish the cultural milieu in which his characters live, so too does he use music in much the same way. For that reason, it was important to employ songs that would have been familiar (and important) to those characters. Indeed, for such a low-budget film, *Mean Streets* has a surprisingly high-profile soundtrack, headlined by the Rolling Stones' 1968 classic "Jumpin' Jack Flash," one of the truly canonical songs in the rock pantheon. The soundtrack also features R&B classics such as The Shirelles' "I Met Him on a Sunday" (1958) and The Ronettes' "Be My Baby" (1963). Finally, it includes two tracks of songs by groups featuring Eric Clapton, Cream's "Steppin' Out" (1966) and "I Looked Away" (1970), by Derek & the Dominos.

The Cream track perhaps provides a direct link to the soundtrack of *Joker*, although what is probably more important as a link between *Mean Streets* and *Joker* is the general fact that the soundtracks of both films are so important to their overall impact. Scorsese certainly uses the songs on his soundtrack as a way to evoke the cultural milieu in which his characters live. But his songs are also carefully chosen to resonate with the scenes they accompany. For example, "Jumpin' Jack Flash" is possibly the highlight of the soundtrack, not just because it is such an important song in rock history but also because of how effectively it accompanies the film's introduction of the swaggering Johnny Boy. Similarly, the film very effectively uses the Chips' "Rubber Biscuit" (1956) to indicate the drunken state in which Charlie finds himself at one point.

This careful match between music and moment is also a characteristic of *Joker*, although *Joker* is much less concerned with using popular music to indicate the cultural background of Fleck or any of the other characters. Indeed, in this sense, the soundtrack of *Joker*, rather than contributing to the representation of a coherent cultural environment, instead contributes to the film's postmodern fragmentation, which is of course entirely appropriate. Despite Johnny Boy's borderline psychosis in *Mean Streets*, which would seem to align him in some ways with Fleck, he and Charlie do belong to a community with a shared culture and worldview. Fleck, though, has little connection with anyone—and certainly lacks any sense of belonging to a coherent cultural subgroup. Sinatra, Cream, and Jackson Frank don't really seem to fit together as part of a specific playlist, but that is largely the point. Few things fit together in the experience of Arthur Fleck.

Formally, Phillips also uses the songs of his soundtrack in some interesting ways that contribute to the fragmentation of the film. I noted in

Chapter 2 some of the moments in *Joker* in which music plays continuously across otherwise jarring cuts. I would argue, however, that this technique of audio matching does not help to smooth out these cuts. Instead, the continuity in the music actually calls attention to the visual discontinuities involved in the action across these cuts. For example, when the Murray Franklin theme begins to play after Fleck has just (apparently) murdered his mother, we naturally assume that we are hearing it on the television in her hospital room, where we have seen Fleck watching the show. That this music plays seamlessly across a sudden cut back to the Fleck apartment is rather startling and disorienting, suggesting the unstable and fragmented nature of Fleck's consciousness.

Indeed, music is one of the principal methods through which *Joker* conveys the mental state of its title character, a state that, in itself, might be regarded as the central topic of this film. Meanwhile, music is also used to help set the tone and mood of individual scenes in the film, which is, of course, what film music is most generally intended to do. This sort of use of music is especially important, though, in the horror genre, which is another aspect of *Joker* that connects it to that genre. Indeed, some of the most memorable music of the films of the years leading up to and including the historical setting of *Joker* has, in fact, been associated with horror films, especially those involving deranged killers. Thus, the crucial importance of music in *Joker* connects it to such predecessors as the screeching violins of the shower-murder scene of *Psycho* (1960), music that would be referenced in so many subsequent slasher films, including John Carpenter's *Halloween* (1978), which features its own extremely effective (and now iconic) theme music that so compellingly announces the approach of super-slasher Michael Myers. Even a film such as *The Texas Chain Saw Massacre* (1974), not particularly noted for its music, is linked to *Joker* not just because Leatherface, its central killer, is driven to murder by family dysfunction, but also because of Leatherface's trademark, weirdly joyful, whirling, cavorting dance with his chain saw, an antic that is made even more absurd because it seems celebratory but does not particularly seem to be related to any particular cause for celebration. I will discuss in more detail the links between *Joker* and the horror film in the next chapter.

Notes

1 See Kerins for a discussion of the ways in which sound other than music (in particular, ambient urban sounds) plays a key role in creating the film's sense of realism.

2 One well-known Sinatra song that does not appear in *Joker* is "New York, New York," which was written for the soundtrack of Scorsese's 1977 film of the same title and performed in the film by Liza Minnelli. Its most famous version, however, is Sinatra's cover, released in 1980. Interestingly, Sinatra's version was used to close Spike Lee's 1999 film about the Son of Sam killings, *Summer of Sam*.
3 On the background and historical evolution of this song, see Zollo.
4 Janelle Monáe's cover of "Smile" in her 2007 concept album *Metropolis: The Chase Suite* is a particularly bleak recent version that emphasizes the sadness of this ever-so-familiar song. On the other hand, an upbeat instrumental version of the song appears at one point in *Joker*, as Ellis Drane and His Jazz Orchestra play a dancing Fleck onto the stage during his entrance for his appearance on *Live with Murray Franklin*.
5 The rendition of the song used in the film was actually recorded by French jazz pianist Claude Bolling.

Part II
Joker and Political History

CHAPTER SIX

"How Can a President Not Be an Actor?"
Joker and the Reagan Era

Evoking the historical context of the 1980s via film references seems highly appropriate given that this decade was so strikingly marked by the ascension of a former film actor to the presidency of the United States. But *Joker* refers to the real world of its historical context in more direct ways as well, locating its events in a Gotham City that is based, in one way or another, on New York City roughly in the late 1970s or early 1980s. Gotham, from the beginnings of Batman in the late 1930s, had always been based on New York, which was very much the center of the early comics industry. Todd Phillips, meanwhile, was born in Brooklyn in 1970, so the New York of the late 1970s and early 1980s is a milieu that he would remember very well from his childhood. It is fairly clear that the film is generally meant to evoke a range of years, rather than any one specific year, even though the film sometimes goes out of its way to suggest that the setting is based on New York in the specific year of 1981. The film thus seems to want to have it both ways by being both vague and specific about the period in which the events are set, which I take as a marker of the postmodern weakness of any genuine historical sense in the film. But the vagueness can also be seen as part of a historical blurring that ultimately suggests important parallels between 1981 and 2019. This complex engagement with the historical context in which *Joker*'s events take place is a crucial part of the film and one of the characteristics that most clearly identifies it as a thoroughly postmodern work.

Joker's Gotham City and New York History

The general atmosphere of Gotham City in *Joker* evokes a particularly difficult time in the history of New York City, which went through a very troubled period in the late 1970s and early 1980s, beginning with the severe fiscal crisis faced by the city in late 1975. This crisis, meanwhile, is perhaps marked most vividly in historical memory by a notorious newspaper headline that dramatised the stated refusal of then-President Gerald Ford to allow the federal government to come to the city's aid. In a speech delivered at the National Press Club in Washington, D.C., on October 29, 1975, Ford announced his intention to veto any bill that might be passed by Congress to dedicate financial aid to the city. The next day, the *New York Daily News* responded with a front-page headline that remains almost legendary in the annals of the city (and of journalism): "Ford to City: Drop Dead."

Interestingly, the *Daily News* revived this famous headline in June 2017 in reference to President Donald Trump's decision to withdraw the United States from participating in the 2015 Paris Climate Accord. On June 2, 2017, the paper's lead headline read "Trump to World: Drop Dead." This repetition seems even more appropriate when one considers that Ford's attitude here toward New York and the administration of Democratic mayor Abraham Beame certainly anticipates Trump's often-expressed disdain for "Democrat-led" cities, especially during his unsuccessful presidential re-election campaign of 2020. Indeed, another aspect that complicates *Joker*'s engagement with history (which I will discuss in more detail in Chapter 10) is that it is so rooted in its own 2019 historical context, despite its close connection to the early 1980s. For now, I will simply note that the double context of *Joker* in both 1981 and 2019 seems to suggest certain parallels and continuities between the two time frames; at the same time, it also suggests a postmodern lack of historical sense because the film itself never really links the two time periods in a narrative way that treats 1981 as the pre-history of 2019. Instead, it merely suggests parallels between the two periods that suggest similarities without establishing such a narrative connection, a connection that I have characterized in this text as arising from the fact that the two times occupy positions on the same historical timeline of the development of neoliberalism.

The difficulties of late 1975 New York were exacerbated as garbage piled up in the streets of the city thanks to an 11-day strike of private company garbage workers in early December, while a wildcat strike of city sanitation works from July 2–4, 1975 also added to the grim atmosphere of the city during that year. Neither of these particular garbage strikes appears, however, to be the most direct inspiration for the one that is going on in Gotham throughout the events of *Joker*. The radio news report that begins the film announces that the Gotham garbage strike is continuing on this day, identified as Thursday, October 15. October 15 was a Thursday in 1981 (while it was a Wednesday in 1975). A quick check of the historical record then shows that there was indeed a garbage strike in New York City in late 1981, though it occurred in December and lasted 17 days, while the film begins on the eighteenth day of its strike and goes forward from there.[1]

Joker is quite careful, then, to link its Gotham garbage strike to the New York garbage strike of 1981, only to undermine that connection by providing details that are simply inconsistent—again, in what I take as a sign of the postmodern attitude of the film toward history as something that can be drawn upon as needed for material but need not necessarily be represented accurately. Meanwhile, the garbage strike of the film *is* linked to 1975 in another, quite postmodern way, because Scorsese's *Taxi Driver* (1976), which also contributes so much to the texture of *Joker*, was in fact partly filmed on the streets of New York during the July 1975 wildcat garbage strike, a fact that helped to contribute to the decaying vision of the city that comes through in that film.

The importance of Scorsese's early New York films to *Joker* is an indication of the heavily mediatized way in which it remembers the New York past. Indeed, while Phillips is a native New Yorker who lived in the city in 1981, he was only ten years old at the time in which *Joker* appears to be set, so that even his memories of New York at the time probably derive largely from media representations. While making *Joker*, for example, he urged crew members to view Chantal Akerman's documentary film *News from Home* (1977), shot in New York in 1976, to get a feel for the atmosphere he hoped to create in the Gotham City of his film (Tangcay).

Joker portrays its Gotham as a city in the midst of widespread urban decay—and also in the throes of violent civil unrest—as well as in the midst of a mayoral election. In the real world of 1981 New York, there was, in fact, a mayoral election in the fall, although that election does not appear to bear much of a resemblance to the election in the film. For one thing, the events of the film take place in the second half of October and perhaps even beyond, which makes it rather odd that Thomas Wayne would only just be declaring his candidacy for mayor this close to the election. For another thing, despite its many problems, 1981 New York was a city experiencing remarkable political unity: popular incumbent mayor Ed Koch easily won re-election on November 3. Not only did Koch receive an astonishing 74.3 percent of the vote, but he also achieved the unusual feat of being the officially endorsed candidate of both the Democratic and the Republican parties. Meanwhile, none of Koch's

129

opponents seems to have had much in common with *Joker*'s Thomas Wayne. The characterization of Wayne, in fact, does not appear to have been much informed by any real-world New York politicians (although New York would have a billionaire, Michael Bloomberg, elected to mayor in 2001). In fact, the real-world politician who seems to resemble Wayne most would be none other than Donald J. Trump, the billionaire president of the United States at the time *Joker* was made and released, something that I will discuss in more detail in Chapter 10 of this study.

As far as the civil unrest portrayed in *Joker* (which is a central topic of Chapter 9 of this study), there is also no direct correspondence in the history of New York City, even though that city does have a long history of violent disturbances, going back to the draft riots of 1863, in which 120 people were killed after protests against new laws designed to draft additional soldiers for service in the Civil War turned violent. Perhaps the best-remembered, politically motivated civil violence in New York history occurred in the 1969 Stonewall Riots, in which demonstrations by the LGBT community turned violent in response to a police raid of the Stonewall Inn, a gay bar. Finally, the most violent civil unrest of the 1980s in New York occurred in 1988 in the Tompkins Square Park riot. Here, the Koch administration imposed a curfew on Tompkins Square Park after complaints that the park had been taken over by homeless people, drug dealers, and the like during late-night hours of the 24-hour park. Protests against the curfew grew violent as a result of heavy-handed police attempts to dispel the protestors—the *New York Times* termed the event a "police riot."

The Tompkins Square Park riot does not correspond all that closely to the riots that break out near the end of *Joker*, with the exception that the riot was, at the time, widely seen as an example of class warfare and as a reminder of the large gap between the rich and poor in the city. On this view, the police were representing the interests of the wealthy and privileged citizens who were participating in the rapid gentrification of the area around Tompkins Square park, while most of the protestors were members of a downtrodden underclass that had become accustomed to calling the park home.[2] This connection calls attention to the way in which the events of *Joker* sometimes refer quite directly to specific events that occurred in or around the year 1981, while at other times the film's events gesture toward events from slightly different times.

Among the events of *Joker* that are based on specific events from the 1980s, one of the most obvious involves the subway shootings that ostensibly begin Arthur Fleck's career as a murderer. It is quite clear that these shootings are based, at least in part, on an incident on December 22,

1984, in which Bernhard Goetz shot and wounded four black teenagers on a subway train. Goetz was arrested and originally charged with attempted murder, assault, and reckless endangerment, though he was eventually convicted only of a lesser charge of carrying an unlicensed firearm. The terms of this shooting incident are clearly quite different than those of the subway shootings in *Joker* in terms of both race and class, as well as physical circumstances—Goetz, for example, was not assaulted by the teenagers, although it is not entirely clear whether they intended to rob him, as he claimed to believe. And, of course, Goetz's case did not trigger a large-scale revolt, though he did receive a great deal of popular support among New Yorkers who felt that the shootings were an attempt to strike back against the very high crime rate that plagued New York in the early 1980s.

The Goetz case received a huge amount of public attention and became one of the signature events of the early 1980s. Dubbed the "Subway Vigilante," Goetz in an odd way came to play something of the same role that Batman (also often described as a vigilante) has long played in American culture—although public support for Goetz tended to wane as more details about the shootings (and their potential racist motivations) came to light. Goetz himself nevertheless became a figure in American popular culture in his own right; he is mentioned by name, for example, in Billy Joel's landmark 1989 song "We Didn't Start the Fire," which sums up many of the most striking events between World War II and that time, including a line that summarizes the dark texture of the early 1980s: "Foreign debts, homeless vets, AIDS, crack, Bernie Goetz."

Goetz's subway shootings were obviously not the only high-profile violent events in New York in the early 1980s. One recalls, among other things, that ex-Beatle John Lennon, one of the biggest stars in global culture in the twentieth century, was shot and killed just outside his New York apartment building in December of 1980. A recognition of New York's high 1980s crime rate clearly provides some of the dystopian texture of Gotham in *Joker*—as well as in a number of Batman works of the 1980s, including Tim Burton's original 1989 film. That period has provided inspiration for numerous other films, as well. For example, J. C. Chandor's critically acclaimed (although commercially unsuccessful) crime film *A Most Violent Year* (2014) is set in New York in 1981. The very title of this film—not to mention its violent narrative—indicates the texture of life in New York in 1981, a texture that is very well captured in *Joker*.

No Joke: Todd Phillips's *Joker* and American Culture

Ronald Reagan, the Movie

This dialogue with the history of New York City is crucial to the overall import of *Joker*. However, what might be even more crucial is the film's broader dialogue with American history in the late 1970s and early 1980s—although, of course, New York is an important part of America, and its history cannot be treated as entirely separate from American history as a whole. For one thing, New York was obviously not the only place in America where violence occurred in the early 1980s. Thus, if the 1980s got off to a rough start in New York with the murder of Lennon, it was only a few months later, on March 31, 1981, that John Hinckley Jr. shot and wounded new president Ronald Reagan in an assassination attempt in Washington, D.C., in the same attack also wounding police officer Thomas Delahanty and Secret Service agent Tim McCarthy. Reagan's Press Secretary, James Brady, suffered a particularly serious head wound and was permanently disabled, eventually dying 33 years later in a death that was ruled directly related to the shooting.

The attempted assassination of Reagan is linked to *Joker* in ways that go beyond the simple fact that it can be taken as evidence of the violent nature of early-1980s America. Hinckley, as it turns out, had become obsessed with young actress Jodie Foster after watching her performance in *Taxi Driver*, a film that also involves a political assassination attempt; Hinckley then attempted to kill Reagan in the hope of gaining Foster's attention (having earlier stalked Reagan's predecessor, Jimmy Carter, for an extended period, with the same possibility in mind). Given the substantial influence of *Taxi Driver* on *Joker* (see Chapter 3), the fact that this film was a crucial part of the background of Hinckley's attack on Reagan already suggests an interesting connection between that attack and *Joker*.

While exact diagnoses at the time were not definitive, Hinckley (much like Arthur Fleck) clearly suffered from a dangerous mental illness (most diagnoses have seen him as principally suffering from untreated schizophrenia) that made him a threat to himself and others. Indeed, Hinckley was found not guilty by reason of insanity when tried for the shootings, subsequently spending the next 35 years under psychiatric care in a mental facility. Hinckley's acquittal was controversial at the time, leading to widespread debate over the general merits of insanity defenses that ultimately led to the Insanity Defense Reform Act of 1984. Ironically, though, while it does seem clear that Hinckley was suffering from a serious, untreated mental illness at the time of the attempted assassination, his case did not lead to a re-examination of America's mental health system or to reforms of a kind that might have prevented the shooting of Reagan in the first place.

In fact, the reverse seems to be true. In 1978, the President's Commission on Mental Health reported to then-President Jimmy Carter that the U.S. mental health system was in need of significant reform and improvement. This report led to one of the signature achievements of the last year of the Carter administration when Carter signed into law the Mental Health Systems Act (MHSA), on October 7, 1980. This act was designed to expand the support provided to state and local mental health systems by the federal government. Before much could actually be implemented, however, Reagan had defeated Carter in the presidential election of November 1980, ascending to the presidency on January 20, 1981. Reagan entered the White House with a strong distrust of psychiatric medicine in general and with no intention of vigorously pursuing the reforms dictated by the MHSA. By August 13, 1981, Reagan would be signing into law a bill that dismantled most of the provisions of the MHSA and substantially reduced federal support for the treatment of the mentally ill.

As Alexander R. Thomas outlines, much of this assault on the mental health system was part of a larger strategy to realign the American economy by dismantling the Welfare State as much as possible and reconceiving the U.S. government as an entity whose principal function was not the provision of services to vulnerable individuals but the maintenance of a socioeconomic system that was favorable to businesses and corporations. This radical restructuring involved, among other things, the intentional undermining of a number of respected government institutions. Thomas summarizes some of Reagan's policies in a way that makes them seem oddly familiar to those of us who can so vividly remember the more recent years of the Trump administration, noting Reagan's appointment to the National Labor Relations Board of officials who were declaredly anti-union, implicitly authorizing employers vigorously to pursue anti-union actions that had long been shunned in America. Further, Thomas notes that

> Reagan himself pursued such a policy when he fired eleven thousand striking air traffic controllers in 1981. Regulations designed to protect the environment, worker safety, and consumer rights were summarily decried as unnecessary government meddling in the marketplace. Programs designed to help the poor were also characterized as "big government," and the people who utilized such programs were often stigmatized as lazy or even criminal. With

the help of both political parties, the administration drastically cut social welfare spending and the budgets of many regulatory agencies.

Thomas argues that Reagan saw the dismantling of the MHSA as part of this same war against big government and the welfare state, in the interest of capital and big business. The effect, however, was to significantly reduce the amount of care for the mentally ill that was provided by the state, including a major reduction in institutionalization in government-run mental health facilities that saw a number of mentally ill patients emptied out onto the streets, often with little or no subsequent treatment or supervision. Thomas summarizes the overall impact of Reagan's social policies, including the dismantling of the MHSA:

> Reagan's economic policy was to adjust government regulation so that it favored business once again, and social policy was merely an outgrowth of this larger issue. While family groups and professional groups and patient groups did clamor for respect, the real struggle was between the state and the business community. Reagan worked to lessen the tax load for the rich, and the social policies were meant to match this goal. Business needed a more favorable corporate climate, and Reagan worked to that end. […] As for the mentally ill, certain changes that their families and practitioners wanted were gained, and the administration pointed this out. Even though these changes came about primarily through state governments and the courts, the Administration would take credit. All in all, business interests were served. Families and doctors were appeased. Patients were forgotten.

At the same time, while Thomas rightly focuses on the larger agenda of the Reagan administration, it should not be overlooked that Reagan himself, with almost no appropriate education and relatively little relevant experience that qualified him for the presidency, had a number of peculiar attitudes that influenced his attitudes, including that toward the mental health system. At first glance, Reagan's lack of belief in federal support for the mental health system seems quite peculiar in light of the fact that he himself had been shot and nearly killed by an untreated schizophrenic. Moreover, former Congressman Allard Lowenstein had been killed by an untreated schizophrenic just over two weeks before Reagan's shooting, while Lennon (three months before that) had also been killed by an untreated schizophrenic. Torrey, meanwhile, notes that the whole decade of the 1980s was marked by a number of high-profile killings committed by untreated or prematurely released mental patients (104).

Given this environment, one might think that the mental health system would have been excluded from Reagan's attempts to dismantle the welfare state, but Reagan, in fact, had a long history of hostility and suspicion toward the whole concept of treatment for mental health. As Gary Wills points out, Reagan had also tried to cut government support for mental health when he was governor of California, although in this case his cuts triggered such a widespread public backlash that the state government was ultimately forced to *increase* spending on mental health (435–436).

Torrey, in his study of the tremendous damage done to the American mental health system by federal government policies (especially during the Reagan administration), points toward one particular reason, beyond a general hostility toward big government, for the special animus that Reagan reserved for the mental health system: "President Reagan never understood mental illness. Like Nixon, he was a product of the Southern California culture that associated psychiatry with communism" (88). Both Nixon and Reagan were, of course, Cold War presidents, so it is not, at first glance, surprising that they would view communism as the enemy. But their unreasoning hatred of communism spilled into paranoid excess. This excess, of course, was sometimes calculated. It was certainly useful. Nixon rose to political prominence as a relatively little-known Congressman who made a name for himself as a communist witch-hunter in the Alger Hiss case, while Reagan's most effective and widely remembered piece of political rhetoric might well be his characterization (delivered, tellingly, in a speech delivered before a convention of the National Association of Evangelicals) of the Soviet Union as an "evil empire."

Reagan's speech, delivered on March 8, 1983, did indeed have an evangelical tone, recasting the political disagreements of the Cold War as a clearly delineated battle between good, God-fearing Americans and evil, godless Soviets. But it also has a pop cultural tone; it reminded many at the time of the evil empire that had figured so prominently in George Lucas's *Star Wars* franchise, at that time a dominant force in the American pop cultural consciousness, thanks to the recent success of *Star Wars* (1977) and *The Empire Strikes Back* (1980), with *The Return of the Jedi* only two months away. Reagan then reaffirmed suspicions that *Star Wars* might have been influencing his thinking with another landmark speech on March 23, when he outlined his science fictionesque plan for an elaborate advanced missile defense system official known as the "Strategic Defense Initiative" (SDI). That system would never become a reality, although the program would not be officially canceled until Bill Clinton became president in 1992, finally ending the Reagan–Bush era.

On March 24, Democratic Senator Ted Kennedy called Reagan's SDI plan a collection of "reckless *Star Wars* schemes," and the *Star Wars* designation was widely used to denigrate the system, which many scientists soon declared to be impracticable and unrealizable. But the phrase caught on in the popular consciousness and came to be widely used, sometimes even by supporters of the SDI. By 1985, television commercials touting the SDI and referring to it as the "Star Wars" defense system were widely shown. Lucas even filed suit in an attempt to prevent his *Star Wars* trademark from being used to characterize Reagan's scheme, with which he did not want to be associated. A judge ruled, however, that the term "Star Wars" was in public domain and that Lucas had no legal recourse to its use in association with the SDI (Rogin 43).

Perhaps it comes as no surprise that the first American president to be a former Hollywood actor would derive rhetoric from a prominent film. Asked while running for president if he thought it was appropriate for an actor to be president, Reagan famously responded, "how can a president *not* be an actor?" Indeed, Reagan seems to have brought a new performative aspect to the presidency. For example, as Rogin points out, Reagan derived a great deal of his rhetoric (and perhaps his worldview) from the movies. Importantly, most of this inspiration came from classic films of the period in which Reagan himself had worked in Hollywood. As Rogin points out, these films "put realism in the service of fantasy, as if movies were mirroring the mundane. [...] For many people, movies functioned as arenas for role playing, and they were the place where the role player who was to become president of the United States discovered his identity" (6). Noting Reagan's tendency to lift material from movies—such as quoting Clint Eastwood's Dirty Harry character in order to make himself seem tough—Rogin concludes that "Reagan's easy slippage between movies and reality is synecdochic for a political culture increasingly impervious to distinctions between fiction and history" (9).

Reagan's personal battle against communism seems to have been one of the key areas in which he may have confused reality with fantasy. As Rogin notes, "the fantasy of Communists taking over Hollywood was delusional, the stuff of a Hollywood movie" (27). Of course, the fact that the narrative of nefarious communists infiltrating and controlling Hollywood was so obviously the stuff of cinematic fiction made the narrative more, not less, attractive to someone like Reagan, whose thought processes were so extensively shaped by the movies. That such a crackpot worldview would propel Reagan to the presidency at first seems far-fetched—about as far-fetched as a television reality game show host known for abusing his contestants being propelled to the presidency. But Reagan's view of the communist threat, however divorced from reality, was widely held (by Nixon, among others); it was, in fact, a mainstream view during the peak Cold War years following World War II, making the road to a Reagan presidency not all that surprising.

Arthur Fleck, the Talk Show

The connections between Reagan and *Joker* are, in fact, numerous and important, and it seems likely that one of the more significant things about the year 1981 as the setting for *Joker* is that this year was the first one of the Reagan administration and the beginning of a Reagan–Bush Republican hegemony that would last through 1992. The most obvious and direct connection inheres in the fact that Arthur Fleck is a former mental in-patient who has been prematurely thrust into the streets just as Reagan's dismantling of the MHSA two months earlier was leading to the early release of mental patients all over the country in real-world America. But there is perhaps a deeper and more telling parallel between the ways in which Reagan and Fleck both find it difficult to distinguish fiction from reality, a difficulty that has informed the texture of American political life from the 1980s to the present day, making Fleck's mental condition not only an allegorization of the fragmented nature of psychic life under late capitalism but an emblem of a growing disengagement from reality that has dogged American politics since the days of the McCarthyite anti-communist witch hunts, culminating in the surreal "post-truth" era of Trumpism.

That Arthur Fleck is one of the forgotten mental patients denied adequate treatment in the early 1980s is established quite early in *Joker*. As Fleck consults that harried "Health Department Social Worker" immediately after the display of the film's title, we are first introduced to his laughing disorder, which seems to strike him whenever he is under any kind of particular emotional duress. Though the name of this disorder is never mentioned in the film, there is a real disorder that involves uncontrolled laughter that is not related to genuine mirth, known as the "pseudobulbar affect," or "PBA." And Fleck's display of symptoms is relatively true to what we know about this disorder, although true sufferers of PBA experience laughter that is not related to their mental state at all and thus is not triggered by stress. The film, though, is not concerned with an accurate portrayal of this condition. Rather, it is simply concerned with establishing that Fleck is mentally and emotionally dysfunctional, in this case using a traditional aspect of the character of the Joker from the Batman comics—his famous unhinged laugh—as an inspiration for one of Fleck's key symptoms.

As this scene continues, it is clear from the shabby decor of the social worker's office that the Department of Health does not have lavish resources with which to support her work. Thus, when Fleck asks his question about whether it is getting crazier out there, and she responds in an economically focused way (leading to the conclusion that "these are tough times"), one can easily imagine that she is referring, not just to Gotham in general, but also to her own underfunded department. The dour social worker does not seem particularly engaged with Fleck's case (and has apparently forgotten that he told her he was attempting to pursue a career as a stand-up comic). Indeed, her questions seem mechanical and scripted. When he tells her that he felt better when he was locked up, she asks him if he has thought more about why he was locked up. His response—"Who knows?"—sums up the general epistemological situation in this film and will remain a question throughout. We will never learn why Fleck had been locked up, and the film does not specify why he has been released, although the fact that this session is apparently occurring in October of 1981 makes it fairly clear that he, like so many others, was released as a result of the Reagan administration's cutbacks in support for mental health. That this release was premature is signaled by the fact that Fleck is now feeling worse, despite the seven medications he is on. In fact, he asks the social worker if she can get the doctor to order even more medications for him, because "I just don't want to feel so bad anymore."

It is clear that one of the principal forces that drives Fleck over the edge is the simple feeling of being unseen, unheard, and forgotten. This situation applies even to his social worker. In a later session, she interrupts Fleck's discourse to inform him that she has some bad news. Fleck shakes his head at the interruption, suggesting that she never really listens to anything he says, merely asking him formulaic questions, such as whether he has any negative thoughts. "All I have are negative thoughts, but you don't listen," he tells her. He's apparently right, because her only response is to note that, due to ongoing budget cuts, she will no longer be meeting with him, thus depriving him of even that meager amount of support. "They don't give a shit" about people like Arthur, or, for that matter, her, she declares, referring most obviously to the Gotham city government, but perhaps also suggesting a critique of the "not-my-problem" attitude of the Reagan administration toward the mentally ill. According to what we see on the screen, this new development will eventually send Fleck off his meds and out of treatment altogether, to the disastrous results that we observe in the film.

Because Fleck receives no real treatment in the film, we have very little in the way of actual medical information about his condition. In fact, in a further reflection of the inadequacy of the system that is supposed to be serving people like him, it is not clear that Fleck himself has ever received an accurate diagnosis of his condition. Fleck's sense of being invisible and forgotten is no doubt partly a result of the lack of available treatment and support, so that this lack of a diagnosis is a powerful commentary. At the same time, it is also the case that the specifics of Fleck's condition are not particularly germane to the narrative of the film. We know enough about his symptoms, about his psychic pain and his difficulty in distinguishing fantasy from reality in order to understand how important these are to the narrative, even if we don't have a specific name for his condition.[3]

I would, in fact, go so far as to argue that the real significance of Fleck's condition is not medical but political. Read allegorically, his condition certainly comments on the breakdown of the American mental health system as a result of the policies of the Reagan administration. But that is only one of many ways in which the film engages with Reagan and his policies. Indeed, Fleck's disengagement from reality is not that far removed from Reagan's seeming tendency to blur the distinction between reality and the movies. As Rogin notes, Reagan would sometimes relate anecdotes that he claimed (and perhaps believed) to derive from actual events. A close check, however, would show that the entire anecdote seemed to have been lifted from a movie. For example, Rogin relates the story of how Reagan once told a mass audience about a courageous bomber captain who won a posthumous Medal of Honor after he chose to go down with his plane so that he could provide comfort to a wounded crew member who was trapped on board. Reagan related this story as if it had really happened, although in fact it actually occurred in the 1944 film *A Wing and a Prayer* (7–8). In fact, Reagan repeated this story frequently during his 1980 presidential campaign, obviously hoping that audiences would somehow associate the story with the kind of American heroic virtue that he himself sought to project to voters. In addition, as David Mikkelson notes in his discussion of this anecdote on the fact-checking site Snopes.com, Reagan even went the extra mile, going so far as to claim that he knew of this story because he himself had worked during the war on the committee that recommended the heroic captain for the Medal of Honor.

Whether Reagan was flat-out lying or whether he himself had somehow come to believe that this tear-jerking story was true is almost

No Joke: Todd Phillips's *Joker* and American Culture

beside the point. Reagan had the kind of reassuring, affable charm that made audiences *want* his stories to be true, even when they suspected that they weren't. Meanwhile, Reagan had spent nearly 30 years of his adult life working in Hollywood, so it perhaps comes as no surprise that so much of his perception of reality was filtered through the movies. And he certainly wasn't the only American of his generation whose understanding of what the world is really like came largely from the movies. One could argue, in fact, that *Joker*, which demonstrates a view of the early 1980s that is so heavily filtered through films of that era, shows some of this same tendency, as, to an extent, does its central character.

As I noted in Chapter 3, it is even interesting to imagine that one reason why so much of Arthur Fleck's world seems like something from a vintage Scorsese movie is that Fleck himself might have seen some of these films—though, of course, it is important to remember that *Joker* does not take place in our reality and that there is no direct evidence that Scorsese or his films even exist in the world of the film's Gotham City. There is, however, direct evidence in the film that many films from *our* 1981 also exist in the 1981 of the film. In addition, we actually see Fleck watching (and responding strongly to) two Golden Age Hollywood films in the course of his activities within *Joker*.

I have already noted the sequence in *Joker* in which Fleck ostensibly attends a screening of Charlie Chaplin's *Modern Times* (1936), a film that certainly could be important to Fleck, both because Chaplin might be one of his comedic heroes and because his Little Tramp character represents precisely the sort of lowly outcast figure that Fleck imagines himself to be. In that sense, the ultimate triumph of the Tramp in *Modern Times* (and elsewhere), keeping his good humor and sweet disposition regardless of the misfortunes that befall him, might have provided a potential model for Fleck, although it is not a model that he is ultimately able to emulate.

The other classic Hollywood film we see Fleck watching during *Joker* (this time on television) is the 1937 Fred Astaire–Ginger Rogers vehicle *Shall We Dance*. We only see a brief snippet of this film, but its appearance is still quite significant. Fleck watches the film just after giving his mother a bath; he seems agitated (perhaps because of her suggestion during the bath that he is not funny enough to be a comedian) and is fondling his revolver, obviously contemplating both suicide and murder, though it is not clear who his contemplated victim (or victims) might be. This time he is watching on the slightly larger, color television in the Fleck living room, although, of course, the film is in black and white, so it is not clear from this scene that this is a color TV. What is clear, though, is that the Flecks, in their meager household, have at least two televisions (and a VCR, still a relative luxury in 1981), suggesting just how thoroughly the medium of television has colonized their lives. As Fleck watches the movie, he begins one of his dances; Astaire, as perhaps America's most famous movie dancer, is clearly another role model for Fleck, who seems to regard dancing as one of his greatest talents. Here, he imagines an exchange with a woman (possibly Sophie) in which she compliments him, noting that he is a really good dancer. "I know," he says, confidently, "You know who's not? *Him*!" He then swings the gun toward an imaginary foe (possibly Astaire, but more likely Murray Franklin, who frequently dances—badly—during his show) and accidentally fires it, blowing a hole in the wall and startling his mother.

That this movie resonates with Fleck's own inclination toward dancing would in itself be a perfectly good reason to include it in *Joker*. In turns out, though, that almost everything in this film is more complex, multi-layered, and carefully chosen than might immediately be obvious. For example, the snippet that we see is the beginning of an upbeat musical number called "Slap That Bass," in which energetic, jazzy music is declared to be a cure for what ails you. Yet, underneath this cheerful surface, there is the opening declaration by a member of the all-black ensemble cast that supports Astaire in the scene, of a situation that not only acknowledges the Depression-era context of this film but also seems to match the dystopian situation we find in the Gotham City of *Joker*:

> The world is in a mess, yes!
> Politics, taxes, and people grinding axes,
> There's no happiness!

Other aspects of *Shall We Dance*, not included in the brief segment we see, also resonate with *Joker*. For one thing, the music for this film was written by George Gershwin (with lyrics by his brother Ira), a sort of musical poet laureate of New York City, his jazzy *Rhapsody in Blue* serving as an unofficial theme song for the city.[4] Near the end of the film, meanwhile, Astaire dances with a troupe of female dancers, all of whom wear masks made from a photograph of the face of Ginger Rogers, signaling the devotion of Astaire's characters to Rogers' character. It's a rather creepy scene, actually, but it connects in an interesting way with the scenes of crowds wearing clown masks in *Joker*. And, finally, *Shall We Dance* ends as Astaire and Rogers are reunited in one final dance as Astaire sings "They All Laughed," which Rogers had sung earlier in the film and which might have served as a theme song for *Joker*, especially as it ends with Astaire looking into the camera and singing, triumphantly, "Who's laughing now?"

This last line, of course, also closely resembles the punch line of the best joke told by Fleck in *Joker*, while at the same time glossing Fleck's seeming rise to power and prominence near the end of *Joker*. Meanwhile, the song "They All Laughed" is a love song, but it is also somewhat of a paean to technological progress; the bulk of its lyrics consists of a catalog of technological innovators whose inventions at first seemed far-fetched, maybe even laughable, until their value finally came to be widely recognized, which is then compared to the quest of the singer to win the heart of his or her loved one. In this, *Shall We Dance* is a sort of counterpoint to *Modern Times*, which shows a strong suspicion toward the potential dehumanizing consequences of technology. That *Shall We Dance* openly embraces the technology of which *Modern Times* is so suspicious can also be seen in the sequence that includes "Slap That Bass." Here, Astaire and his supporting cast perform in the engine room of an ocean liner and so are surrounded by massive, pumping machinery. But the song, despite its beginning, is a happy one, assuring listeners that music can make them happy, despite the apparently sad state of the world. Moreover, unlike the dark, menacing, and ultimately enslaving machinery that fills the factory in *Modern Times*, this art-deco engine room is gleaming in all white and chrome, looking more like art than technology. Astaire dances to the rhythm of the massive machines around him, as if to say that it is possible to find joy in the music of modernity. Meanwhile, as opposed to the harried factory workers of *Modern Times*, the workers in this engine room, clad in spotless white shirts, seem totally carefree. The machines do all the work, while the all-black cast of workers is free to dance and sing along with Astaire's character, a famous faux-Russian ballet dancer who has deigned to slum it in their midst.

Shall We Dance resonates with *Modern Times* in other ways as well. *Modern Times* is, in a sense, Chaplin's surrender to the new technology of integrated sound, which he had resisted for so long. Indeed, one of the film's most famous sequences shows the Tramp being caught up and fed through the gears of the machinery at the factory in which he works, very much as film is fed through the sprockets of a projector. The implication is clear: Chaplin's concerns about the dehumanizing consequences of an excessive reliance on technology include (and even perhaps focus on) the increasing reliance on technology in filmmaking, of which the new integrated sound technologies are the most spectacular recent example. To emphasize this concern, *Modern Times* (Chaplin's first sound film) still contains very minimal dialogue, taking advantage of the new technology most effectively through music, perhaps most memorably in Chaplin's performance of the nonsense song *"Je cherche après Titine,"* in which the famous comedian shows off his skills from his younger days on the London music hall stage. He might not be able to dance like Fred Astaire, but he can perform with the best of them.

Shall We Dance is a key example of the kind of escapist musical that was so popular in the 1930s, clearly designed to provide audiences with fantasy respite from the miseries of the Great Depression. The musical genre, of course, was also the one that embraced sound most enthusiastically, depending on integrated sound for its very existence. Thus, while Chaplin struggled ever to attain in the sound era the lofty status he had enjoyed in the silent film era, it is difficult to imagine that Astaire could have ever become a major movie star had the coming of integrated sound not enabled the development of the genre of the Hollywood musical.

Finally, however impressive Chaplin's dancing and singing might be in performing *"Je cherche après Titine,"* his most impressive set-piece in *Modern Times* just might be that department store roller-skating scene that Fleck ostensibly watches in Wayne Hall. Interestingly, if Chaplin's dancing and singing in *Modern Times* seem almost like a reminder that he can match musical stars such as Astaire if he so chooses, one dance segment of *Shall We Dance* reads almost like Astaire's response to Chaplin. That segment, performed to the now well-known song "Let's Call the Whole Thing Off," features Astaire and Rogers dancing together *on roller skates*.[5]

Such scenes are not all that unusual: they would become almost like standard tests of agility in musical films: for example, famed movie dancers Donald O'Connor (in the 1953 film *I Love Melvin*) and Gene Kelly (in the 1955 film *It's Always Fair Weather*) would eventually dance on roller skates on film as well. Nevertheless, this roller-skating scene in *Shall We Dance* participates in a complex web of interconnections among *Joker*, *Modern Times*, and *Shall We Dance* that demands interrogation. At the most obvious level, the inclusion of these films within *Joker* reminds us of just how much *Joker* draws upon the films of the past for examples of both style and content, including a reminder that *Joker*'s use of past films goes well beyond its heavy reliance on films of the period in which its action takes place.

One of the things the presence of these Golden Age films reminds us of is that a large part of the American worldview in the 1980s had been constituted by such films. Ronald Reagan might have been a special case, both because of his prominence and because of his professional background in the movies, but he was clearly not the only American of his generation to have had his notion of what the world is like strongly influenced by what he had seen in the pointedly unrealistic movies produced by Golden Age Hollywood. Meanwhile, by including both *Modern Times* and *Shall We Dance*, two movies that at first glance seem so ideologically dissimilar, as examples of films that have influenced the evolution of the American worldview, *Joker* suggests that the Golden Age Hollywood vision of America was so powerful that it could function over a wide range of perspectives.

Chaplin's Tramp, in *Modern Times*, is a lowly factory worker who is jailed as a suspected communist agitator, becomes unemployed, yet remains unbowed and emerges triumphant, walking happily into the future with his beautiful true love as the film ends. In *Shall We Dance*, Astaire plays the prominent Russian ballet star Petrov, although we quickly learn that he is something of an impostor. Though certainly a talented dancer, he is in fact Peter P. Peters, who comes from a relatively humble (and very American) background in Philadelphia. Meanwhile, he falls in love with the American tap dancer and musical stage star played by Rogers. They, of course, wind up happily together despite their seeming cultural mismatch, a mismatch that is complicated by the fact that "Petrov" is neither a foreigner nor a fundamentally highfaluting artist. As in *Modern Times*, love conquers all, and the ordinary man prevails, even if he has assumed an identity that makes him seem anything but ordinary.

Both Chaplin and Astaire, two of the biggest stars in Hollywood history, would seem to verify this vision of the triumph of the common man, given that both originated from humble beginnings as the children of parents who put them to work on the stage at a very young age. Ultimately, though, both became rich and famous and widely admired thanks to their performances in the movies, even if Chaplin, a British national, would ultimately be driven into exile from America in 1952 due to the repressive political climate fostered by politicians such as Nixon and supported in Hollywood by anti-communist crusaders such as Reagan. Thus, while Chaplin's fate would ultimately reveal the dark side of the Hollywood dream machine, both he and Astaire still stand as images of one of the notions that Golden Age Hollywood films attempted to convey, suggesting that anyone can be a star and that true love conquers all, both of which are key elements of a distinctively American individualism that emphasizes the basic goodness and capability of the common man, traits which combine to give him access to upward mobility and a fulfilling heteronormative patriarchal relationship.

Arthur Fleck, then, has grown up in a world infused with the notion that men (especially *American* men) can achieve a happy life with a beautiful, but subservient, woman at their side by sheer force of determination and perseverance. And, given his background and psychological condition, it comes as no surprise that Fleck might take this notion literally and might feel that he has been shortchanged and mistreated because he has achieved none of the rewards promised by the Hollywood version of the American dream. Fleck, after all, would have been born around 1950, when Golden Age Hollywood was still very much alive, although poised on the precipice of a coming decline, with the Paramount anti-trust case having broken the hegemony of the big studios in 1948 and television just about to emerge as a major competitor for cultural power in America.

Interestingly, the two classic films that Fleck watches in *Joker* were released in 1936 and 1937, which means they are roughly from the same period that seems to have inspired Reagan. In fact, Reagan began his own Hollywood career in 1937 (after a stint as a sportscaster), so that *Joker* looks back through the inclusion of these two films to precisely the moment when Reagan's life began to be shaped so strongly by the movies. I am not suggesting that the inclusion of these films is a conscious allusion to Reagan himself; I am, however, suggesting that it is not insignificant that these two films represent the same era of Hollywood film that went into the shaping of Reagan's particular consciousness—and of much of the American consciousness in general.

From this point of view, it is important that the events depicted in *Joker* can be taken, not only as reflecting Fleck's personal disillusionment at having been excluded from the American dream depicted by Golden Age Hollywood, but also as suggesting the way in which this vision was beginning to lose its purchase on the popular American imagination in light of the fact that it was becoming increasingly obvious that the vision of America put forth in Golden Age Hollywood films was simply not an accurate representation of reality. Meanwhile, the transition that began at the start of the 1950s—roughly contemporaneous with the birth of Fleck—was by this time pretty much complete. Scorsese and the other directors of the New Hollywood movement had transformed American film in the 1970s, producing a much darker and less idealized vision of America.

As numerous observers have detailed, the New Hollywood phenomenon was enabled by a number of historical transformations in the American film industry, including the declining power of the older studio system and the demise of the Production Code, partly fueled by the social movements of the 1960s. I would argue, however, that this new cinematic version of America, which could be quite subversive relative to the Golden

No Joke: Todd Phillips's *Joker* and American Culture

Age version, was also made possible by the fact that film was simply no longer the dominant force in establishing the official fictionalized version of America. That role had by this time been taken on by television, a fact that *Joker* acknowledges in a variety of ways.

Television factors much more prominently in *Joker* than in most American films, which tend to ignore the existence of television altogether unless they happen to be specifically *about* television, as in the case of Sidney Lumet's *Network* (1976), the most important New Hollywood film in this category. I have noted elsewhere that *Network* is a "scathing cynical commentary on the venal, corrupt, and thoroughly commodified nature of American culture in the postmodern era of late capitalism. It focuses on the cheerful willingness of television network executives to stoop to any level of exploitation in the interest of higher ratings—and thus higher profits for their corporate bosses" (*Postmodern Hollywood* 158). *Network* is unusual in the realism with which it critiques the attempt of television news to convert reality into entertainment, but it is not unusual among the films of its time in maintaining a largely critical attitude toward the medium of television.

Joker depicts a world that is thoroughly saturated by television. However, one of the ways in which it is clearly a work of 2019, rather than 1981, is that it depicts this situation without comment or criticism: it is simply treated as a given. At least one of the two televisions almost always seems to be on in the Fleck household. When we first see Fleck in the apartment, for example, he comes home to find Penny watching the news on television. The program continues to play in the background as Fleck feeds his mother her TV dinner, conveying a report about the fact that Gotham seems to have been invaded by a new strain of "super rats" that are very hard to kill, thus adding to the film's depiction of a dystopian, decaying Gotham. The co-anchors treat the report essentially as a joke (one of them quipping that the city apparently needs to find a Pied Piper). Just as this quip is heard in the background, Penny announces that Thomas Wayne "will make a great mayor," almost as if the billionaire might be just the Pied Piper Gotham needs, although it is clear that neither of the Flecks is really listening to the news.

Immediately after the news, the Murray Franklin show comes on the television (with Franklin beginning his opening monologue with a rather lame joke about the super rats, suggesting that they might be battled with super cats). This opening then leads to the scene in which Fleck fantasizes himself in the show's audience, being acknowledged and called down to the stage by Franklin. This scene makes it clear early-on that television is a key source of Fleck's fantasy life. Meanwhile, that the Flecks watch this scene on a small black and white television in Penny's bedroom, while Fleck vividly imagines it in color, indicates just how powerful his imagination can be. As the scene ends, with Franklin hugging Fleck on his colorful stage, we cut back to the Fleck apartment, where Arthur and Penny now appear to be in black and white (perhaps because of the light from the TV), suggesting the relatively impoverished nature of their material existence relative to what Arthur imagines the world of Franklin's show to be.[6]

The next time we see Fleck returning home, he meets Sophie in the elevator, which sends him strolling down the hall to his apartment to the sound of Lawrence Welk and His Orchestra playing the romantic song "The Moon Is a Silver Dollar." Welk and his orchestra, of course, are best known for their appearances on *The Lawrence Welk Show*, which began airing locally in Los Angeles in 1951 (again, about the time of Fleck's birth), and then ran nationally (either on ABC or in syndication) from 1955 to 1982. It would have been on essentially all of Fleck's life, and it is not unlikely that his mother might have been a fan, so that the show might have played often in the Fleck household. It is easy to imagine, then, that Fleck might have heard "The Moon Is a Silver Dollar" on the show, although it had first been recorded by Welk in 1939 and is thus close to contemporaneous with films such as *Shall We Dance*. It's a romantic song about dreams coming true, and so it is easy to see how Fleck's meeting with Sophie might have triggered it in his head, although it is also a song whose lyrics couch dreams in the language of money, inadvertently suggesting the way in which love, like everything else, has become a commodity in modern-day America.

When Fleck enters the apartment and bathes his mother, we can still hear "The Moon Is a Silver Dollar" faintly playing on the soundtrack, as if coming from the television in the next room—although we might also be hearing the soundtrack inside Fleck's head. There is, in this film, a very fine line between the world of television and the world inside Fleck's head, so much so that even he (not to mention we viewers) sometimes cannot tell the two worlds apart. Then follows the moment in which Fleck watches *Shall We Dance* on television, suggesting that the boundary between the worlds of film and television, as well, is at this point collapsing.

A bit later, soon after the subway shootings, Fleck watches Thomas Wayne commenting on the crime on a morning television program (*Good Morning, Gotham*), seen in color on the living-room TV. Among other things, given their penchant for watching Franklin's late-night show, that the Flecks are now watching a morning show suggests that they watch television virtually around the clock. In any case, they clearly have a special interest in this program, given Wayne's appearance, in which he reveals that the three shooting victims had all been employees of Wayne Investments. This is the point at which Wayne inspires Penny with his declaration that all Wayne employees are like family to him. Arthur, though, is more interested in the host's suggestion that, amid the rising tensions between the rich and the poor in Gotham, "it's almost as if our less fortunate residents are taking the side of the killer." Wayne responds that this situation is a shame and is one of the reasons why he is considering a run for mayor.

Wayne's class-based haughtiness and absolute disdain for the 99 percent are key to the political texture of this film. Such attitudes on the part of the rich are also key to Fleck's growing animosity toward the Gotham establishment, something that is clear in his nervous reaction to this televised interview. Meanwhile, Penny's ongoing loyalty to Wayne is clearly a sore point with her son (and might well be a key reason why he ultimately commits matricide, or at least fantasizes about it). The next time Fleck sees Wayne on TV, Fleck is watching from Penny's bed, with Penny away at the hospital. Wayne is now officially running for mayor, with the "kill-the-rich" protests building around him. Wayne, of course, regards the protestors with contempt, claiming that they don't realize he is their "only hope." Fleck takes it all in, wheels clearly turning inside his head, but we have no access to what exactly is going on in there.

What we can tell is that Fleck's inner life has been strongly constituted by the constant watching of television—perhaps even more than Reagan's had been constituted by the movies, given that television penetrates daily life more thoroughly than the movies ever had. Indeed, one of the key ways in which *Joker* engages with its context in the early 1980s is its clear suggestion of a sociohistorical movement through which television has, by that time, replaced film as the dominant cultural force in American life. This movement, in fact, is emphatically announced near the end of the film in that moment when those 24 television screens expand to overwhelm the entire *mise en scène* of the film, suggesting the way in which the fragmented, postmodern world of television, with many different representations being broadcast simultaneously side-by-side, is now the dominant form through which Americans receive representations of reality.

Among other things, television during the period in which *Joker* is set called attention to real-world events in a way that was unprecedented in the extent to which the representation of these events penetrated the popular consciousness. In addition, certain aspects of television news coverage not only tended to favor sensational events but to sensationalize these events even more. One key aspect of the historical context of the 1970s and 1980s that both illustrates this phenomenon and provides important context for *Joker* concerns the fact that this period was a sort of Golden Age of American serial killing, as I explore in the next chapter.

Notes

1 This radio report also provides another to the real world of 1981 New York. The announcer on the radio identifies himself as Stan L. Brooks, which is likely a reference to Stan Z. Burns, a prominent announcer on New York radio station 1010 WINS from the mid-1940s through the 1980s.

2 For details concerning this riot and its historical background and aftermath, see the collection of essays edited by Patterson and Ferrell. In his essay in the collection, for example, Joshua Rothenberger argues that the "police brutality" that was central to the riots was really a signifier of a larger class war in which the gentrification of the Lower East Side displaced the working class from their traditional homes in the historic district.

3 In an interview with Josh Rottenberg of the *Los Angeles Times*, Phillips was clear that he was not concerned with depicting Fleck as suffering from some specific mental illness: "Me and Scott and Joaquin, we never talked about what he has—I never wanted to say, 'He's a narcissist and this and that,'" Phillips said. "I didn't want Joaquin as an actor to start researching that kind of thing. We just said, 'He's off.' I don't even know that he's mentally ill. He's just left-footed with the world."

4 In *Shall We Dance*, a brief passage from *Rhapsody in Blue* can be heard when Gershwin's name is shown in the opening credits, emphasizing its central place in his work.

5 This roller-skating scene was, however, apparently Rogers' idea, or at least so she claims in her autobiography (213). Elsewhere in her autobiography, Rogers brags about the critical success of a film she starred in with Reagan—*Storm Warning* (1951), a supposedly anti-KKK film that somehow manages to exclude the topic of racism (343–344).

6 We will later see snippets of the Franklin show on the color TV in the Fleck living room, which explains why Fleck can easily imagine the color scheme of the show even when watching it in black and white.

CHAPTER SEVEN

"Clowns Can Get Away with Murder"
Joker and the Golden Age of American Serial Killing

In *Joker,* Arthur Fleck is depicted as a serial killer. However much the film might do to provide sympathetic explanations for the psychological problems that drive Fleck to murder in the film, however much the postmodern aesthetics of the film might make us question the "reality" of his murders, the fact is that he is shown committing a series of killings in the film. Moreover, many of these killings are of an especially shocking nature, even by the standards of violence to which we have become accustomed in contemporary film. Fleck smothers his own mother with a pillow as she lies in her hospital bed; he stabs a co-worker in the throat and the eye with a pair of household scissors; he shoots his own personal hero and role model point-blank between the eyes (Figure 6). Moreover, all of these killings occur suddenly and out of the blue, which makes them all the more shocking, even as it increases our suspicion that these might merely be Fleck's fantasies. These killings also help to contextualize *Joker,* in terms both of its historical setting and its cultural positioning. For example, these killings are all highly cinematic, placing *Joker* itself in the company of a number of different kinds of films. But they also place the events depicted within *Joker* squarely within what one might call the "Golden Age" of American serial killing.

Serial killers as a recognized phenomenon first arose to widespread public consciousness around the time of the 1981 setting of the action of *Joker,* and the killing spree (real or imagined) of Arthur Fleck resonates with this fact. Fleck himself is a serial killer (at least in his own mind) by any reasonable definition of the term, including the official, but extremely basic, FBI definition of serial murder as the "unlawful killing of two or more victims by the same offender(s), in separate events" (Morton and Hilts). The characterization of Fleck, in fact, seems to have been directly influenced by what we know about serial killers, especially the former

151

No Joke: Todd Phillips's *Joker* and American Culture

Figure 6. Fleck shoots his hero Murray Franklin on live TV.

rent-a-clown John Wayne Gacy. More importantly, though, a recognition of the more general link between Fleck and the phenomenon of serial killing—which experienced a sort of gruesome Golden Age of high-profile media-star serial killers between the Manson murders in 1969 and the end of the killing career of notorious cannibal necrophiliac Jeffrey Dahmer with his conviction in 1992—helps us to understand *Joker* as a commentary on certain dark elements of American culture during that same time span. It is, after all, now widely accepted that serial killing is not merely an individual phenomenon, but a social one. As Keppel and Birnes put it, "In a macabre way, looking at the changing face of a serial killer is like looking at the changing face of America" (214–215).

In his survey of the phenomenon of American serial killers, Peter Vronsky notes that such killers had been around for some time as the 1970s began but that it was only during this decade that the serial killer emerged in the American popular consciousness as a distinct cultural phenomenon with a specific name. It was, for example, in 1972 that the FBI founded the Behavioral Science Unit, which, by the end of the decade had established a special unit charged with gathering data in an attempt to understand the characteristics and motivations of serial killers.[1] Vronsky further notes that David Berkowitz, the "Son of Sam" killer who murdered a string of young New York City women in 1976 and 1977 might have been the first true serial killer to gain widespread attention in the American media and the American mind. Even then, according to Vronsky, serial killings were typically regarded as "isolated acts of animalistic depravity," rather than as signs of some larger social phenomenon (6).

However, the emergence of Ted Bundy—whom Vronsky calls the first "postmodern" serial killer—would begin to change all that by making serial killers the objects of extensive, often sensationalized media coverage, coverage that essentially made serial killers in commodities for marketing via the media, just as everything else was commodified by the rise of neoliberalism.

John Wayne Gacy and Arthur Fleck

Chicago's Gacy was one of the most notorious of the several high-profile American serial killers of the 1970s. Indeed, Vronsky places Gacy on the same level of prominence as Bundy by characterizing the serial killers of the era as the "Ted Bundy–John Wayne Gacy generation of serial killers" (387). Gacy became an object of popular fascination partly because he seemed to present a relatively normal face to the world, raising the titillating possibility that anyone's suburban neighbor might be a crazed serial killer. A suburban husband and (step)father, Gacy ran his own construction company and was active in Chicago-area Democratic politics. He was locally renowned for the summer parties he hosted with jovial aplomb in his home and yard. Yet he was also a particularly prolific serial killer whose ultimate conviction for the murder of a total of 33 individuals is still a record. His crimes, which typically involved the homosexual rape and then murder by strangulation of young men and boys (his victims ranged in age from 14 to 21), were also particularly lurid, made more so by the fact that Gacy was given to dumping the corpses of his victims, covered with lime, in the crawl space beneath his house.

The investigation into Gacy's crimes, aided by Gacy's own confessions, ultimately led to the discovery of 29 bodies on Gacy's property, most of them in his crawl space. Four more bodies had been dumped in the Des Plaines River. The murders Gacy is known to have committed occurred from January of 1972 to December of 1978. He was arrested on December 21, 1978, and eventually brought to trial on February 6, 1980. On March 12, 1980, he was convicted of the 33 murders, then sentenced to death, with an initial execution date set as June 2, 1980. His career as a serial killer thus essentially spanned the 1970s, though (due to appeals) he would not actually be executed (by lethal injection) until 1994.

During his 14 years on death row, Gacy took up painting as a hobby, executing dozens of paintings (including portraits—from photographs and memory—of such subjects as Elvis and Charles Manson) that became

No Joke: Todd Phillips's *Joker* and American Culture

Figure 7. Fleck performs as a clown in a children's hospital.

valuable collectors' items after Gacy's death, winding up in the hands of several famous people, such as actor Johnny Depp and film director John Waters (Rosewood and Lo 148). Gacy's most famous paintings are actually self-portraits; the best-known of which are portraits of one "Pogo the Clown," which just happens to be the persona adopted by Gacy, during his stint as a "respectable" Chicagoan, when he performed as a voluntary clown for gigs such as entertaining children at parties or amusing the young patients at children's hospitals.[2] Indeed, when Gacy (like most famous serial killers) was given a "serial-killer name" in the media, he was dubbed the "Killer Clown."[3] "Clowns," Gacy has been quoted as saying, "can get away with murder."

At the beginning of *Joker*, of course, Arthur Fleck also works as a part-time clown—although he does it for money and seems to regard it largely as a stepping-stone toward his real goal of becoming a stand-up comedian. Still, Fleck's key performance as a clown in the film occurs precisely at a children's hospital, although this performance goes badly wrong when the firearm he is hiding inside his costume comes loose and goes clattering to the floor—leading to a swift end to Fleck's clown career (Figure 7). This link between Fleck and Gacy does not appear to be coincidental; there are several indications within *Joker* that the general parallels between Fleck and Gacy as clowns-turned-killers are intentional and that the characterization of Fleck in the film was directly influenced by the career of Gacy.

Fleck designs and applies his own clown makeup, as did Gacy. And it is quite possible that the look of Fleck's makeup was influenced by the

Joker and the Golden Age of American Serial Killing

Figure 8. Fleck performs his comedy routine at Pogo's Comedy Club.

somewhat sinister look of Gacy's "Pogo" makeup. For example, Gacy's makeup featured sharp points around both his mouth and his eyes, which runs contrary to the received wisdom that such points should be avoided lest the makeup be frightening to children. And, lest these similarities in makeup be deemed coincidental, *Joker* includes at least one clear clue to the Gacy influence that is difficult to see as a coincidence (Figure 8). In one crucial scene, Fleck is shown trying out his stand-up act at a Gotham City comedy club, and the film clearly displays a sign identifying the name of the club as "Pogo's."[4]

The Problematic Parentage of Arthur Fleck

It seems fairly certain, then, that Todd Phillips wants his viewers to make the connection between Gacy and Fleck, although there is no indication that Fleck shares any characteristics with Gacy other than being a somewhat sketchy individual whose psychological problems drive him to murder (or, in Fleck's case, at least to fantasies of murder). There are also clear indications in the film that Fleck had been the victim of childhood abuse, as had Gacy, so it is possible that the link to Gacy is intended to call attention to the importance of Fleck's childhood trauma as a source of his adult mental illness.

As with most things in *Joker*, the details of Fleck's experiences in his childhood are a bit complex to piece together, partly because his memory of those experiences is rather sketchy and partly because his mother seems to have misrepresented those experiences, perhaps because her own mental instability makes her memories of that time unreliable as well. In any case, whether as a result of intention or of delusion, Penny seems to have created (and shared with her son) an entire mythology of Fleck's happiness in childhood. Indeed, she has nicknamed him "Happy," an appellation by which she continues to address him in adulthood and which she claims captures his generally sunny disposition. For his part (although presumably with his mother's approval, or even at her instigation), Fleck had initially developed his own narrative about wishing to be a clown and a comedian so that he can make other people as happy as he is.

One crucial bit of information that Fleck's mother conveys (and seems genuinely to believe) is that Thomas Wayne is his biological father and that Fleck is the product of an affair that occurred while Penny was one of Wayne's household servants. Wayne vehemently denies this connection, and what documentary evidence we are shown in the film seems to substantiate his claim, although we are also reminded (by Penny, who might herself not be all that reliable) that a man of Wayne's wealth and power could easily have had the historical record changed. Thus, in keeping with the overall air of interpretive indeterminacy that runs through the entire film, we can simply not be sure of the facts, even when they are backed by official documentation.

In the case of Fleck's childhood, the documentary evidence presented in the film consists primarily of Penny's case file from her own time as an inmate at Arkham State Hospital, which Fleck apparently manages to steal from a clerk whom he has convinced to dig it up from Arkham's archives. According to the records in this file, Fleck is neither Wayne's son nor Penny's: he had been found abandoned as an infant and was subsequently adopted by Penny. The file also shows that young Arthur had been repeatedly physically abused by one of Penny's boyfriends, while Penny stood by and did nothing—though the boyfriend had battered Penny, as well. The file even includes newspaper clippings that appear to verify these events. We are shown a flashback scene of an interview between Penny and a psychiatrist that enacts the information in the file (while an adult Fleck looks on in the background, possibly suggesting that the file might be triggering his memories of his childhood abuse). "Penny," says the psychiatrist, "your son was found tied to a radiator in your filthy apartment, malnourished, with multiple bruises across his body and severe trauma to his head." The shot then returns back to Fleck in the present, reading the file and laughing, snot dripping from his nose, in a strained way that reveals, rather than hides, his pain—possibly because he is now beginning to remember the abuse he had tucked away into his

JOKER AND THE GOLDEN AGE OF AMERICAN SERIAL KILLING

unconscious mind all these years (or possibly just because the information is inherently painful).

Again, though, the notion that Wayne might have somehow planted the information in this file is not entirely beyond belief. In addition, this whole sequence in Arkham seems a bit far-fetched. For example, would a clerk really be likely to dig through decades-old records to come up with Penny's file and then bring the file to Fleck, just because Fleck asked him to do so? And would Fleck really be able to successfully make off with the file and subsequently exit the high-security facility?[5] As with most things in the film, it is impossible to tell with certainty if this whole sequence of events really occurs within the world of the film or whether it simply emanates from Fleck's fevered mind. Similarly, we cannot know if Fleck's strong emotional reaction to this sequence of events comes about because he has discovered painful new information about his past or whether it simply comes about because his own fantasies are feeding upon themselves by causing him to imagine the discovery of this information.

What we do know is that Fleck has gone to Arkham (or imagined going there) seeking information about Penny's time there as part of an ongoing investigation into his own origins—and especially into Thomas Wayne's role in those origins. Much of the action of *Joker*, in fact, is driven by Fleck's search for his father, whose absence seems crucial to Fleck's psychopathology, again placing him very much in the same situation as many serial killers. For example, Vronsky suggests that the generation of serial killers who committed their crimes roughly from the late 1960s to the early 1990s were psychologically formed decades earlier in their childhoods, which occurred at a time when the generation of their American fathers had been traumatized by the experiences of the Great Depression and World War II. The result was a wave of absent or abusive fathers in the 1940s and 1950s, contributing in a crucial way to the development of a generation of serial killers decades later. Vronsky wonders, meanwhile, whether events such as the 2001 bombings of the World Trade Center and the 2008 financial collapse might contribute to the rise of a new wave of serial killers in the near future, although the latest version of his book was published just before the 2020 Coronavirus pandemic would become the most traumatic event of the twenty-first century to date.

Soon after the subway killings, Fleck rides on a crowded commuter train in which many passengers, Fleck included, are reading newspapers featuring front-page accounts of the killings. Fleck, though, focuses on an article about Thomas Wayne and his plan to run for mayor of Gotham City. He tears out a picture of Wayne, his wife Martha, and their young son Bruce and stuffs it inside the spiral-bound notebook that he carries around with him so he can have a place to jot down any "jokes" that might occur to him. He then heads straight to the Wayne estate, whose richly landscaped grounds stand in such stark contrast to the decaying urban environment of the bulk of Gotham City as presented in the film. There, Fleck encounters young Bruce Wayne, whom most viewers of the film will surely recognize as the boy who will grow up to become Batman. For now, though, he is just the privileged son of a wealthy father, living the life that Fleck seems to feel should have been his own, thus providing a neat explanation for the Joker's later animosity toward Batman. Here, though, Fleck simply tries to get Bruce's attention with bits of his clown act (including one gag with an alternately drooping and stiffening magic wand that could have clearly inappropriate sexual connotations). He then reaches through a gate and puts his hands on the boy's face and uses his thumbs to contort the boy's mouth into an awkward smile. Then an unidentified Englishman (clearly the Wayne butler Alfred Pennyworth, another figure well known to Batman fans, though he is not named within the film),[6] comes to the rescue and orders the boy away from the fence. "I know about the two of them," Fleck whispers to Alfred, in reference to his mother and Thomas Wayne. Alfred sternly rebuffs the insinuation and assures Fleck that there was nothing between Penny and Wayne and that Penny "was delusional; she was a sick woman." When Fleck insists that Wayne is his father, Alfred laughs in his face, at which Fleck reaches through the iron bars on the gate and starts to choke the surprised butler, before ultimately turning and running away in a panic (Figure 9).

When Fleck returns home from this encounter, he finds an ambulance outside his building and then finds them loading Penny, who has apparently had some sort of attack, inside it. He rides with her to the hospital, then sits outside the emergency room smoking while they treat her inside, having determined that she has had a stroke. He is clearly thinking of her possible death, wondering if he will soon be all alone in the world. Despite the problematic way she has carried out her duties as a mother, she is still the only person in the world to whom he has a real connection. Then he is approached by Detectives Garrity (Bill Camp) and Burke (Shea Whigham), two cops who will play an important role in the second half of the film. They had been questioning Penny about Fleck shortly before her stroke, and now they want to question Fleck himself about the subway killings. He rebuffs them, turns to go inside, crashes into the door (which he had expected to open automatically, not realizing he is entering through an exit), and is then next shown suddenly sitting beside his mother in her hospital room, with Sophie at his side (although her presence, we will eventually discover, is a mere fantasy).

Joker and the Golden Age of American Serial Killing

Figure 9. Fleck grabs Alfred Pennyworth through the iron gate that separates Wayne Manor from the rest of Gotham City.

In Fleck's world, insult is continually added to injury. While he sits with his mother after Sophie ostensibly leaves, Murray Franklin comes on the TV and shows a clip of Fleck's recent (disastrous) performance at Pogo's. At first, Fleck is delighted, but then he realizes that Franklin is mocking him. Then he is back home watching television in the apartment he had shared with his mother, pleased to see that the "Kill the Rich" movement is gaining strength in the streets of Gotham and that the participants in the movement, many of them wearing clown makeup or clown masks, seem to have identified Thomas Wayne as a particular object of their ire. Fleck stares thoughtfully into the distance, as if descending into fantasy. Then we immediately cut to a scene in which Fleck is in the middle of a demonstration (or is he?) in which police battle protestors outside of Wayne Hall, inside which Wayne and other members of Gotham's elite are viewing that special charity benefit showing of Charlie Chaplin's 1936 classic *Modern Times*.

When Wayne slips out to go to the restroom during that screening, Fleck follows him there to confront him. When Wayne insists that he is not Fleck's father, Fleck insists that he is, but assures him that he wants nothing from him, except "maybe a little bit of warmth. Maybe a hug, *Dad*." It seems a preposterous request, given the circumstances of the encounter, but it is perfectly in keeping with Fleck's quest for a father (or at least acknowledgement and affection from *someone*) that runs through the film, a quest that will culminate in his (real or imagined) appearance on *Live with Murray Franklin*, in which Fleck has a nasty encounter with

159

still another father figure. At the same time, it also points back to the early scene in which Fleck watches *Live with Murray Franklin* with Penny and imagines Franklin actually *giving* him a hug, while declaring of all the showbiz trappings of his life, "I'd give it all up in a heartbeat to have a kid like you."

Of course, Fleck's second appearance on the Franklin show doesn't end so well. The encounter with Wayne doesn't end well, either. When Fleck reverts to his habitual uncontrolled, pained laughter, Wayne abruptly punches him in the face. "Touch my son again, I'll fucking kill you," grumbles Wayne on his way out of the restroom. It's an important moment, and one that is doubly hurtful: not only has Fleck been rejected in his quest to be regarded as Wayne's son, but Wayne unequivocally identifies young Bruce as his true son, and a true son that Wayne, as a loving father, will do anything to protect from the usurper Fleck. Fleck is thus identified as the son rejected by his father, whether literally or figuratively, placing him in somewhat the same psychological position as Gacy, who was apparently beaten, abused, and rejected by his own father.

Granted, the following match cut calls into question whether any of the events just depicted at Wayne Hall actually occurred, but the scene still helps to emphasize the way in which Wayne (like Franklin, in a less literal sense) clearly serves as an absent father figure for Fleck, pointing clearly (almost *too* clearly, as if in parody) to the importance of seeking a father as a part of Fleck's search for a viable identity for himself. That both Wayne and Franklin ultimately reject and even humiliate Fleck only makes his situation worse; that these rejections and humiliations might well occur only in Fleck's imagination suggest just how troubled he is by his lack of a functioning father figure. It also suggests parallels between Fleck's psychological condition and one that has frequently been attributed to serial killers such as Gacy.

Fleck's problems, of course, are connected in *Joker*, not only to the absence of a viable father figure, but to the problematic *presence* of his mother. Penny's obsession with Thomas Wayne hovers over her entire relationship with her son, whom she at times seems to regard as a sort of surrogate for Wayne, which could explain the fact that she might have invented/fantasized the entire narrative involving an affair with Wayne that produced Arthur as an offspring. In any case, there is a clear sexual charge to the relationship between Arthur and Penny, such as in a brief, but somewhat uncomfortable, scene in which Arthur bathes his mother while she sits nude in the bathtub in their shabby apartment. There is, of course, absolutely nothing wrong or inappropriate about Arthur bathing his mother in this way; it should, in fact, be a touching moment of filial devotion. I would argue, however, that it seems uncomfortable because it reveals a private moment that most viewers are not accustomed to seeing in films, certainly not in superhero films, a moment that involves a reminder of the ravages of old age, which might make it difficult for Penny to bathe herself, a reminder that is enhanced by a brief partial view of Penny's aged, naked body. During the bath, meanwhile, she continually talks about Thomas Wayne and the possibility that he will rescue them. They don't need Wayne's money, explains Arthur, because he's about to hit it big as a stand-up comedian. Penny dismisses this notion by asking, "Don't you have to be funny to be a comedian?" The film then cuts to Arthur alone in the living room, bitterly fondling his Smith and Wesson and aiming it at the screen of their small TV, on which Fred Astaire is dancing to the song "Slap that Bass" in the film *Shall We Dance* (1937).

The seemingly unnatural closeness of Fleck to his (possibly adoptive) mother perhaps recalls the relationship between Son-of-Sam killer Berkowitz and his adoptive mother. In Fleck's case, however, this relationship soon turns dark, as this closeness turns to murder—or at least to a fantasy of murder. We are not meant, I think, to be able to determine whether this matricide is real or imagined, but this scene (which occurs shortly after Fleck has either read Penny's Arkham file or fantasized that reading) surely indicates that Fleck at least harbors powerfully antagonistic feelings toward his mother, feelings that might conceivably lead to murder. While this does not seem particularly to have been the case with Gacy, real-world serial killers have also frequently been found to harbor violent resentment toward their mothers, sometimes to the point of matricide. Berkowitz didn't kill his mother, although he did kill her pet bird. But Henry Lee Lucas, the so-called "Confession Killer" (because he confessed to thousands of murders, though he was only convicted of committing 11) began a killing spree that stretched from 1960 until his final arrest in 1983 with an initial victim who was his own mother. Meanwhile, Edmund Kemper, the so-called "Co-Ed Killer," killed his grandparents in 1964, then committed a string of grisly murders of young women in 1972 and 1973, and topped it off with the murder of his own mother.

The Mediatization of American Serial Killing

Such parallels between Fleck and real-world serial killers, carefully established in *Joker*, would seem to point toward something larger than simple similarities between Fleck and specific real serial killers, especially as Fleck's career is a sort of amalgam that only matches parts of the careers of individual real-world serial killers. What the link between Fleck and serial killers such as Gacy really calls attention to is the fact that *Joker*'s 1981 setting places the events of the film smack in the middle of that period from the late 1960s to the early 1990s that might be called the "Golden Age" of American serial killers, at least in terms of public fascination with such figures. In particular, I would argue that the very existence of such a grim Golden Age highlights the extent to which the period beginning roughly with the collapse of the 1960s counterculture with the inauguration of Richard Nixon in 1969 and extending through the Reaganite 1980s (and on through 1992 and the end of the first Bush administration) was in a number of ways one of the darkest times in American history.

Of course, there were serial killers—even fairly well-known ones—in America before the beginning of the Nixon administration in January of 1969. Some of these even had a direct impact on the American film industry, perhaps most prominently in the case of Ed Gein, the so-called Butcher of Plainfield, Wisconsin, who ghoulishly fashioned trophies of various kinds from the bones and skin of bodies he exhumed as a graverobber and body snatcher, although he also committed multiple murders. Gein's exploits inspired Robert Bloch's 1959 novel *Psycho*, which itself inspired Alfred Hitchcock's 1960 film of the same title, which still stands as a crucial work of American cinema. It also stands as the first American film centrally inspired by the crimes of a serial killer, partly because the Hollywood Production Code made it so difficult to depict such crimes on film. Later, after the collapse of the Code, many other films would be inspired by serial killers, and Gein himself would be at least a partial inspiration for the characters Leatherface in *The Texas Chain Saw Massacre* (1974) and Buffalo Bill in *The Silence of the Lambs* (1991).

The identification of Gein as an inspiration for such well-known cinematic serial killers has kept his name in the popular American memory to this day, even though his crime spree ended in 1957. Meanwhile, although Gein's activities were especially and spectacularly macabre, his success as an inspiration for so many important horror films suggests that there is something particularly cinematic about the serial killer figure in general, perhaps because serial killers represent an embodied and easily identifiable figure upon whom to focus the otherwise amorphous and vaguely defined anxiety and sense of peril that have become such a common part of life in the precarious world of late capitalism. From this point of view, it makes perfect sense that the phenomenon of serial killers would be part of the inspiration for Joker, while it also makes sense that the truly prominent "superstar" serial killer would be prefigured by the appearance of Charles Manson in the dark year of 1969, soon after the

JOKER AND THE GOLDEN AGE OF AMERICAN SERIAL KILLING

heady utopian dreams of the 1960s counterculture had come crashing to earth in 1968 with the assassinations of Martin Luther King Jr. and Robert Kennedy, followed by the Chicago police riots and the presidential election of Nixon, bête noire of the counterculture and harbinger of the neoliberalism that would begin to emerge in full force with Reagan.

The dark events of 1968 also had a direct impact on American film, as can perhaps be seen in the shocking end of the countercultural classic *Easy Rider* (1969). Meanwhile, Kendall Phillips has noted that George A. Romero's groundbreaking horror film *Night of the Living Dead* (1968) appeared shortly after events such as the assassinations of King and Kennedy had put a damper on the utopian hopes of the oppositional political movements, ushering in a new era of skepticism and pessimism. Phillips thus argues that theatrical audiences viewing the film in the late 1960s must have identified with the doomed plight of the trapped humans inside the farmhouse of *Night*: "Sitting in movie theaters in inner-cities and near college campuses in the immediate aftermath of this dissolution, the resonance with the desperate and divisive group surrounded by chaos and violence must have been palpable" (99).

The ascent of Nixon to the presidency in January of 1969 essentially served as an exclamation point that punctuated the dark turn taken by American society in 1968. Nixon's assumption of office did not, of course, directly *cause* the subsequent rise of serial killing as a prominent media phenomenon in American culture. One does, however, wonder how much the sensationalized accounts of an America being overrun with violent crime put forth by Nixon during his presidential campaign might have actually excited and inspired would-be violent criminals. Meanwhile, it is also worth noting that, other than Nixon, the most prominent purveyor of law and order political rhetoric in the United States in the late 1960s was his fellow California Republican, Ronald Reagan, providing an important link between the Nixon–Ford years (1969 through 1976) and the Reagan–Bush years (1981 through 1992), suggesting that, at least in this sense, the 24 years from the beginning of 1969 to the end of 1992 were very much of a piece, with a brief respite during the Carter years at the end of the 1970s. It is thus all the more interesting that this same period was also very alike in terms of both the rise of neoliberalism and the prominence of serial killers as a social/media phenomenon in America. Donald Trump's attempts to revive this same law and order rhetoric (but with a more hysterical and fanatical—one might say performative—turn) thus link his ill-fated administration to those years as well, making it entirely appropriate that *Joker*, one of the most telling cultural products of the Trump years, would place its action in the midst of the Republican hegemony of 1969–1992, while tying that action to the serial-killer phenomenon of those same years.

It is certainly the case that the Nixon presidency marked a significant turn toward a darker national outlook that made the general population more receptive to serial killing as a media "event." Indeed, by the time of Nixon's election, American television audiences had already received detailed reports (and sometimes, as in the case of Jack Ruby's shooting of Lee Harvey Oswald, live broadcasts) of a stunning sequence of violent events, with the 1968 killings of Kennedy and King preceded by the 1963 assassination of President John Kennedy and the 1965 shooting of Malcolm X, and with daily accounts of the carnage in Vietnam coming to be a staple of the nightly television news.

One could, in fact, argue that televised accounts of Chicago police busting the heads of unarmed demonstrators outside the Democratic National Convention in late August of 1968 made a crucial contribution to the election of Nixon, making that election the result rather than the cause of the mediatization of violence in America. In any case, it was less than seven months into the Nixon presidency when, in the early hours of August 9, 1969, members of the "Manson family" invaded the Los Angeles home of prominent film director Roman Polanski and his 26-year-old wife, the actress and model Sharon Tate, and committed multiple bloody murders with which the American popular imagination has been fascinated ever since. That the victims had prominent show-business connections made the killings all the more fascinating as a media event. That the murderous communal "family" built by the charismatic Charles Manson was largely based on a sort of obscene perversion of the values of that 1960s hippie counterculture contributed to its lurid appeal as well. For one thing, the sex, drugs, and rock 'n' roll agenda pursued by Manson and his family initially convinced some in the surviving counterculture to see them as heroes. At the same time, this agenda served, for those already horrified by the "hippie" lifestyle associated with the counterculture of the 1960s, as a demonstration of the dangers of that lifestyle. In any case, the extensive public fascination with Manson and his followers made it clear that the story of the Manson family resonated with many popular concerns and anxieties of the time.

Manson's minions, arriving at the Polanski–Tate home, found that Polanski, working on a project in Europe at the time, was not home, but the eight-and-a-half-months' pregnant Tate was brutally murdered, along with her unborn son. Also present in the house (and also murdered) were prominent hair stylist Jay Sebring (Tate's former lover), coffee heiress Abigail Folger, and aspiring screenwriter Wojciech Frykowski, a friend of the Polanskis who was also the lover of Folger. Eighteen-year-old Steven Parent, who had been visiting the property's caretaker, ran into the killers as he was leaving and was shot to death in the driveway, bringing the death toll to six, including the unborn infant. The following night, the Manson family invaded the home of Leno and Rosemary LaBianca, killing the couple in a similarly bloody fashion.

Partly due to the gruesome nature of the killings and partly due to the high-profile nature of the victims, these killings became the object of intense media attention. But, as the investigation and its press coverage unfolded, public fascination became increasingly focused on the bizarre collection of killers and especially on Manson, their Svengali-like leader. Some left-wing newspapers, confused by Manson's apparent endorsement of countercultural values, proclaimed him a hero. In June 1970, the more mainstream (but still vaguely countercultural) *Rolling Stone* published a cover story entitled "Charles Manson: The Incredible Story of the Most Dangerous Man Alive," furthering his mystique. To this day, Manson (who died of natural causes in prison in 2017) remains one of the most notorious criminal figures in American history, even though he apparently did not physically commit any of the Tate–LaBianca murders for which he is best known. Manson's ongoing fame was furthered by his antics after his arrest and even during his long years of imprisonment prior to his death in prison in 2017.

The story of the Manson killers was also kept alive in the popular imagination by media coverage of their arrest and trial—including such sensationalisms as Manson's appearance at the first day of testimony during his trial in July 1970 with an "X" carved into his forehead. Then, later in his trial, he converted the "X" into a swastika, one of the most charged images in Western culture and one that was sure to garner considerable attention, furthering his notoriety. Manson was, in many ways, made for the American media, so perhaps it was no surprise that the 1974 account of the case by prosecutor Vincent Bugliosi (with Curt Gentry), entitled *Helter Skelter: The True Story of the Manson Murders*, became a major best-seller.[7] In fact, more than half a century after the initial murders, *Helter Skelter* remains the best-selling true-crime book of all time, even as true crime has become an increasingly popular genre over the years.

Manson's rise to fame was, if anything, accelerated by Nixon's famous denunciation of him, including a sort of high-profile jury-tampering that occurred when Nixon publicly declared Manson to be guilty of murder— *in the midst of Manson's murder trial*. As Jeff Guinn notes, Nixon, speaking during a trip to Denver in August 1970, complained that the media's extensive coverage had made Manson a "rather glamorous figure." For Nixon, this was an outrage, given that Manson was "guilty, directly or indirectly, of eight murders without reason" (qtd. in Guinn 362). As Guinn further notes, news of these comments spread through the wire services like wildfire—nearly causing Manson to be granted a mistrial.[8]

Carl Freedman sees this incident as more than a slip of tongue, as something that connects Nixon, the proponent of law and order, with certain darker elements in American history. Noting that the United States is widely known as the land of "free speech and due process," Freedman reminds us that

> America is, after all, also a country of lynch law and vigilantism: an aspect of his culture that Nixon seemed clearly to embrace when, as president, he pronounced Charles Manson to be guilty of murder while the trial was still taking place and, during the same week, praised the John Wayne film *Chisum*, in which those who Nixon identified as "the good guys" take the law into their own hands. (*Age of Nixon* 100)

John Wayne himself, of course, was regarded as a good guy by Nixon, despite (or perhaps because of) the fact that the actor was a racist, an apologist for the genocide of Native Americans, a member of the extreme right-wing John Birch Society, and a strong advocate for American participation in the Vietnam war. Wayne was also one of the great stars in the history of American cinema, a larger-than-life figure whose fame and influence went well beyond the world of film. As Richard Slotkin—in his study of the ways in which the Western film helped to shape a mythic national American identity—notes, Wayne by 1960 had become "a kind of folk-hero, his name an idiomatic expression, a metaphoric formula or cliché that instantly invoked a well-recognized set of American heroic virtues—or, from a different perspective, inflated American pretensions" (518–519).

Manson, meanwhile, was a very different sort of folk "hero," although one who nevertheless became a very prominent media presence. He was not, strictly speaking, a classic serial killer, in that the killing spree for which he is famous only lasted approximately 24 hours, while the actual killings were committed by others at his instigation.[9] Even if one considers him to belong among serial killers, he was not the first of the "Golden Age" serial killers of the "1970s." That distinction would probably go to the most mysterious (because never definitively identified) "Zodiac Killer," who apparently began a killing spree right at the end of 1968 that extended into the 1970s. It was Manson, however, who paved the way for the intense media attention paid to serial killers in the 1970s, which saw a sudden and unprecedented increase in the public profile of serial killing in the United States. Indeed, it is his status as a media star that makes Manson relevant to *Joker*, more than any particular parallels between Manson and Fleck as killers. Indeed, the mediatization of violent crime is one of the crucial topics of *Joker*, although *Joker*'s consciousness of violence as media spectacle is probably a sign more of its 2019 release date than its 1981 setting.

In any case, it is probably no coincidence that serial killers first came to true prominence in the American consciousness just as events such as the Watergate scandal and the war in Vietnam produced one of the most anxious climates in American history. Most serial killers seem primarily motivated by their private personal histories and pathologies, but it is logical to assume that the personal problems that drive individuals to become serial killers would, if anything, be exacerbated by a widespread mood of anxiety. Moreover, the anxieties of the 1970s likely contributed to the media attention and public fascination granted to the superstar serial killers of the 1970s, while the very attention that was focused on these figures could only have intensified the mood of anxiety that informed American society during the decade.

Given the media attention granted to serial killers in the 1970s and 1980s, it was probably inevitable that serial killers would soon draw the attention of the Hollywood film industry, with the connection of the Manson murders to the world of film providing an especially direct point of intersection. Indeed, some of America's leading filmmakers have made films based on the stories of real-world serial killers, whose murderous careers have become a form of intellectual property amid the neoliberal commodification of everything. For example, David Fincher's *Zodiac* (2007), based on the Zodiac Killer, merges the slasher film with the police procedural to produce what is one of the greatest of all serial killer films. Before that, Spike Lee's *Summer of Sam* (1999) had drawn upon the Son of Sam killings to produce a film with similarly high aesthetic aspirations. Lee's film, in fact, is perhaps the serial-killer film that resembles *Joker* most extensively. This film, set in New York City in the summer of 1977 against the background of the Son of Sam killings, goes to great lengths to capture the texture of life in the city at that time. Indeed, David Berkowitz is actually a rather minor character whose killings provide background for a picture of the city that suggests a violent society so intolerant of difference that it almost inevitably produces serial killers. *Summer of Sam* thus anticipates *Joker* in the way it uses a serial killer narrative to produce social commentary, buoyed by extensive use of references to contemporary popular culture (especially music, in this case).

Given the lurid nature of the Manson murders—and given their connection, through Tate and Polanski, to the film industry—it should perhaps come as no surprise that those murders have been the direct inspiration for a number of films over the years. *Helter Skelter* itself was adapted as a two-part television film of that title in 1976, then again as a TV film in 2004. And numerous other works have been inspired by Manson over the years, including both documentaries and dramatizations. Numerous books on Manson have appeared as well, including the recent book, *The Last Charles Manson Tapes* (2019), based on interviews with Manson in prison shortly before his death. According to authors Dylan Howard and Andy Tillett, in those interviews Manson reveals that he followed the careers of at least some of the serial killers of the 1970s and 1980s, seeming especially jealous of Ted Bundy, whom he calls a "coward," declaring that he, Manson, is the greatest serial killer of all time. Manson even seems to have resented diagnoses of Bundy as suffering from bipolar disorder (and possibly multiple personality disorder), claiming that he himself was far more mentally ill than Bundy had ever been.[10]

Manson was no doubt responding to the widespread attention gained by Bundy due to his murderous career as a serial killer. Handsome, charismatic, and articulate, Bundy became a major object of media fascination, both because of the lurid, sex-related nature of his crimes and because of his unusual exploits, including multiple escapes from police custody and serving as his own attorney in the Florida murder trial that, in 1979, became the first criminal trial to be nationally televised, adding to Bundy's mystique. This trial led to Bundy being sentenced to death on February 10, 1980, a sentence that would ultimately be carried out on January 24, 1989. As is often the case with serial killers, it is not entirely clear how many murders Bundy committed, although he did ultimately confess to a series of 30 grisly murders of young women and girls in seven different states between 1974 and 1978, typically raping his victims before killing them and sometimes later performing additional sex acts with their decomposing corpses.

The contrast between Bundy's boyish good looks and the shocking nature of his crimes only served to make him even more an object of public fascination, both in the immediate revelation of his crimes and in subsequent years. He has, for example, inspired a particularly interesting array of films over the years, beginning with the two-part television film *The Deliberate Stranger* (1986), based on a 1980 book published in the immediate aftermath of Bundy's final arrest and subsequent trial.

Subsequent films based on Bundy include the black comedy *Ted Bundy* (2002), the dark television drama *The Riverman* (2004), the police-procedural *The Capture of the Green River Killer* (2008), and *Bundy: An American Icon* (2008, also known as *Bundy: A Legacy of Evil*), which recasts Bundy's career essentially as a low-budget horror film.[11]

Bundy has also been the subject of several documentary films (some with such lurid titles as the 2006 *Ted Bundy: Natural Porn Killer*), as well as featuring prominently in a number of documentaries covering broader topics, beginning with *The Killing of America* (1981). However, perhaps the most striking aspect of Bundy's media career is his recent emergence as a popular "star" on streaming video platforms such as Netflix and Amazon Prime Video. For example, the four-hour documentary mini-series *Conversations with a Killer: The Ted Bundy Tapes* premiered on Netflix on January 24, 2019—which just happened to be the thirtieth anniversary of Bundy's execution. This series, directed by Joe Berlinger, is based on taped interviews with Bundy while he was on death row in the 1980s and thus largely shows the face he wanted to show, without ever quite capturing the ugliness of his crimes and the depths of his depravity. Berlinger then followed with a dramatized film that also related Bundy's story in a somewhat sanitized form, with Zac Efron playing the serial killer in *Extremely Wicked, Shockingly Evil, and Vile* (2019), the title of which was taken from the assessment of Bundy by his Florida judge (played here by John Malkovich).[12] Amazon Prime Video then followed in early 2020 with a five-part documentary mini-series about Bundy. *Ted Bundy: Falling for a Killer*, based on the memoir of a woman who had been Bundy's fiancée, draws upon public fascination with the fact that Bundy, even during his extensive career as a rapist and murderer and corpse abuser, was able to carry on relatively conventional romantic relationships with women—including his notorious "wedding" during his murder trial in Florida.

The Manson family has also gained renewed attention in recent years, with no fewer than three dramas based on the Tate–LaBianca murders being released in 2018–2019 alone. Mary Harron's *Charlie Says* (2018) is a compelling film that dramatizes the efforts of social worker Karline Faith (played by Merritt Wever) to help several members of the Manson family overcome the cult-like conditioning that led them to follow Manson in the first place. *The Haunting of Sharon Tate* (2019), written and directed by Daniel Farrands, is essentially a horror film (though not a very good one) that emphasizes the nightmarish aspects of the killings, focusing on Tate, played here by Hillary Duff. By far the highest profile film to be inspired by the Manson family, however, is Quentin Tarantino's *Once Upon a*

Time in Hollywood (2019), which combines a satire of the Hollywood film industry with an alternate history retelling in which Manson's minions find themselves on the receiving end of deadly violence, while Tate and her houseguests are unharmed.

Once Upon a Time in Hollywood was a commercial hit that took in more than $370 million in worldwide box-office receipts, while also garnering ten Oscar nominations, a total exceeded in the 2020 Oscar season only by *Joker*. The texture of Tarantino's film, with its combined focus on the film industry and on the Manson family, perhaps suggests that the family themselves were the product of certain violent tendencies in American culture and society, although the violence of the film itself (and of all of Tarantino's films) certainly complicates any attempt to read it as a critique of violent content in films. What the success of *Once Upon a Time in Hollywood* does clearly indicate, however, is that the popularity of violent films and the public fascination with serial killers might perhaps arise from a common source.

The Epix network television mini-series *Helter Skelter: An American Myth* (2020) was another sign that popular fascination with the Manson killings was still alive and well. One sign of a broader renewed fascination with 1970s–1980s serial killers in our own contemporary culture is the Netflix series *Mindhunter*, which premiered in October 2017 with a first season that focuses on the genesis of a new unit within the Behavior Science Unit of the Federal Bureau of Investigation (FBI) that is organized in 1976 in response to the seeming epidemic of serial killing then sweeping America. This first season focuses primarily on the agents within this unit as they seek better to understand the phenomenon of serial killing, at the same time doing a great deal to define serial killers as a distinct phenomenon. Indeed, one of the lead characters in *Mindhunter*, FBI Special Agent Bill Tench (Holt McCallany), is directly based on Special Agent Robert Ressler, who used the term "serial homicide" in a 1974 lecture and who is often credited with coining the term "serial killer," although it is difficult to document the actual first use of that now common term. In season 1, Tench and fellow agent Holden Ford[13] (Jonathan Groff), along with psychologist Wendy Carr (Anna Torv), seek to understand the phenomenon of serial killing via interviews with imprisoned serial killers, gaining particular insight from interviews with the towering Edmund Kemper (Cameron Britton), the "Co-Ed Killer." Season 2 (which debuted on August 16, 2019, just two weeks before the premiere of *Joker* at the Venice Film Festival) features appearances by a who's who of serial killers, including Manson, Berkowitz, and Richard Speck, among others. The season focuses, however, on the attempts of the protagonists to use their newfound knowledge to help investigate the notorious Atlanta Child Murders of 1979–1981, in which a series of at least 28 people, mostly black children and adolescents, were killed.

The 1981 conclusion of this series of killings (which ended with the arrest of Wayne Williams, who was convicted of the murder of two adult victims but has yet to be convicted of any of the child killings) can be taken as the end of the remarkable sequence of serial killings that marked the 1970s, although serial murders have, of course, continued to be committed ever since. For example, Jeffrey Dahmer, the last of the "big-name" serial killers of the 1970s and 1980s, had begun his career as a serial killer in 1978 and would extend that career into 1991. *Joker*'s setting in 1981 thus places it almost exactly at the midpoint of the sequence of high-profile serial killers that began with the Manson murders in 1969 and ended with the Dahmer conviction in 1992, just as the release of the film in 2019 places it within the midst of a tidal wave of American cultural products that deal with the phenomenon of serial killing.

These temporal correspondences are surely more than mere coincidence. The "boom" in serial killing between 1969 and 1992 is a key part of the historical background of the events of *Joker*, while *Joker* itself is a key contribution to the flurry of serial-killer dramas and documentaries that flooded American culture at the end of the 2010s, marking a different kind of "Golden Age" in American serial killing. When discussing *Joker*, it is important continually to remind ourselves that the psychological condition of Arthur Fleck makes it difficult to know what is actually occurring within the world of the film, as opposed to what might simply be the product of Fleck's troubled imagination and uncertain grip on reality. It is clear, though, that the events related within the film identify Fleck as a serial killer—or at least as someone who *believes* he is a serial killer.

The rash of high-profile serial killings that occurred between 1969 and 1992 is thus a crucial part of the historical background to *Joker*, just as these serial killings have inspired a rash of films over the years. Moreover, that *Joker* appeared in the midst of an upsurge of media representations of serial killers once again shows its dual historical context as rooted in both 1981 and 2019. Meanwhile, given that *Joker* is so rooted in the world of *film* as much as it is in the world of historical reality, it should come as no surprise that *Joker* seems informed as much or more by films about serial killers than by the serial killers themselves. And these films include not only ones that are obviously and directly based on the careers of specific serial killers but also ones that are more influenced by the general awareness of serial killers on the part of the general American population. The relevance to *Joker* of these films—especially the slasher films that became such a dominant phenomenon in American horror film in the 1970s and 1980s—was discussed in Chapter 4. But the more mainstream films of the New Hollywood era often involved serial killings and other dark crimes as well—and might have exercised an even more direct influence on *Joker*. That phenomenon will be discussed in the next chapter.

Notes

1 The evolution of the FBI's study of serial killing is detailed in the 1995 non-fiction book *Mindhunter: Inside the FBI's Elite Serial Crime Unit*, written (with the help of Mark Olshaker) by John E. Douglas, an FBI Special Agent who was centrally involved in this project.
2 The children's hospitals are an often-repeated part of Gacy lore, although there seems to be no definitive evidence for these hospital performances other than Gacy's own claims.
3 It might also be noted that, according to his entry in the *Biography* website, Gacy's performances as Pogo the Clown were carried out under the auspices of a clown club known as the "Jolly Joker" club.
4 In the kind of strange connections that abound in *Joker*, as Fleck prepares to perform at the club, he overhears from backstage part of a routine delivered by real comic Sam Morrill, who can be seen performing that same routine on *The Late Show with Stephen Colbert* in 2016 in a video currently available on YouTube at https://youtu.be/A8ikF6Kjg3s. Ironically, as that routine ends, Colbert can be seen on the video touting Morrill's upcoming performance at "Gotham Comedy Club."
5 It might also be noted that the file indicates that Penny, back in the early 1950s, was diagnosed with "narcissistic personality disorder." But this terminology was not introduced into the medical lexicon until 1968, when it was first used by Heinz Kohut.
6 The film's ending credits, in fact, explicitly identify the character as "Alfred Pennyworth" (played by Douglas Hodge).
7 Bugliosi's title derives from Manson's own claim that the murder spree was inspired by the 1968 Beatles song "Helter Skelter," the chaotic imagery of which was supposedly interpreted by Manson as an anticipation of the inter-racial warfare he hoped to trigger with the murders.
8 Manson also one-upped Nixon by issuing a statement of his own: "Here's a man who is accused of murdering hundreds of thousands in Vietnam who is accusing me of being guilty of eight murders" (qtd. in Bugliosi 431).
9 Manson was also convicted of instigating the murder of Gary Hinman in late July 1969 and the murder of Donald Shea in late August, so that the total

killing spree lasted a full month. These killings, however, were the objects of much less public fascination than were the killings of August 9–10.

10 Interestingly, John Hinckley Jr., while incarcerated in a mental facility after his attempted assassination of President Ronald Reagan, actually corresponded with Bundy during the 1980s, while Bundy was also in prison awaiting execution.

11 Bundy was also an important inspiration for the character of Patrick Bateman in Mary Harron's *American Psycho* (2000), a film that will be discussed in more detail as a predecessor to *Joker* in the next chapter.

12 See Sims for a skeptical assessment of *Extremely Wicked* based on its failure, despite the title, to capture the dark side of Bundy's crimes.

13 Ford's character is loosely based on Douglas, the FBI Special Agent whose book *Mindhunter* provided the initial inspiration for the series.

CHAPTER EIGHT

Joker, Performance, and the Society of the Spectacle

Two of the film genres to which *Joker* is most obviously connected (the superhero film and the horror film) are also among the most spectacular of American film genres, in the sense of "spectacle" as applied to describe certain films whose razzle-dazzle, attention-gathering visual flair is key to their appeal to mass audiences. And *Joker* certainly joins superhero films and horror films in its tendency to be visually impressive to the point of excess. But "spectacle" often has very specific implications as a tool of social criticism, usually as a way of describing certain characteristics of late capitalist society, emphasizing the ways in which the commodification of everything in late capitalism leads to an emphasis on appearances, in which marketing is all, especially as neoliberalism become more and more dominant as a framework within which to conduct capitalism.[1] This use of the term spectacle became prominent in social criticism after the 1967 publication of Guy Debord's *The Society of the Spectacle*, although it also a describes the kind of society that would eventually, thanks to the work of Fredric Jameson, come to be associated closely with postmodernism. The society of Gotham City in *Joker* (and, by extension, the society of Reagan-era America) certainly resembles the kinds of societies described by Debord and Jameson.

In short, *Joker* deals quite extensively in both the kind of spectacle that has long been a key element of Hollywood film and the kind of spectacle that Debord (with later elaborations proposed by Jean Baudrillard and Jameson) associates with the fundamental texture of life under late capitalism. At the same time, it should be emphasized that these two types of spectacle are not independent of one another. Film spectacle and other deployments of spectacle in popular culture (especially in advertising) made major contributions to the evolution of the society of the spectacle throughout the twentieth century, ultimately leading to a mediatization of all experience that essentially collapses the boundary between pop cultural fiction and material reality, each of which simply becomes a source of images for popular consumption.[2]

Joker and Film Spectacle

The notion of spectacle in film has taken different forms at different times in the history of film. In film's earliest days, for example, film technology itself provided amazement for impressed audiences who were unaccustomed to the very idea of moving images. During the 1930s, when Hollywood film was still taking on its sound-era form, one of the key purposes of film as a medium was to provide escapist entertainment that could offer at least a brief respite from the struggles of life during the Great Depression. Later, with the rise of television, Hollywood film began to tend more and more toward spectacle as a way of competing with the small-screen, black and white entertainment that was suddenly being broadcast directly into American homes. Then, with the rise of computer-generated imagery, it became possible to produce more and more spectacular images on the screen, leading ultimately to the superhero film explosion of the early twenty-first century.

By 1981, when the action of *Joker* is set, the notion of film itself as a technological marvel was long past, although the digital special effects explosion that began with *Star Wars* only four years earlier was still a novelty. *Joker*, though, does not particularly address this aspect of its 1981 setting, and the numerous contemporary films referenced within *Joker* do not include the kinds of films (mostly science fiction) that were central to the special effects revolution of the day. *Joker* does, however, show signs of its own spectacular nature through its connections to Hollywood film as early as the 1930s, when a turn to spectacle in the film industry—which solidified the notion of Hollywood as a "dream factory"—took on a number of forms, in addition to the content of the films themselves.

For example, the screening of *Modern Times* in the posh environs of Wayne Hall directly recalls the "movie palaces" mostly associated with the 1930s (although this phenomenon actually dates back to the early 1920s). Through the construction of these elaborately decorated venues (many of them, such as Hollywood's own Grauman's Egyptian Theatre, opened in 1922, built upon exoticist themes), the film industry allowed moviegoers to attend films in lavish surroundings that were far more luxurious than anything they would be likely to encounter in their everyday lives, although these environments sometimes threatened to spill over into garish bad taste by attempting to materialize popular fantasies of the luxurious. These theaters thus helped to promulgate the notion of filmgoing as a temporary escape from the poverty of the Depression.

This function of movie theaters as places where filmgoers could escape the material hardships of the Depression was often quite literal. After the first theater (the Rivoli Theatre in New York's Times Square) was air conditioned in 1925, air conditioning in movie theaters quickly spread, often making them an ideal place to escape summer heat at a time when few homes were air conditioned. Though not especially large, the Rivoli itself was one of the grandest movie palaces on the East Coast, among other things famed for its excellent acoustics. It also happened to be the site of the world premiere of *Modern Times* on February 5, 1936, providing a link to *Joker* and to the screening of Chaplin's film in the posh setting of Wayne Hall. Meanwhile, the theater itself ceased to operate in its original form in 1981, its conversion into twin theaters a sign of the hard times that obtained in New York in the early 1980s. The theater was eventually closed in 1987, then demolished to make way for a black glass skyscraper that sprang up as part of the 1980s New York real estate boom, the same boom that brought Donald Trump to prominence in the business world. Fittingly, in terms of *Joker*, the most famous tenant of this new building (both at the beginning and still, in 2021 as I write) is Caroline Hirsch's famed comedy club Carolines on Broadway, originally established at another location in 1981 (clearly a key year in New York history) and the place where a number of stand-ups (including Jerry Seinfeld) worked to launch their careers.

The Depression-era film industry also provided Depression-era escapist entertainment of a sort through an extensive and high-powered public relations effort that helped to promote the notion of Hollywood stars as fantasy figures whose exciting lifestyles could provide vicarious adventures for their fans. This aspect of Hollywood spectacle seems relatively unimportant in *Joker*, although it does provide an important impetus to the sort of celebrity culture that would lead Fleck to adopt Murray Franklin as his personal hero, while also contributing to Fleck's notion that entering show business might be his best path to achieving a more fulfilling life. And, of course, one of the key reasons why *Joker* was such a huge box-office success was that many moviegoers were lured into theaters simply by reports of the virtuoso performance of Joaquin Phoenix in the title role.[3]

Indeed, Debord specifically addresses this aspect of the spectacle, noting that media stars essentially serve as images of human beings that provide a sort of compensation for the lack of connections that media's consumers have with real human beings:

> Media stars are spectacular representations of living human beings, distilling the essence of the spectacle's banality into images of possible roles. Stardom is a diversification in the semblance of life—the object of an identification with mere appearance which is intended to compensate for the crumbling of directly experienced diversifications of productive activity. Celebrities figure various styles of life and various views of society which anyone is supposedly free to embrace and pursue in a global manner. (*The Society of the Spectacle* 38–39)

And, of course, the talk show, a form that figures so prominently in *Joker*, is the perfect venue for this sort of celebrity culture. As Booker and Daraiseh note of the typical talk show,

> This tried and true format provides a comfort zone in which viewers can relax into a familiar setting almost as if visiting with the host as a friend (or even family member)—a friend who has particularly interesting or attractive guests with whom the viewer can also visit. Talk shows thus form a sort of simulated community that might be seen as substituting for the lack of genuine community in the modern societies of late capitalism. Talk show audiences are thus treated to an experience analogous to that of Mildred, the wife of the protagonist of Ray Bradbury's 1953 dystopian classic *Fahrenheit 451*, who considers the characters she watches on television to be her "family." (*Consumerist Orientalism* 168)

In short, Arthur Fleck's fascination with Murray Franklin can be taken not only as a sign that he sees Franklin as someone who gets the kind of visibility and attention that he himself so craves, but also as a sign that Fleck yearns to join the manufactured community of Franklin's show to compensate for his own almost total lack of real connection with other actual human beings.

In terms of the films themselves, the most important aspect of film spectacle during the 1930s involved the rise of elaborately staged and choreographed musicals of the kind often associated with the work of choreographer and director Busby Berkeley, whose distinctive designs of elaborate production numbers involving the arrangement of large troupes of dancers into intricate geometric patterns remain a standard against which such production numbers are measured to this day. Meanwhile, the biggest star to emerge from the Hollywood musicals of the 1930s was Fred Astaire, whose relevance to *Joker* has already been discussed, although it should be noted that there is also a clear element of spectacle in that roller-skating scene from *Modern Times* that Fleck observes in Wayne Hall.

In the postmodern era, some of the films that have served most clearly as spectacles have involved revved-up and digitally enhanced versions of the elaborate musical production numbers of the 1930s—as in the case of Baz Luhrmann's *Moulin Rouge!* (2001) or *The Great Gatsby* (2013). Many recent films have also featured spectacular violence. However, despite its reputation in some circles, *Joker* actually includes relatively few scenes of spectacular violence. Instead, the most spectacle-like scenes of the film are the scenes of Fleck's dancing, especially that crucial jaunty dance down those stone steps, which clearly links back to the musicals of the 1930s and 1940s, which depended so heavily on the virtuoso dancing of Astaire, Gene Kelly, and others to achieve their effects as spectacular entertainment. Such dancers (and I would include here Chaplin's roller-skating scene in *Modern Times*) often performed in seemingly dangerous or precarious settings, with James Cagney's famous tap-dance down a flight of stairs in *Yankee Doodle Dandy* (1942) perhaps providing the closest analogue in classic Hollywood film to Fleck's stair-dance in *Joker*.

By the end of the 1930s, however, new forms of spectacle began to gain importance in Hollywood film, as 1939 saw the release of the two landmark Technicolor films that presaged the large-scale, full-color epics of the 1950s. One of these, *The Wizard of Oz*, is a musical of sorts, but it moves beyond the earlier emphasis on large-scale production numbers, introducing an important element of fantasy and adventure. The other, *Gone with the Wind*, is an elaborate historical epic that mixes romance with the American Civil War. *The Wizard of Oz* would take a while before it became the beloved film that it now is, but *Gone with the Wind* was an immediate hit that remains the biggest box-office draw of all time in terms of inflation-adjusted dollars, although its potential romanticization of the slave South has become increasingly controversial over the years.

The success of *Gone with the Wind* pointed toward the biblical epics and other grand, large-scale Technicolor productions of the 1950s, as Hollywood studios sought to deliver types of entertainment that could successfully compete with the much more convenient format of television. At this point, film content and film technology became closely allied in the attempt to produce impressive spectacles. All of the important spectacle films of the 1950s were in color, and many of them employed new widescreen technologies, because, with spectacle, bigger is better. For example, producer Michael Todd had a giant curved screen installed in the Rivoli Theatre to accommodate the world premiere run of his musical spectacle *Oklahoma!* (1955) in his own 70 mm Todd-AO process.

No Joke: Todd Phillips's *Joker* and American Culture

A number of other Todd-AO films eventually ran on this screen as well, including the legendarily spectacular *Cleopatra* (1963), whose premiere at the theater included the temporary replacement of the theater's traditional Greek-column façade (already spectacular in its own right) with an Egyptian-themed façade.

The spectacle films of the 1950s and 1960s, eventually boosted by the digital special-effects revolution that took off with *Star Wars* in 1977, would eventually lead to the superhero films of the twenty-first century, perhaps the most spectacular films ever made. I have already discussed in Chapter 1 some of the ways in which *Joker* gains energy (and, especially, box-office appeal) from the popularity of superhero films and from the fact that audiences clearly thought of it as such a film. But *Joker* largely eschews the computer-generated violence and mass destruction that have helped to make recent superhero films such huge box-office hits. Indeed, while there are scenes of graphic violence (especially Fleck's shocking murder of his former co-worker Randall) and large-scale mayhem (such as the violent mass demonstrations at the end of the film), the spectacular aspects of *Joker* tend more toward more subdued instances such as the scenes of Fleck dancing (typically, and tellingly, without an audience). This emphasis helps to make *Joker* seem more like a realistic drama than do most superhero films (reportedly pitched by Phillips as a "real movie" disguised as a comic book movie), while also lending itself to the film's intense focus on the personal travails of its protagonist. However, this personal focus also allows the spectacular aspects of the film to produce a coherent social commentary free of the distractions that would have been produced by the high-action scenes typical of other superhero films. This commentary suggests a vision of the society of Gotham City (and, by extension, the United States) very much in accord with the analysis of late capitalist Western society presented in Debord's *The Society of the Spectacle*, an analysis that would later be extended by thinkers such as Jameson in ways that remain quite consistent with Debord's fundamental ideas. In particular, Debord's notion of "spectacle" is closely congruent with Jean Baudrillard's notion of "hyperreality," a notion that also seems to have significantly influenced Jameson.

Joker and Social Spectacle

Much radical thought of the past half century or so (including that of Debord, Baudrillard, and Jameson) can be understood as an attempt to update and refocus Marx's original analysis of capitalism to account for the immense structural changes undergone by capitalism in the course of the twentieth century. Most of these were driven by the initial fundamental shift at the beginning of the century from the classical production-oriented capitalism of the nineteenth century to the marketing-oriented consumer capitalism that has become increasingly dominant ever since.[4] One eventual crucial consequence of this transformation was the globalization of capitalism, although that aspect of the shift is relatively unimportant to *Joker* (or to Debord's original work),[5] other than as a way of accounting for the global commercial success of the film. More pertinent to Debord's work and to the society depicted in *Joker* is the fact that this shift in capitalism leads in obvious ways to a shift from the material considerations of factory production to the image-related considerations of advertising and marketing, in which what a commodity can be made to *appear* to be or do becomes more important than what it actually is or does.

Debord's analysis of the spectacle includes a thumbnail sketch of the history of capitalism as proceeding from an emphasis on "being," through an emphasis on "having," and, finally, with the emergence of the spectacle in all its power, to an emphasis on "appearing" (*The Society of the Spectacle* 16). It is important to note, however, that the society of the spectacle described by Debord is not a departure from Marx's description of capitalism. Instead, it is a rather faithful extension of Marx's analysis dictated by the fact that capitalist tendencies already noted by Marx had proceeded to new levels in the era of consumer capitalism. In the first volume of *Capital*, for example, Marx discusses what he calls "the fetishism" of the commodity, in which the realities of the human labor and human social relations that go into the production and distribution of commodities are obscured by a sense that the commodity has somehow been produced, fully formed, as if by magic. Moreover, the magical properties of commodities become even more mysterious and seemingly metaphysical because

> A commodity appears, at first sight, a very trivial thing, and easily understood. Its analysis shows that it is, in reality, a very queer thing, abounding in metaphysical subtleties and theological niceties. So far as it is a value in use, there is nothing mysterious about it, whether we consider it from the point of view that by its properties it is capable of satisfying human wants, or from the point that those properties are the product of human labour. It is as clear as noon-day, that man, by his industry, changes the forms of the materials furnished by Nature, in such a way as to make

them useful to him. The form of wood, for instance, is altered, by making a table out of it. Yet, for all that, the table continues to be that common, every-day thing, wood. But, so soon as it steps forth as a commodity, it is changed into something transcendent. It not only stands with its feet on the ground, but, in relation to all other commodities, it stands on its head, and evolves out of its wooden brain grotesque ideas, far more wonderful than "table-turning" ever was. (Marx and Engels 319–320)

In particular, for Marx, the commodity, because of the way it functions within the capitalist economic system, takes on a mysterious value that is largely disengaged from its practical usefulness. This "exchange value" is related, not to what the commodity can provide in terms of practical benefits, but simply to the price that it can demand on the open market, in competition with other commodities. Economically, then, commodities have a tendency to operate in a world of their own, divorced from the real world of the humans who made them or who purchase and use them. In this way, humans are estranged from the products produced by their labor, ultimately alienated from those products, from other people, and even from themselves.

Debord's society of the spectacle is essentially a world in which this process is being pushed toward its logical conclusion, anticipating the postmodern world of Jameson where that conclusion has essentially been reached. This world is informed by the absolute victory of exchange value over use value. Moreover, as the exchange value is determined by factors such as marketing and advertising, rather than by the inherent properties of the commodity itself, the commodity becomes more and more divorced from use value and even from material reality, which is thus replaced, for all practical purposes, by a world of images.

Debord himself notes the importance of Marx's theorization of commodity fetishism to his own work by noting that "the principle of commodity fetishism" is "absolutely fulfilled in the spectacle, where the perceptible world is replaced by a set of images that are superior to that world yet at the same time impose themselves as eminently perceptible" (*The Society of the Spectacle* 25–26). In the society of the spectacle, for Debord, the image reigns triumphant over real lived experience: "The commodity world is thus shown *as it really is*, for its logic is one with men's estrangement from one another and from the sum total of what they produce" (26).

The emphasis here on "estrangement" is an important one, and Debord insists throughout *The Society of the Spectacle* that the situation he is describing leads to increasingly radical alienation. Debord insists that the prevention of direct and meaningful intersubjective contact between individuals is not an accidental by-product of capitalism but is in fact one of capitalism's central goals. For him,

> The reigning economic system is founded on isolation; at the same time it is a circular process designed to produce isolation. Isolation underpins technology, and technology isolates in its turn; all *goods* proposed by the spectacular system, from cars to televisions, also serve as weapons for that system as it strives to reinforce the isolation of "the lonely crowd." (*The Society of the Spectacle* 22)

Debord here refers to (without specifically mentioning) David Riesman's 1950 book *The Lonely Crowd* (1950), indicating his tendency to refuse to adhere to academic norms for documenting sources, although he often does (as here) provide clear pointers. For Riesman, in an analysis that was first and foremost a study of alienation, individuals can be characterized via "personality types" that cause them to act in certain ways and that contribute to the inability of individual Americans to develop any distinctive sense of personal identity. In particular, Reisman argues that America, at the beginning of the 1950s, was in the process of a fundamental shift from the dominance of "inner-directed" personality types (who act out of a sense that what they are doing is right) to the dominance of "other-directed" personality types (who act primarily out of the hope that others will approve their action), especially among the affluent middle classes.

Arthur Fleck's desire to be seen is clearly also a desire for the approval of others, a desire that also drives his aspiration to be a successful stand-up comedian. In his case, though, his alienation is so radical that, however much he wants others to approve of him, he also finds it virtually impossible to relate to others. For Jameson, as I noted in Chapter 2, this alienation that is a natural consequence of capitalism had ultimately, by the 1980s, become so radical that it transcends the original Marxist/modernist definition of alienation, spilling over into what he calls "psychic fragmentation," a notion that certainly describes Fleck's plight quite well, while also providing an excellent explanation for the dysfunctional nature of his "other-directed" behavior.

Fleck's struggles in *Joker* can be described as an ongoing attempt to establish and maintain a stable sense of his own identity—not just to establish the nature of his identity, but to establish that he has any identity at all, that he even *exists* at all. Given the centrality of images to the society of the spectacle, it comes as no surprise that Fleck's sense of his own tenuous identity is centered on the way he appears to others—or on whether he appears to them at all. When we catch a glimpse of his journal and joke diary in his session with the social worker near the beginning of the film, one of the lines within it that stands out is the notation that "I want people to see me."

This desperate desire to be seen, this desire to be *acknowledged*, is a crucial driving force for all of Fleck's actions in *Joker*, although the fact that he would focus specifically on being seen suggests the primacy of the visible in the spectacle, which also makes film a perfect venue for conveying ideas that illustrate the spectacle.[6] Fleck's desire here also partakes of the emphasis on image and appearance that Debord sees as a central characteristic of the society of the spectacle. What is particularly telling, though, is that Fleck primarily envisions himself becoming known by being seen on television rather than directly. As Maria Flood suggests, even the cinematography of *Joker* features an unusual number of shots that deviate from the usual Hollywood close-up on the protagonist, involving instead indirect views of Fleck's face as it appears on "a range of distorted surfaces, such as windows, mirrors, and television screens." This penchant for indirect representation suggests the separation of Fleck from others, as does the fact that he must don a costume and play an invented character in order to solidify his sense of his own existence.

Even when Fleck performs live in Pogo's Comedy Club, it is clear that he views this venue as a stepping stone that might someday take him into television, though of course he could not have foreseen how (or how quickly) this move actually happens in the film. But, as we are reminded throughout *Joker*, the society of Gotham City is thoroughly mediatized—as is Debord's society of the spectacle. Most of what Fleck himself sees of the outside world comes to him through television, film, or radio, with television clearly being pre-eminent among these different media. As a result, it is not surprising that he might imagine being seen in the same way.

Similarly, it is telling that Fleck's most spectacular performances are carried out when he is alone, so that no one actually observes them. This fact is entirely unsurprising, given his radically alienated (or fragmented) condition. It does not, however, indicate that Fleck is insincere in his stated desire to be seen. Rather, it is an indicator of the fact that he is so radically disconnected from other people that performing in front of them is extremely difficult for him, almost unthinkable, however much he might crave attention. Thus, while his unobserved dancing performances are sometimes quite impressive, they can be so because they are not carried out in front of an audience—except for that last dance atop a cop car amid the riot near the end of the film, which is probably imaginary. Meanwhile, when Fleck performs at Pogo's, in front of a live (though sparse) audience, he is partly able to do so at all because he imagines Sophie in the audience, imaginary people apparently being, for him, much easier to deal with than real people. But, at that, his performance is so embarrassingly clumsy that even he seems to realize it, sending him into one of his paroxysms of stress-induced laughter.

It is not surprising, of course, that Fleck is never able to succeed in his attempt to become a stand-up comedian, just as his own mother predicted. After all, success as a comedian would presumably require some sort of ability to connect with his audiences, but Fleck seems unable to connect with anyone, including his mother. Indeed, *Joker* indicates that the condition of radical alienation that afflicts Fleck when he is out in the world follows him home as well, as Debord's characterization of the spectacle would predict. Beginning with Lewis Mumford's analysis of the alienating effect of life in the modern city, Debord notes that the fundamental characteristics of modern capitalist society are built on maintaining a separation between individuals that allows them to co-operate when needed for the operation of the economic system without building any genuine sense of solidarity with others. Meanwhile, this separation in the public world of work and commerce then extends into private space as well:

> These imperatives pursue the isolated individual right into the *family cell*, where the generalized use of receivers of the spectacle's message ensures that his isolation is filled with the dominant images—images that indeed attain their full force only by virtue of this isolation. (*The Society of the Spectacle* 122)

Those scenes of Arthur and Penny huddled together watching television in their apartment illustrate Debord's observation quite clearly. Consuming the same images, they are not brought together, but pushed apart. When they see Murray Franklin or Thomas Wayne on their television screen, they see very different things. Each of them relates to the world through their own interpretation of the images on the screen, which has the effect that each of them, in a very real sense, lives in a different world. Penny lives in a world in which Wayne, for example, is a "good man" who thinks of his employees like family and treats them accordingly. Arthur, on the other hand, is much more skeptical of Wayne, while seeing Franklin as much more of a potential role model (or father figure).

Fleck's view of Franklin will, of course, change in the course of the film, as Fleck sheds his hero-worship of Franklin and instead essentially evolves into his own hero by donning the invented Joker persona. *Joker* is very much a study of the personal development of its protagonist, but it is by definition a highly unconventional character study because Fleck, rather than undergoing the traditional character development that one might associate with something like the *Bildungsroman*, instead undergoes a spectacular development into an anti-character who is almost pure image (and may, in fact, be literally imaginary).

That so much of this development is captured visually in the film is a sign of its spectacular, performative nature, especially as so much of Fleck's development can be specifically traced through his dancing performances. Fleck's shirtless dances in his apartment, putting on display his emaciated state, are a key aspect of spectacle in *Joker*, providing a vivid visual image of his longtime struggles with poverty and illness. The fluid movements of that ravaged, abject body, performed so smoothly in concert with music, make this spectacle even more effective, introducing a sort of poetic pathos that would almost certainly be unachievable in mere still photos—or, for that matter, in a moving image that was not synchronized with music. And abject is the perfect term here, especially as influentially theorized by Julia Kristeva in *Powers of Horror*. For Kristeva, the experience of abjection is largely one of horror at the realization of one's own mortality, a realization that occurs when confronted with aspects of one's physical existence (such as viewing a corpse or one's own excrement) that serve as reminders of one's mortality. I'm not sure I would go so far as Bainbridge, who quite explicitly links Fleck's physique to the kinds of images that are normally associated with abjection when she notes that "Phoenix's twisty, contorted body makes Arthur Fleck into a turd-like being" (60). I would, however, argue that Fleck's emaciated body, with those protruding ribs on such full display, clearly serves as a reminder of the physicality—and perhaps of the fragility—of the human body, coming very close to spilling over into the realm of "body horror," which so clearly performs a similar function.[7]

These private performances are worth reviewing in detail in terms of their contribution to the spectacular aspects of *Joker*, because the dances are not of a consistent piece. In fact, they evolve through the film, providing a spectacular representation of Fleck's character development through the film.[8] Fleck performs four main dances in *Joker*, which occur in two closely spaced pairs, each consisting of one dance shirtless in his apartment and one in clown costume in the world outside his apartment, and each punctuated by a murder scene that falls between the private

Joker, Performance, and the Society of the Spectacle

dance and the "public" (but unobserved) one. Fleck's first performance establishes him as a rather pathetic figure, someone who is to be pitied more than feared. This performance occurs just over 20 minutes into the film, as Fleck watches "Slap That Bass" from *Shall We Dance* and is moved to start dancing to the music. This moment immediately evokes the past of the Hollywood musical as spectacle, inviting us to consider *Joker* in relation to that legacy. Fleck's dancing is not particularly impressive in this scene, however, and his fantasy of impressing a woman with his dancing seems sad and pathetic given the shocking condition of his body and given the fact that he performs this dance with a gun in his hand. This gun, in fact, will interrupt the performance by going off after only a few seconds in a sort of symbolic premature ejaculation, emphasizing the futility of Fleck's romantic fantasies. In the meantime, his emaciated physique combines with the role played by this gun to set up a powerful contrast between the predicament of Fleck and the romantic spectacle of Hollywood musicals and stars such as Fred Astaire.

To an extent, then, this scene is a sort of anti-spectacle that reveals the emptiness at the heart of the more conventional spectacles that are, for Debord, the very stuff of life under late capitalist society. The same might also be said for Fleck's second dance, which occurs only ten minutes of runtime later, after the subway shootings that seem to mark a watershed in Fleck's movement toward his eventual emergence as either a real or an imagined supervillain. In this scene, his dancing is much more fluid and graceful than in the previous one, perfectly synchronized with the solemn beauty of Guðnadóttir's music. It probably helps that Fleck is now fully clad, so that we cannot see the spectacle of his starved physique, although the fact that he is still partly in his clown costume (including oversized clown shoes that dominate the first shot of the dance sequence) interrupts the aesthetic spectacle of the performance, as does the fact that it is taking place in the surroundings of that grimy public restroom, creating a stark, almost Brechtian, contrast between the grim reality of the setting (both the physical setting in the restroom and the post-murder plot moment) and the synchronized beauty of the music and Phoenix's movements.

Phoenix's performance in this scene is also highly introspective, robbing it of the collective energies of a truly Brechtian estrangement effect. He literally dances as if no one is watching, and it is significant that much of the dance is performed directly in front of a mirror, indicating that this performance is meant for his own consumption and also suggesting the way in which his radical loneliness and alienation separate him from others. Still, the dance, which seems so surprisingly skillful, does serve as a visual marker of Fleck's development as a character (Figure 10). Without

No Joke: Todd Phillips's *Joker* and American Culture

Figure 10. Fleck dances in a grimy public restroom.

dialogue, without comment, without any real action that is actually part of the plot, this scene is able to convey that the blow struck against the Wall Street guys (whether or not he is the real perpetrator) has given Fleck a newfound sense of self and self-worth that potentially make him a much more formidable and dangerous figure. The scene thus serves as character development by pure spectacle, suggesting that *Joker*, however much it might be read as a commentary on late capitalism as spectacle per Debord, is also itself implicated as an example of spectacle. Indeed, in this film, it would seem that the only alternative to spectacle is more spectacle, which might not be any alternative at all.

Fleck's second shirtless dance occurs a little over an hour after the first in terms of runtime and at another key moment, just after he is shown killing his mother and just as he is beginning to suit up for his performance on the Franklin show. This dance, performed to Sinatra's "That's Life," adds to Fleck's preparations for the show, given that the song is Franklin's personal theme (Figure 11). We still see only a few seconds of actual dancing, but, during this hour of runtime, in which so much has happened, Fleck seems to have evolved considerably as a dancer in comparison with his first shirtless dance. This dance lacks the slow, solemn beauty of the restroom dance, but (in keeping with the change in the music), Fleck seems to have gained considerably in the confidence and flamboyance of his movements in comparison with his dance in response to "Slap That Bass." His body even appears less abjectly thin, even if his baggy briefs undermine any attempt to see him as the impressive figure he wishes to be. Indeed, the visual of this underwear

Joker, Performance, and the Society of the Spectacle

Figure 11. Fleck dances alone in his apartment, accompanied by Frank Sinatra singing "That's Life."

helps to emphasize the contrast between Fleck and Sinatra, who here plays somewhat the same role as Astaire in the earlier scene by standing as an exemplary emblem of the "official" spectacle, in sharp contrast to the outcast Fleck, who is now evolving into an emblem of "oppositional" spectacle, even though the lack of an audience once again renders the dance politically inert.

This more defiant shirtless dance, of course, is followed by still another murder scene, the bloodiest in the film and one that clearly takes *Joker* into the realm of horror as Fleck murders Randall with an outburst of spectacular and excessive violence, even repeatedly bashing his victim's head against the wall, blood flying, after the man is obviously already dead. And then, only six minutes of runtime after the second shirtless dance, comes Fleck's final and most spectacular dance performance, as he jauntily bounces down those steps to the strains of "Rock and Roll Part 2." This dance, in keeping with the music that accompanies it, is overtly demonstrative and declarative, punctuated by high kicks and exaggerated pelvic thrusts that signify his newfound sense of masculine power. Now in full Joker costume, Fleck for the first time presents a fully fleshed-out visual performance, clearly imagining himself thrilling a crowd, even though there is no crowd present. It can thus be considered his final rehearsal before his one truly public performance, the appearance on *Live with Murray Franklin*, which apparently (at least in his own mind) makes Fleck the adored leader and figurehead of the crowds venting their pent-up rage in the streets of Gotham.

No Joke: Todd Phillips's *Joker* and American Culture

The crucial part played by those stone steps indicates the key role played by Gotham City itself in the visual spectacle of *Joker*, the city becoming a sort of public manifestation of the same energies that are contained at a personal level in the character of Fleck. In particular, the dilapidated condition of the city mirrors Fleck's emaciated physical condition, with all those sidewalks stacked with bags of garbage that almost seem to be threatening to burst open and spill out, revealing the hidden reality of the wastefulness of consumer society. Indeed, this garbage plays very much the same role for the society as excrement does for the individual, representing a repressed element of abject reality. We should recall that the very word "abjection" literally means a state of being cast off, like so much garbage, and so the concept of abjection seems highly relevant to the role played by garbage in *Joker*. Meanwhile, Kristeva, while working principally within a psychoanalytic framework, also sees the abject as playing a crucial sociopolitical role. For her, abjection is central to the "demarcating imperative" through which modern societies are built upon systems and hierarchies, and especially on the desire to separate the "clean" from the "filthy" and thus to suppress abject images (*Powers* 68). From this point of view, *Joker*, by bringing abject images into full view, plays a clearly subversive role. All those mounting garbage bags that we see everywhere in *Joker* clearly represent a spectacle of their own sort that adds a great deal to the characterization in the film of Gotham as a city on the verge of boiling over into violence.

The use of garbage in such a way is essentially a form of "poverty porn," which has recently received considerable discussion in film criticism and which clearly points to the fascination that Kristeva associates with abjection. Discussions of poverty porn in film studies have typically focused on the representation of urban squalor in the Global South, as in discussions of Danny Boyle's *Slumdog Millionaire* (2008) and its representation of poverty in Mumbai, a representation that, as Gonzaga notes, has been accused, especially by Indian critics, of "reducing the rich complexity of everyday life in Mumbai to stylized stereotypes of an impoverished India" (113).

Such representations of non-Western cities, either by Western directors or by indigenous directors, clearly contribute to a Western othering of these cities as a different, inferior, and underdeveloped reality against which Western cities can favorably be compared. Thus, as Gonzaga notes, "cinematic representations of the Global South cannot be extricated from prevailing discourses of urban poverty, which measure the circumstances of developing nations against the norms of industrialized countries" (103). At the same time, similar imagery can be directed at American cities as well, and sometimes in clearly subversive ways. Steven Shaviro, for example, has discussed the representation of a blighted Detroit in Jim Jarmusch's *Only Lovers Left Alive* (2013) as an example of "ruin porn," which is essentially a version of poverty porn, without the typical teeming masses. But, as Booker and Daraiseh note, the representation of a ruined Detroit in this film—as opposed to a much more functional and livable Tangier—can be seen as a reversal of the typical Orientalist dynamic that opposes the clean, modern, well-lit Western city to the dark and crumbled slums of the East ("This Is the Bloody").

The representation of Gotham in *Joker* also plays a political role by undermining stereotypes. In particular, one of the functions of the emphasis on urban squalor in *Joker* is to provide a realistic counter to the current movement in American popular culture toward nostalgic, idealized visions of the 1980s. Thus, rather than oppose the urban squalor of the Global South to the clean, smoothly functioning cities of the Global North, *Joker* instead asks us to oppose the grim realities of life in American cities in the 1980s to the nostalgic representations of the 1980s as a time of youthful innocence—the latter typically enacted in small-town or suburban (and mostly white) settings.

One thinks here of the Netflix series *Stranger Things* (2016–), whose nostalgia is tellingly focused less on real life in the 1980s than on the pop culture of the 1980s (such as the films of Steven Spielberg or the music of The Clash), suggesting the thoroughly mediatized nature of our memories of the past in the era of the spectacle. The series reads very much like a pastiche of several well-known cultural products of the 1980s, such as Spielberg's *E.T. the Extra-Terrestrial* (1982) and Rob Reiner's *Stand By Me* (1986)—with a dash of *The X-Files* (1993–2002) thrown in as well. There is an occasional nod to the real 1980s, as when one family displays a Reagan–Bush yard sign in the second season, which is set during the 1984 presidential campaign. The series is filled with direct references to the culture of the 1980s, including a liberal helping of 1980s popular music, often heard diegetically, but also included as background music either to scenes or to the closing credits. Snippets of various television programs or commercials are also seen, while numerous films of the decade are referred to as well, either in passing (as in the inclusion of movie posters on the kids' walls) or even as part of the plot, as when a group of the kids in the show go trick-or-treating dressed as the gang from *Ghostbusters* (1984). Finally, a number of specific commodities (toys, snack foods, sodas) that one might associate with the 1980s appear within the series.

All of these items make *Stranger Things* seem like a spectacle of 1980s nostalgia objects, pointing toward the way in which nostalgia in general is a fundamentally spectacular phenomenon built on the replacement of actual memories of the past with images of a past time that might well have little or no connection with the material reality of that time. In the case of *Stranger Things*, the nostalgia value of the series is enhanced by the fact that it is primarily set in a small Indiana town and is dominated by characters who are children or teenagers. The series features numerous scenes of things such as kids riding around town on bikes or inexperienced teenagers exploring the dynamics of sex and love for the first time, creating a sense of the 1980s as a simpler and more innocent time, much in the way the 1950s had long been portrayed in popular culture, including in 1980s works such as *Stand By Me*. Even the adult characters in *Stranger Things* are often played by actors (Winona Ryder, Matthew Modine, Sean Astin) who had first risen to prominence as cultural icons playing children or teenagers in films of the 1980s, adding an additional nostalgia effect.

Indeed, in addition to the obvious echoes of *Stand By Me*, *Stranger Things* calls attention to the similarities between its depiction of the 1980s and the depiction of the 1950s in earlier nostalgic works in other ways. For example, the secret government experiments that set the events of the series in motion are modeled on the actual "MKUltra" CIA mind-control experiments, which were officially authorized in 1953. MKUltra is, in fact, directly mentioned several times in *Stranger Things*, and in ways that acknowledge the link to the experiments that drive *Stranger Things*. In addition, even some of the products that are used to create a "1980s" atmosphere for the series are actually products of the 1950s. Eggo frozen waffles, for example, play an especially prominent role, but these products (which were quite popular in the 1980s) actually date to 1953 and were first marketed under the "Eggo" brand label in 1955.

The pastoral setting of Hawkins, Indiana, meanwhile, is further emphasized in the second season episode "Chapter Seven: The Lost Sister," which involves an excursion to a dark and dangerous industrial Chicago that would be very much at home in the squalid urban world of *Joker* and that contrasts sharply with the small-town environment of Hawkins. On the other hand, Hawkins is also the site of the Hawkins National Laboratory, where sinister secret experiments are underway, suggesting the existence of nefarious official forces that threaten the tranquility of this pastoral 1980s world. Those dark forces, however, are treated with a light touch, as drivers for the science fictional plot more than as objects of political commentary. Indeed, while Ronald Reagan is occasionally mentioned in the series, there is no real interrogation of his policies and little is done to pursue the fact that the national laboratory is administered by the Department of Energy, a cabinet-level organization within the Reagan administration (though the sinister experiments date back an unspecified number of years). Instead of identifying Reagan as the person ultimately responsible for the operations of Hawkins Lab, the lab instead seems to be an almost autonomous organization run by Modine's sinister character and his successors. Reagan is not really regarded as a political figure at all but is instead simply treated as part of the furniture of the 1980s, just another nostalgia object like the Bangles, or *Masters of the Universe*, or rabbit ears and corded telephones.

It is tempting to see the current wave of nostalgia for the 1980s as a simple generational change in which the Culture Industry simply shifts its nostalgic target to maintain a focus on a time that roughly corresponds to the childhood years of individuals now in their prime adult years. And this explanation no doubt contains some truth. However, I think that the current nostalgic focus on the 1980s also has a particularly postmodern aspect that Jameson has described as a "nostalgia for nostalgia" (*Postmodernism* 156). One might also describe this phenomenon as a sort of meta-nostalgia. We are now, I would argue, no longer able to maintain a genuine nostalgia for the past; instead, we are faux-nostalgic for the 1980s because that was the last decade in which we were still able to feel a *genuine* nostalgia for the 1950s.

Seen in this way, it is not surprising that *Stranger Things* is only one of numerous recent pop cultural products to have employed nostalgic visions of the 1980s to connect with audiences in the twenty-first century. Steven Spielberg's own *Ready Player One* (2018), for example, contains a veritable barrage of references to the popular culture of the 1980s, a culture to which Spielberg himself was a central contributor. Particularly telling as an example of 1980s nostalgia is the "San Junipero" episode of the Netflix series *Black Mirror*, in which the year 1987 is chosen as the setting for an idealized simulated environment, with the music of that time used with particularly good effect to help create that environment. Isra Daraiseh and I have discussed this episode in detail elsewhere ("Unreal City"), but for now I would simply like to point out that the nostalgic vision of 1987 featured in this episode is overtly specifically a simulation designed, not to be realistic, but to replace reality with a more pleasant simulation, so that the episode shows a clear analysis of just how nostalgia works.

Of course, this nostalgic fascination with the 1980s, presumably built on a sense that the 1980s were very different from the 2010s, might very well be based instead on a sense of recognition, on a realization (conscious or not) that the 1980s and the 2010s have a great deal in common. I will address this possibility at more length in the final chapter. For now, I will simply note that nostalgic visions of the 1980s (like all nostalgic visions) can only function at all by obscuring and repressing certain unpleasant realities concerning the past. *Joker*, then, stands in stark opposition to these nostalgic visions by dragging the dark elements of the 1980s out into plain view. In this film, the 1980s consists not of innocently horny teenagers and children riding bikes, but of subway shootings, garbage strikes, soaring unemployment, and the collapse of the mental health system. However, *Joker* does not counter the spectacle of nostalgia with hard-headed reality; instead, it opposes the spectacular nostalgia for the "good" 1980s with a counter-spectacle of the "bad" 1980s. Once again, the only alternative to spectacle would appear to be more spectacle, suggesting that the society of the spectacle envisioned by Debord in 1967 seems to have established itself all the more firmly over time.

Of these "bad" aspects of the 1980s, the garbage makes for the most spectacular imagery, and its constant presence in the visual representations of the streets of Gotham is crucial to the effect of *Joker*. It is, of course, the function of the waste collection system, shut down in the film due to the garbage strike, to remove the garbage generated by daily life under late capitalism and transport it somewhere out of sight. When this system breaks down, as in a garbage strike, the realities of this garbage suddenly become difficult to deny because the garbage is now piling up in plain sight, even if contained within plastic bags that still provide at least some protection from the abject reality of what is inside.

As Debord points out, excess and waste do not represent inefficiencies within the society of late capitalism; instead, they represent organic necessities that are a crucial part of the society of the spectacle, inevitable results of "the commodity form itself" (*The Society of the Spectacle* 140). Indeed, at the most basic level, the shift from the classical production-oriented capitalism of the nineteenth century to the consumer capitalism that is the basis of the spectacle was a shift from emphasis on producing enough goods to meet the needs of consumers to convincing consumers to buy more than they actually need. But this basic fact is one of the crucial characteristics that late capitalism seeks to keep hidden from view, not only because of the environmental destruction wrought by this excess production and consumption but also because this reliance on excess consumption exposes elements of late capitalism that reveal the fundamentally meretricious nature of the entire system.

The garbage bags littering the sidewalks of Gotham are, in fact, the film's principal representation of consumerism, calling attention to its dark side, as opposed to the shiny, seductive side presented in advertising,

Joker, Performance, and the Society of the Spectacle

perhaps the quintessential consumerist spectacle. Advertisements, in fact, play a relatively minor role in this film—as opposed, for example, to the spectacular advertisements that famously dominate the cityscape of the postmodern Los Angeles in *Blade Runner* (1982). On the other hand, the career of Arthur Fleck in the film is bookended by advertisements, beginning with his sign spinning in the first dramatic scene and ending with the advertisements that are included in that sudden proliferation of television screens that momentarily colonize the film's *mise en scène* after the shooting of Murray Franklin. Indeed, that moment, when those 24 television monitors engulf the screen can be taken as the film's quintessential representation of the Debordian spectacle.

Given *Joker*'s status as a postmodern cultural artifact, it should come as no surprise that so many aspects of the film seem to exemplify Debord's comments on the society of the spectacle, a phenomenon that, Debord notes in his *Comments on the Society of the Spectacle*, had only intensified and become more total in its extent by the 1980s, when Jameson was formulating his theorization of postmodernism as the cultural logic of late capitalism. Indeed, the complete triumph of exchange value described by Debord is simply a slightly different way of stating Jameson's understanding of late capitalism as the result of the completion of the historical process of capitalist modernization, accompanied by the commodification of everything, including culture, once a relatively autonomous sphere within bourgeois society. Indeed, Jameson, to an extent, acknowledges Debord as a predecessor when he quotes Debord to the effect that, in the spectacle, the image has become "the final form of commodity reification" (*Postmodernism* 236). Indeed, Jameson mentions Debord only six times in his seminal book on postmodernism, and five of them are approving references to this one phrase (which he variously calls "extraordinary," "powerful," and "remarkable"), while the other is to rather vaguely lump Debord in with Baudrillard and unnamed others as theorists who have warned us that, "in the process of becoming an image and a spectacle, the referent seems to have disappeared" (414–415). Jameson here does, in fact, capture in capsule form what is the central insight of *Society of the Spectacle*, even if his lack of elaboration suggests that Debord's work has not been especially formative of his own.

Jameson engages with Baudrillard more extensively than he does with Debord, although he takes issue with Baudrillard's pessimism over the possibility of mounting any effective resistance to late capitalism. Noting a number of thinkers who have seemingly envisioned late capitalism as a total system that makes it impossible to find a position from which to mount a telling critique, Jameson concludes that Foucault (who has been widely accused of this viewpoint), is actually less pessimistic than Baudrillard, whom Jameson sees as giving

> the most dramatic and "paranoiac-critical" expression of this dilemma, in his demonstrations of the ways in which conscious ideologies of revolt, revolution, and even negative critique are—far from merely being "co-opted" by the system—an integral and functional part of the system's own internal strategies. (*Postmodernism* 203)

I have suggested in this chapter some of the ways in which *Joker* seems able to oppose spectacle only with more spectacle, which suggests very much the same notion that Jameson is here attributing to Baudrillard. I might also point out that, in *Comments on the Society of the Spectacle*, Debord adopts a similarly pessimistic tone in which he sees the power of the spectacle as having become so total as to be unopposable in the 20 years since his original work. In the next chapter, I will explore this notion much more extensively by looking carefully at the representation of the popular rebellion that occurs within *Joker*—and for which Arthur Fleck ostensibly serves as a symbolic inspiration.

Notes

1 See, for example, Jackson, for a discussion of the congruence between neoliberalism and spectacle.
2 One thinks here of Baudrillard's notorious argument that the Gulf War "did not take place," in the sense that what occurred in Iraq in 1991 was not a war but an atrocity that was packaged as a media spectacle and presented as a war in the media (*Gulf War*).
3 And, of course, Phoenix has a history of literally making a spectacle of himself, as in his public impersonation of himself in support of the mock documentary *I'm Still Here* (2010), which purported to document Phoenix's retirement from film acting so that he could pursue a new career as a rap artist, accompanied by a variety of strange behaviors.
4 For a detailed, and even riveting, account of the rise of consumer capitalism in America at this time, see Leach.
5 In *Comments on the Society of the Spectacle*, Debord's update written in the late 1980s and with the benefit of an additional 20 years of the historical development of late capitalism (years in which actually existing capitalist society came only more to resemble Debord's society of the spectacle), Debord does show more awareness of the phenomenon of globalization as a natural consequence of the spectacle.

6   Debord indicates the importance of the visible in the spectacle when he notes that "the spectacle is heir to all the weakness of the project of Western philosophy, which was an attempt to understand activity by means of the categories of vision" (*The Society of the Spectacle* 17).

7   For comparison here, see Gough's discussion of abjection and body horror in Dario Argento's *Suspiria* (1977), another film that employs dancing as a means of conveying the physical vulnerability of the human body. The 2018 remake of *Suspiria* involves some of the same issues. And, for another recent film that features dancing as a spectacle that turns to horror, see Gaspar Noé's *Climax* (2018).

8   I should note that even Fleck's dancing has been seen differently by different critics. Jürgens, for example, sees Fleck's dancing as relating back to a type of (largely comic) dancing that was popular on the music hall stage of the early twentieth century, which involved "performances featuring convulsive and eccentric, madly dancing bodies" (322). This observation may well be partly true, but it does not capture the fact that Fleck's dancing can at times be so graceful, adept, and highly serious.

CHAPTER NINE

"Kill the Rich"
Joker and the Politics of Rebellion

Given its immense box-office success, *Joker* clearly struck a chord with viewers around the world. Even viewers who seemingly received the film as pure entertainment surely found the film entertaining for reasons that went beyond its aesthetic achievements, however impressive those might be. And, even if many moviegoers might have been attracted by the notion that *Joker* was some sort of superhero film, it seems unlikely that the huge audiences that attended the film worldwide did so merely out a blindly automatic urge to see superhero films. Indeed, any number of contemporary reviewers, as well as early academic critics of the film, felt that the film taps into something fundamental about the experience of life in the contemporary world. Many of these critics seem to have sensed political energies in the film, even while finding it difficult to articulate just what the politics of the film might be. In this chapter, I will attempt to unpack some of the film's political implications by focusing specifically on the popular rebellion to which the film's political logic builds.

Given the consistency with which critics have sensed political energies in this film (and given some of the overtly political material contained within the film), it seems clear that any adequate understanding of *Joker* requires an interrogation of the film's politics. However, the exact political orientation of *Joker*, like most things about the film, is difficult to pin down, no doubt partly because the film inadvertently touches on some matters that the filmmakers did not particularly intend to explore. For example, in the previous chapter, I explored some of the ways in which *Joker* resonates with the radical critique of late capitalism contained in Guy Debord's *The Society of the Spectacle*. Elsewhere, in conjunction with Isra Daraisch, I read *Joker* within a continuum of texts from Dostoevsky's *Notes from Underground*, through T. S. Eliot's "The Love Song of J. Alfred Prufrock, and on through the early films of Martin Scorsese to track the increasingly radical alienation experienced by individuals in a world moving through the historical process of capitalist modernization from the rise of bourgeois hegemony into the era of late capitalism and postmodernism (Daraiseh and Booker, "Jokes"). Other critics have focused more specifically on the contemporary moment of late 2019 in global politics in reading the film. Caroline Bainbridge, for example, sees *Joker* as a

> popular cultural object that evokes the lived experience of the neoliberal conjuncture, its collapse, and the rise of a new wave of populism. The film provides a cultural window onto the distillates of splitting, anxiety, fear, dread, and the ideological breakdown that threatens as the intensities of neoliberalism deepen and implode, and as ecological collapse, structural racism, and health inequalities emerge as the driving issues of our time. ("Cracking Up" 54)

It is clear that Fleck's plight potentially suggests profound aspects of modern urban experience, placing him within the company of any number of modern protagonists who feel adrift in urban environments, unable to connect with the city around them. Sean Redmond thus reads the film within the context of modern works such as Georg Simmel's classic sociological study of the position of the "stranger" as an outsider in modern societies. But, as Redmond notes, even if one focuses specifically on one aspect of the film, such as Fleck's status as a lonely outsider, diametrically opposed readings are possible. In particular, for Redmond, the film leaves open two opposed readings of the character's lonely, isolated predicament. Reading the film within the context of a number of theorizations of life in the modern city, Redmond concludes that, on the one hand, *Joker* clearly evokes any number of Hollywood representations of lonely, white, male protagonists, tapping into the convention of seeing the loneliness of these characters as the result of their personal pathologies. But Redmond also notes that the film potentially "radicalizes" Fleck's loneliness, not only attributing it to the effects of the late capitalist society around him, but also seeing his reaction, especially in his moments of dancing, as a form of resistance to being shaped by those effects (66).

I have already suggested that Fleck's dancing can be taken as an attempt on his part to declare an identity for himself apart from the external forces that he feels to be shaping him against his will. But is this dancing really an effective form of genuinely political resistance? The crowds that rampage through the streets of Gotham by the end of *Joker* certainly seem to see Fleck very much as a figure of resistance to official authority in the city, but Fleck himself seems to disavow that role, insisting that he is "not political." In his dressing room backstage at *Live with Murray Franklin*, before his appearance on the show, Fleck tells

Franklin that he doesn't believe in the values espoused by the anti-rich movement currently sweeping through the streets of Gotham. "I don't believe in anything," he adds. On the program itself, he subsequently declares that "I'm not political. I'm just trying to make people laugh." He then openly confesses to the subway killings on the air and argues that the Wall Street guys deserved to die. Murray asks if Fleck committed the murders to start a movement or to become a symbol, but Fleck replies that he simply did it because the Wall Street guys (and, by extension, their ilk) were so "awful." "Why is everybody so upset about these guys? If it was me dying on the sidewalk, you'd walk right over me. I pass you every day and you don't notice me."

If Fleck's sense of seemingly class-based grievance seems to contradict his claim not to be political, it should also be noted that he has very little in the way of class consciousness. One might say that he has class *un*consciousness, in that he vaguely senses that his separation from the Wall Street guys is a matter of class, even if, on a conscious level, he seems to take it as a purely personal matter. It is certainly the case that *Joker* has two different fundamental plot arcs. I have already described in some detail some of the ways in which the film represents Fleck's seeming personal development into a more confident and formidable figure in the course of the film, while acknowledging that this development might well be occurring only in Fleck's fantasies. But the film also contains a second plot arc in which vague resentments bubbling beneath the surface of Gotham society gradually evolve into an all-out violent revolt. Moreover, these public and private plot arcs are extensively intertwined. While it is clear that, within the confines of the film, Fleck never really develops the kind of class consciousness (or any other group consciousness) that would make him an effective political leader, it is equally clear that the participants in the rebellion portrayed in the film seem more and more to turn to Fleck, or at least to his Joker/clown persona, as a symbol around which their anger coalesces into action.

Fleck himself, I should note, does little or nothing to encourage the people of Gotham to see him as the embodiment of their grievances against the rich. And yet, as he looks around him in amazement at rioters wearing clown masks, it is clear that he is pleased to imagine that he might be important enough to help inspire this violent revolt. It is impossible, of course, to determine from internal evidence in the film whether Fleck's role in inspiring the Gotham riots is real or whether it simply resides in his own fantasies. But the riots themselves do seem to be "real" within the (fictional) world of the film, in that they are one of the few aspects of the film that seems to proceed independently of Fleck's perception of them and thus cannot be fully explained as emanating from his troubled imagination. Thus, in examining the political implications of the film, I will assume that these riots are meant to be interpreted as actually occurring, whatever Fleck's role in them might be; I will consequently focus primarily on the political implications of the riots themselves rather than on Fleck's role in inspiring them.

I should say, though, that some commentators have seen Fleck as integral to the rebellion in Gotham and impossible to separate from it. For example, Jeffrey Brown takes *Joker*'s connection with the Batman universe quite seriously in his reading of the politics of the film. In particular, he notes the critical tradition of reading the Joker character as a sort of inversion of Batman. Thus, while Batman has traditionally been seen as a champion of justice, morality, social order, and official authority, Joker has been seen as the arch-enemy of all of these. However, given that the Batman figure is absent from *Joker*, this tendency to read Joker as the antithesis of everything Batman represents is not immediately available for this film. For Brown, the absence of Batman thus enables a profound reformulation of the social role of Joker. In particular, the removal of Batman—an essentially conservative figure—as the protagonist, opens the way for Joker now to become the protagonist, rather than the antagonist, accompanied by a fundamental shift in political sympathies. In particular, the systems of official authority in Gotham City that are traditionally defended by Batman now become the antagonist, a corrupt and dysfunctional force that is responsible not for maintaining order but for oppressing Gotham's citizens and driving Arthur Fleck to madness and murder. For Brown, the film's

> sympathetic focus on the Joker positions him as a hero for the subaltern, a champion of a justifiable chaos. Rather than the traditional valorization of Batman as a heroic enforcer of the status quo, the Joker emerges as a wretched but galvanizing figure against all the injustices and hypocrisies that the modern city state has heaped on the disenfranchised. ("City without a Hero" 12)

Brown here touches upon the fundamental political implications of the superhero, a topic of much recent critical discussion. Among superheroes, Superman's famous claim to be a champion of "truth, justice, and the American way" may be the paradigm of the role of superheroes as defenders of official ideology. Batman, meanwhile, has sometimes been depicted (as in *The Dark Knight Returns*) as a less pro-establishment figure, and even as an enemy of Superman. On the other hand, Batman has also sometimes been seen as a more right-wing, authoritarian figure even than Superman, as when Pearson and Uricchio argue that the effect of Batman's heroic exploits is "to gain consent for political authority and the system of property relations it enshrines, and thus support the dominant hegemonic order" (207). For his part, Brown expresses some skepticism that *Joker* might inspire genuine political change in the real world, but he does note that its challenge to the traditional value structure has important real-world implications. In particular, he notes that consumers of superhero narratives are encouraged to equate superheroes with all that is good and admirable, so that these narratives serve as ideological support for conservative, even authoritarian political agendas. In turn, for Brown, *Joker*'s reversal of the normal terms of the superhero narrative potentially challenges those agendas.

The eponymous protagonist of Bertolt Brecht's *Galileo* (1943) famously declares that any land that needs a hero must needs be an unhappy one. Galileo here, it is safe to say, speaks for the communist Brecht, making the anti-individualist point that any healthy society must be built on co-operative collective action, not on the heroic intervention of remarkable individuals. Brecht's point, of course, is precisely the opposite of the motivation behind the typical superhero narrative. Meanwhile, the Gotham City of *Joker* is decidedly an unhappy land—and one that would appear to need a hero. The fact that its two "hero" figures (Arthur Fleck and Thomas Wayne) are so disastrously unhelpful would seem not only to support Brecht's point but also to present a subversive challenge to the superhero genre as a whole, thus making the engagement of *Joker* with that genre all the more meaningful.

For Brown, on the other hand, Fleck *is* a hero. Indeed, he sees Fleck as a champion of Gotham's underclasses, who becomes the symbolic leader of a rebellion against the status quo in Gotham City, a rebellion that arises, Brown suggests, from some of the same frustrations that have driven recent political protests such as those associated with the Black Lives Matter (BLM) movement. He notes, for example, that protestors wearing Joker costumes, apparently inspired by the film, appeared at a number of the 2020 BLM protests, apparently in solidarity with the other protestors (16). Indeed, as David James has documented, one demonstrator in Minneapolis, who appeared in a "*Joker*-inspired Arthur Fleck getup" while carrying a sign reading "Justice for George," explained his costuming by noting that Fleck's Joker "has become a model of social injustice, the recognition of the tragedies that occur. I have fallen in love with this character and I think today it serves to push the message" ("Batman and Joker").

No Joke: Todd Phillips's *Joker* and American Culture

Of course, there is no sign within *Joker* that Fleck or the protestors he seems to inspire within the film have any sort of anti-racist agenda, which raises the question of whether the Joker character from the film is really an appropriate emblem for BLM. Indeed, in addition to those early reviewers who saw Arthur Fleck as a potential icon of incel culture, there were also those who saw him as an emblem of white supremacy, despite his own lowly status within the society of Gotham City. Lawrence Ware thus rightfully argues in the *New York Times* that, had Fleck been black, he would have been in a far more disadvantaged position than he already is. Among other things, Ware notes Fleck's series of problematic encounters with black women in the film, although he perhaps overstates the importance of these encounters given that nothing is really made of the race of these women and given Ware's own emphasis on his conclusion (unsubstantiated by anything we see in the film) that Fleck murders Sophie. He then goes on:

> There are other ways that whiteness informs Fleck's character. He anticipates he'll be treated as a son by the Wayne family, and assumes he'll be given medical records just by asking the hospital orderly (played by the great Brian Tyree Henry). The privileges that come with Fleck's race set him up for these unrealistic expectations. When they're not met, the consequences are deadly.

Ware's reading of the film might be a bit problematic, given that he seems to assume that all of Fleck's apparent murders really occurred within the world of the film. It is also the case that the expectations of being acknowledged by the Waynes have been drilled into Fleck by his mother and that the character played by Henry is a clerk, not an orderly, while it seems odd that Ware does not mention the fact that this orderly is black. Where Ware is definitely correct is in sensing that there is an element of white grievance that is built into Fleck's character and that Fleck lives in a society that has taught him to expect that, as a white male, he should have more status and privilege than he actually does. Or, as Ware puts it, "Whiteness may not have been on the filmmakers' minds when they made *Joker*, but it is the hidden accomplice that fosters the violence onscreen."

Ware appears (although he does not make this point very clearly) to believe that this aspect of *Joker* makes the film dangerous, implying that it might inspire other aggrieved white males to take similarly violent action. Ware was writing only a few days after the premiere of the film, and there is no subsequent evidence that any such white supremacist violence was inspired by it. Indeed, one could easily argue that the representation of

Fleck's whiteness in *Joker* potentially makes the film a powerful critique of white supremacy, because it shows some of the awful consequences that this heinous ideology could bring about. Moreover, Fleck is depicted as so thoroughly disempowered that it is perhaps not entirely surprising that BLM protestors might see Fleck/Joker as the very antithesis of a white supremacist. Of course, that does not imply that these BLM protestors were literally *inspired* by the film, but rather only that they chose to co-opt its protagonist as an emblem of their own agenda.

Similarly, within weeks of the release of *Joker*, protestors around the world were already using him as an emblem of opposition to oppressive or corrupt political authority. As Harmeet Kaur notes (in an article posted on November 3, 2019), protestors in such far-flung places as Hong Kong, Iraq, Spain, Lebanon, and Chile were already either showing up at protests in Joker makeup and costumes or using the Joker image on signs, posters, or other forms of political art. This geographical range suggests the global reach of the film and of the Culture Industry as a whole. However, that these protestors were deploying this image in support of a diverse array of causes also perhaps suggests the unspecific nature of the Joker as a political image, although he certainly functions as a symbol of a vague sense that the have-nots have reason to be furious with the haves (even if they have all too often taken out this resentment on those who have even less than themselves).

This widespread appropriation of the Joker character obviously suggests that supporters of a number of different causes have experienced a sense of identification with the grievances that made Fleck's Joker a hero to the protestors in the film, even though the only real issue they espouse in the film is a vaguely stated hostility toward the "rich." Of course, the film gives little real voice to these protestors, who have no spokespeople to articulate their position, which must be deduced from their actions and tersely worded signs on placards. In fact, the most detailed information we get about the protestors in the film comes from statements made *about* them, either by the media or, especially, by Thomas Wayne, who is explicitly *opposed* to the protestors.

While the immediate announcement of the garbage strike in the opening seconds of *Joker* helps to suggest a sense of crisis in Gotham from the very beginning, there is no indication of anything like popular political unrest in the city until the subway shootings of the Wall Street guys trigger widespread sympathy for their killer. The first indication of this sympathy occurs in a scene in the dressing room at Ha-Has, as some of the clowns are reading newspaper accounts of the shootings and their aftermath, suggesting among themselves that the event might be good publicity for their business, given that "they got clowns on the front of every newspaper." Exactly what they are talking about then becomes more clear only seconds of runtime later, when Wayne appears in a television interview decrying the killings of his employees, who were "good, decent, educated" people. His interviewer then notes that "there now seems to be a groundswell of anti-rich sentiment in the city. It's almost as if our less fortunate residents are taking the side of the killer." Wayne responds with the arrogant suggestion that this development is one of the reasons why he is considering a run for mayor, so that he can help Gotham "find its way." Asked about reports that the killer wore a clown mask, Wayne responds with his haughty declaration that it seems appropriate to him for a cowardly killer to hide behind a mask, followed by his suggestion that the protesters who seem to find these killings inspirational are nothing but clowns themselves.

Fleck, ribs protruding prominently as he lies back on the couch after watching this interview, is clearly weighing Wayne's supercilious remarks carefully. These remarks, meanwhile, only make the protesters more likely to wear clown masks, in defiance of his attitude toward them. The next sign that we see of the clown-based political movement that is building in Gotham occurs as Fleck rides the train on his way to Wayne Manor, surrounded by commuters who themselves look a bit like "Wall Street guys," but who are reading newspapers with headlines that give this movement a name and a motivation: "Kill the Rich: A New Movement." Fleck himself, meanwhile, is reading about the beginning of Wayne's mayoral campaign, which is thus once again set in direct opposition to the "Kill the Rich" movement.

We next see evidence of this movement as Fleck again watches television, as a news report specifically sets the protest movement in opposition to Wayne's mayoral campaign, including shots of crowds of protesters carrying anti-Wayne signs bearing statements such as "Wayne = FASCIST." The report also includes an on-air snippet of Wayne declaring paternalistically and condescendingly that he hopes, as mayor, to make life better for "those people." "They may not realize it," he proclaims, "but I'm their only hope." We can again see that Fleck is weighing all of this very carefully, clearly pondering what his own role in this political movement might be. The film then immediately cuts to the showing of *Modern Times* at Wayne Hall, outside of which an unruly crowd of protesters, many wearing clown masks or makeup, bears homemade signs with text such as "Fuck Wayne" and "Clown for Mayor," while chanting, "Down with Wayne!" Fleck wanders through the crowd in seeming amazement at what he is clearly imagining himself to have wrought, although some of the signs (such as "Punishing the Poor for the Sins of the Rich") suggest some deep-seated resentments that go well beyond whatever inspiration might have been supplied by the subway shootings.

This demonstration outside the hall adds irony to the political dissonance of screening Chaplin's film, so sympathetic to the poor, for the rich audience inside the hall, while Fleck's unfortunate (but possibly imaginary) encounter with Wayne inside a posh restroom in the hall clearly adds to the sense that his own grievances are more personal than political, as Fleck will soon proclaim on the Franklin show. Meanwhile, on his way to his appearance on that show, we see another scene on a train that can be taken as a counterpoint to the earlier one involving the newspaper-reading commuters. This time, the train is largely filled with clown-masked protesters, suggesting that they are beginning to become more and more of a presence in the city. Moreover, their attack on the two detectives in that scene suggests that they are growing more angry and violent as their movement gains momentum.

Our most important look at the popular rebellion in *Joker* occurs in the sequence near the end of the film as Fleck is being transported in a police car through streets clogged with violent protesters. Again, this entire sequence might well be occurring only in Fleck's imagination, but (from what we see on the screen) Fleck looks in wonderment at the crowds, laughing genuinely for once, clearly feeling that he might have at least helped to inspire this violence. One of the cops transporting him agrees, angrily grumbling that "the whole city's on fire because of what you did." "I know," responds Fleck, in what might be his most satisfied moment in the entire film, "Isn't it beautiful?" Importantly, though, the crowds we see in these final scenes are not portrayed as protesters with a coherent political agenda but as looters and rioters driven partly by rage (and also perhaps partly by sheer malice), although in an almost carnivalesque mode that breaks down the distinction between comedy and tragedy that seems to trouble Fleck through the film.[1] The masked figures in the streets seem, in fact, to be wreaking havoc in a way that is both angry and celebratory, dancing through the streets as Gotham burns. In fact, these rioters seem to represent very much the kind of chaos that has often been associated with Joker in Batman narratives, perhaps most famously with Heath Ledger's Joker in *The Dark Knight*.

Ledger's Joker certainly hopes to foment chaos in the streets of Gotham, but the Batman film that contains the most in the way of what seems like a political uprising would surely be the next one, *The Dark Knight Rises* (2012), in which the antagonist Bane (Tom Hardy) clearly wants to figure his attempt to take over (and, ultimately, destroy) the city of Gotham as an attempt to liberate the people of the city from corruption and oppression. Indeed, given the timing of this film, there was much initial critical discussion of the parallels between Bane's uprising and the Occupy Wall Street protests of September 2011.[2] Indeed, the politics of this film are highly problematic, possibly even reactionary; after all, the film features an aging Batman (Christian Bale) who essentially leads an army of heroic Gotham policemen in a battle against Bane and an army of depraved "ordinary citizens," with suggestions that chaos and disaster would ensue were those citizens to be allowed to take control of the city. Thus, this film is one of the clearest enactments in the entire Batman franchise of the notion, noted by Brown, of Batman as a proponent of official power.

As Slavoj Žižek has pointed out, while the highly conservative implications of the film's depiction of its popular uprising are obvious, there may be some progressive political value in the very fact that the film at least acknowledges a popular uprising as a possibility. Moreover, Žižek notes that the film endows Bane with a number of very positive characteristics (as when he is presented as motivated more by love than by hate), so that the movement he leads cannot be seen in an entirely negative light. For Žižek, while reading the uprising within the film as an allegory of the Occupy Wall Street movement may produce a "ridiculous caricature" of that movement, the fact is that the film must be read on its own terms and not simply in comparison to the real world. Thus, while we don't really see in the film any sort of functioning people's postrevolutionary government, the fact still remains that the popular uprising in the film, "the event—the 'People's Republic of Gotham City', a dictatorship of the proletariat in Manhattan—is immanent to the film. It is its absent centre" ("Politics").

Moreover, as Žižek also points out, if there is a real-world event that seems to be represented by the rebellion in *The Dark Knight Rises*, it is not Occupy Wall Street, but the French Revolution, something that is signaled by the fact that Commissioner Gordon (Gary Oldman) reads the famous last lines of Dickens' *A Tale of Two Cities* (1859) at the ceremonial burial of Bruce Wayne/Batman after he has ostensibly sacrificed himself in order to save Gotham from a neutron bomb. *A Tale of Two Cities*, of course, is surely the best-known English-language novel about the French Revolution, and it is also a famously negative depiction of that revolution as an outburst of terroristic mob violence.

When first we see the people of Paris in Dickens' novel, it is well before the revolution, but horrible poverty is already driving the people of the city toward rebellion. A barrel of red wine rolls off a wagon and bursts in the muddy street, and a swarm of starving Parisians dive into the resultant mire and starts slurping up whatever wine they can, mud and all. Meanwhile, in a strong harbinger of the revolution itself, one onlooker (simply referred to as "the joker," oddly enough), uses some of the muddy wine to scrawl one ominous word on a wall: "BLOOD" (61). Then, once the revolution begins, Dickens' favorite metaphor for the surging crowd is a sea, the rebels caught up in a mindless tide of fury, losing all sense of individuality:

> The sea of black and threatening waters, and of destructive upheaving of wave against wave, whose depths were yet unfathomed and whose forces were yet unknown. The remorseless sea of turbulently swaying shapes, voices of vengeance, and faces hardened in the furnaces of suffering until the touch of pity could make no mark on them. (249)

Meanwhile, showing a particular fascination with the guillotine, Dickens provide a colorful array of descriptions of the mayhem wrought by the revolution.

In short, using a quote from this novel to link the rebellion in *The Dark Knight Rises* to the French Revolution would seem to suggest a very negative view of both of these uprisings. Indeed, at a July 8, 2012 press conference held in conjunction with the release of the film, both director Christopher Nolan and his brother and co-writer on the film, Jonathan Nolan, made it clear that they saw the French Revolution as represented in *A Tale of Two Cities* as the direct inspiration for the popular rebellion in *The Dark Knight Rises*. Jonathan, in particular, dismissed connections between the film and Occupy Wall Street, noting that the basic outline for the film was developed before Occupy Wall Street, or even the 2008 recession: "Rather than being influenced by that, I was looking to old good books and good movies. Good literature for inspiration." That literature, of course, was *A Tale of Two Cities*, which he went on to describe as "one of the most harrowing portraits of a relatable, recognizable civilization that completely folded to pieces with the terrors in Paris in France in that period. It's hard to imagine that things can go that badly wrong" (qtd. in Lesnick).

Nolan's figuration of the French Revolution in these terms makes clear his own intention to portray the rebellion in *The Dark Knight Rises* as a negative event. This view of the French Revolution as an example of the collapse of "recognizable civilization," of course, was one that gained widespread currency in the West during the Cold War, when it became common, even on the part of professional historians, to suggest parallels between the French Revolution and the Russian Revolution, parallels that required the refiguration of the former (once seen mostly positively in America) in a negative light in order to provide a correspondingly negative vision of the latter.

Of course, negative reactions to the French Revolution have a long history, with Edmund Burke's *Reflections on the Revolution in France* (1790), written when the revolution was still in its early stages, providing what might be considered the founding text in the genre. Burke's horrified reaction to what he saw as the excessive violence of the revolution and the rude treatment of the French king and queen by the revolutionary crowds came well before the 1793–1794 "Reign of Terror." It also came three years before Louis XVI and Marie Antoinette would suffer the ultimate indignity at the guillotine. But later critics of the revolution would focus on these violent events as evidence that the revolution was not a coherent social or political movement so much as an outburst of uncontrolled mob violence and class hatred. Even Thomas Carlyle, whose *History of the French Revolution* (1837) treats the revolution relatively positively, as a popular revolt and as an important predecessor of British Chartism (to which he was sympathetic), included excessively colorful descriptions of the element of terror associated with the revolution that gave his work an almost novelistic quality. In fact, Carlyle's descriptions of revolutionary violence provided a crucial inspiration for Dickens' similar descriptions in *A Tale of Two Cities*.

This is not the place to provide a full survey of reactions to the French Revolution.[3] It is, however, important to note that negative depictions of the revolution, especially in America (where it had largely been viewed positively when it was happening and for some time afterward), became especially prominent in the years of the Cold War, when it became common to depict the revolution as an outbreak of bloody mob violence, while at the same time de-emphasizing its importance in history. This simultaneous condemnation and dismissal of the French Revolution was, however, largely aimed at discrediting the Russian Revolution and was part of an effort, in tune with the ideological climate of Cold War America, to denounce that later revolution (and, to an extent, revolutions in general) as offenses against civilization itself.[4]

Jonathan Nolan's statements suggest that he and his brother accepted such views of the French Revolution, filtered through *A Tale of Two Cities*, uncritically when they were envisioning the popular rebellion in *The Dark Knight Rises*. For my purposes, though, what is important is that the uprising in *Joker* is represented in much the same way, even though the rebels are not shown actually taking charge of the city. The "kill the rich" slogan of the movement in *Joker* already indicates the parallels between this movement and the French Reign of Terror, in which so many of the rich were, in fact, killed. Moreover, a closer look at the actual representation of the insurrection in *Joker* shows that this rebellion is largely portrayed as an outbreak of enraged violence, rather than as a class-based revolution.

There are actually two portrayals of the rebellion within *Joker*. The first involves the demonstration outside Wayne Hall, which is a bit unruly, but does not seem all that different from actual demonstrations, such as the BLM demonstrations in the summer of 2020. Fleck walks through this crowd, amazed and clearly pleased. He wears no clown makeup, and most of the demonstrators have also yet to don clown masks, although many do wear them. It is, however, the second portrayal of the rebellion, the one that Fleck is seemingly driven into by police near the end of the film, that is the more striking and memorable. And it becomes even more so after Fleck experiences that moment of satisfaction at the thought that he might have inspired the riots, when the police car in which he is riding is hit by an ambulance that has apparently been hijacked by one of the clown-masked rioters (unless, of course, its regular driver has joined the uprising), suggesting the extent to which the rioters are taking over many of the city's resources. Seemingly crazed rioters dance in the streets around the scene of the crash, streets that have been set ablaze with multiple fires. Three rioters pull an unconscious Fleck out of the police car and lie him on its hood. Another rioter then literalizes the "kill the rich" agenda by murdering Thomas and Martha Wayne (now playing the roles of Louis XVI and Marie Antoinette) in that alley. At the same time, this literalization reminds us that "the rich" are people too, and potentially discourages sympathy with their killing. Fleck regains consciousness and climbs atop the police vehicle, surrounded by a cheering crowd of clown-masked, weapon-bearing rioters, looking almost like the notorious mob of villagers from *Frankenstein* (1931), except that this time they are rooting *for* the monster (Figure 12).

Fleck looks around him and slowly starts to dance, much as he had in the public restroom after the subway shootings. Guðnadóttir's slow, haunting score accompanies the dance, which is so out of tune with the violence in the streets, indicating that Fleck, even at his moment of (probably imagined) triumph is still out of step with the chaotic and violent world around him. Fleck then uses his own blood to paint the famous Joker grin on his face, presumably signaling his complete assumption of the Joker identity, an identity literally written in blood. Then, as the crowd reaches a climax of crazed celebration, the screen cuts to black, after which we suddenly find Fleck back in Arkham State Hospital.

No Joke: Todd Phillips's *Joker* and American Culture

Figure 12. Fleck overlooks a riotous crowd of his admirers, who have taken over the streets of Gotham City.

Joker's "Kill the Rich" movement grows out of a genuine rage against a corrupt system that has a led to a dramatic inequality in the distribution of the city's wealth, an inequality that obviously mirrors the growing wealth gap that marks American society like a festering sore, a sore that has been there all along but that took a dramatic step in the wrong direction thanks to the policies of the Reagan administration in the 1980s. Indeed, via the wealth redistribution model that came to be known as "Reaganomics" (but what was really just an early form of neoliberalism), Reagan and his administration specifically sought to shift as many resources as possible into the hands of the rich (mostly by sharp cuts in the taxes paid by wealthy taxpayers and corporations), arguing that the rich would be better able to use this wealth to stimulate the economy as a whole, using the power of the market to produce a "trickle-down" effect that would lead to greater prosperity for all.

Of course, this plan (famously labeled by George H. W. Bush himself as "voodoo economics" during his 1980 Republican primary run against Reagan) was highly successful in diverting wealth to the rich and highly unsuccessful at producing wealth for everyone else. For example, a 1992 study conducted by the Federal Reserve Board concluded that the 1980s saw a dramatic rise in the wealth of more affluent Americans, but very little such rise for average- or lower-income Americans. Between 1983 (when such wealth data first became easily available) and 1989, they found, the average accumulated wealth for families earning more than $50,000 yearly grew from $176,100 to $186,500, while the average accumulated wealth for families earning less than $10,000 per year actually dropped from $3,800 to $2,300. Those in between these two levels saw their average accumulated wealth stay approximately the same over this period (Risen). Furthermore, a recent, broader study of the effects of tax cuts for the rich extending over the period 1965–2015 in a number of countries concluded that

> the incomes of the rich grew much faster in countries where tax rates were lowered. Instead of trickling down to the middle class, tax cuts for the rich may not accomplish much more than help the rich keep more of their riches and exacerbate income inequality. (Picchi, "50 Years of Tax Cuts for the Rich")

In the United States, in particular, the wealth gap between the rich and poor has only grown more dramatic in recent decades, becoming particularly dramatic during the years of the Trump administration, whose agenda began with massive tax cuts for wealthy individuals and corporations. More recent numbers published by the Federal Reserve Board show that, in America, in the third quarter of 1989, $4.78 trillion dollars was held by those in the top 1 percent, in terms of wealth, while only $0.76 trillion was held by those in the bottom 50 percent. By the first quarter of the Trump administration, in early 2017, these numbers had grown to $29.05 trillion and $1.23 trillion, respectively. By the fourth quarter of 2019, when *Joker* was released, an astonishing $34.58 trillion in wealth was held by those in the top 1 percent, while only $2.02 trillion was held by those in the bottom 50 percent (Board of Governors of the Federal Reserve System). Put differently, from the beginning of the Trump years until the release of *Joker*, the top 1 percent of Americans gained approximately 7 times as much wealth as the bottom 50 percent combined, which means that the very wealthiest Americans gained approximately 350 times as much per person as did Americans on the lower half of the income scale. And these numbers only got worse in the final year of the Trump administration, so that, during the four Trump years as a whole, the top 1 percent of Americans gained approximately 9 times as much wealth as the bottom 50 percent combined, which means that the very wealthiest Americans gained approximately 450 times as much per person as did Americans on the lower half of the income scale.[5]

My point in citing all of these numbers is to suggest that, while the kind of wealth gap that so angers the people of Gotham in *Joker* was bad and getting worse in the United States in 1981, the real American wealth gap was only beginning to expand at that time and would reach far worse levels during the Trump years. In short, assuming that economic conditions in Gotham are meant to be interpreted as mirroring those in the real world of the United States, there is a very real way in which the political movement portrayed in *Joker* seems to respond more to conditions when the film was made than to conditions when the action is set.

This phenomenon can, I think, be taken as another of the many ways in which *Joker* essentially elides the differences between the early 1980s and the late 2010s, thereby suggesting parallels between the period of its action and the period of its release. In this case, I believe the popular rebellion portrayed in *Joker*, by responding to conditions that are more representative of 2019 America than 1981 America, helps to link those two time periods by suggesting that many of the social and political problems that have been associated with the Trump administration had their roots in the Reagan administration, or possibly even as far back as the Nixon administration.

Of course, the members of the riotous crowd at the end of *Joker* do not seem to have done a lot of detailed analysis of just what they are protesting against. Because of their masks, they are reminiscent of another cinematic predecessor, the crowds wearing Guy Fawkes masks in the 2005 film *V for Vendetta*, which (like *Joker*) has its roots in the world of DC comics—in this case the 1988 limited series of the same title by Alan Moore and David Lloyd. These masked rebels have also inspired real-world protestors to wear Guy Fawkes masks. However, the parallels end there. The protestors of *V for Vendetta* are inspired by an actual leader (the "V" of the title, played by Hugo Weaving), as opposed to the leaderless rioters of *Joker*, for whom Fleck might be imagined to be a galvanizing symbol because they have no other leadership. Moreover, the rebels of *V for Vendetta* have a much more coherent agenda in terms of their anarchist opposition to a clearly dystopian government.

The rebellion of *Joker*, seemingly driven by an incoherent lust for violence, resembles that of *V for Vendetta* less than it resembles the French Revolution as portrayed in *A Tale of Two Cities*. Indeed, by suggesting that Fleck's turn to violence is driven by mental illness, rather than by political outrage, *Joker* makes him the perfect symbolic leader of that film's popular uprising, which seems similarly crazed, even as it gives lip service to a perfectly understandable protest against class inequality. Meanwhile, the portrayal of the film's rebellion in this way undermines any attempt to see the film as a sharp critique of this inequality and as clearly sympathizing with the rebellion.

What is at stake here is not just representations of the French Revolution but representations of revolution in general, something with which American popular culture has had a great deal of difficulty, especially since the years of the Cold War, when "revolution" came more and more to mean "the Russian Revolution." Of course, it is not quite fair to call the events depicted in *Joker* a "revolution," as the participants seem to have no coherent plan for overthrowing the current social and political system and establishing a new one. But American popular culture has difficulty handling any sort of political insurrection (whether it be coherent or not) unless the revolt depicted is substantially removed from reality, as in the case of *V for Vendetta*—or even more for such highly successful films as *Star Wars* (1977) or the four films of the *Hunger Games* sequence (2012–2015).

Again, the uprising in *Joker* does not represent an actual revolution. It is simply an outburst of violent civil unrest confined to a single city and not likely ever to overthrow the current government. Such localized outbursts have, of course, occasionally occurred in the United States, as we saw with the BLM protests in the summer of 2020, protests that were clearly aimed at stimulating reform, not at overthrowing the government. And such real-world protests have sometimes turned far more violent than the BLM protests, which never reached the level of violence depicted in *Joker*. The most prominent example of real-world American protests-turned-violent were the race riots that occurred in a number of American cities in the late 1960s. Again, though, these outbursts were localized in specific cities and were aimed at the specific issue of racism, not at overturning the government.

Race-related violence has also been a central topic of a number of fictional films, such as Spike Lee's *Do the Right Thing* (1989), perhaps the most respected of such films. But American filmmakers have generally had trouble portraying even these sorts of events. For example, Kathryn Bigelow's *Detroit* (2017) deals with the real event of the 1967 Detroit Rebellion, in which heavy-handed, racially charged actions by Detroit police triggered a widespread uprising that became the most violent of all the events that marked the violent summer of 1967 (widely known as the "long, hot summer"). Yet the film ignores that rebellion almost entirely and instead focuses on the Algiers Motel incident, a related event in which Detroit police murdered several African American men inside the Algiers Motel while the riots raged outside.

In *Joker*, no such official actions trigger the riots that sweep through the streets of Gotham. If anything, the subway killings of the Wall Street guys act as a catalyst to ignite resentments that were already brewing in the troubled city. These resentments seem to grow from a vague sense of grievance among the protestors, who seem to be multiracial (although mostly white) and almost exclusively male. This grievance seems to be mostly related to class-based inequality, both in terms of economic injustice and in terms of a generalized sense of being disrespected, a sense that is, of course, exacerbated by Thomas Wayne's imperious and insensitive reaction to their complaints. Indeed, the rebellion appears to be galvanized as much by Wayne as by Fleck, because of the way Wayne's comments on the initial protests directly feed the anger that was driving them.

The 2020 BLM protests differed dramatically from the insurrection within *Joker* in that they were triggered by specific official actions (such as the police killing of George Floyd) and had specific goals in terms of police reform and racial justice. Nevertheless, for any number of commentators, the protests of 2020 made *Joker* seem a prescient film, suggesting that it tapped into the budding anger that was bubbling up beneath the surface of American society.

Of course, *Joker* would appear to have sensed the political mood of American society even more profoundly when a violent mob breached the U.S. Capitol building on January 6, 2021, in an attempt to prevent the certification of Joe Biden as the newly elected U.S. president, thus preserving that office for their hero and inspiration, Donald J. Trump. That particular "revolution," as it turned out, was televised, and millions of viewers around America watched in shock and horror as it unfolded, although some others, no doubt, watched with glee, including Trump himself, who was reportedly "loving watching the Capitol mob."[6] Of course, it was not until later, as more and more video shot on the spot began to emerge, that we began to appreciate just how vicious and violent that assault really was.[7]

The January Capitol insurrection, I would argue, resembled the one depicted in *Joker* far more than had the BLM protests of a few months earlier. The Capitol insurrectionists displayed a high level of rage and willingness to do harm to both people and property, driven by a sense that some sort of injustice had been done to them and their ilk. They also seemed dedicated to the notion of doing possibly deadly harm to specific individuals, with Mike Pence and Nancy Pelosi now playing the role played by Thomas Wayne in *Joker*. There was also a certain carnivalesque aspect to the Capitol insurrection. Despite the rage displayed by many members of the mob, some seemed to be greatly enjoying themselves, many of them proudly displaying their MAGA merchandise and wearing costumes and masks somewhat in the spirit of the clown masks of *Joker*, causing multiple commentators to see them as "cosplaying" rebellion.[8] Interestingly, though, none of the insurrectionists appears to have worn a Joker costume, that garb perhaps having been discredited for them via its use by the BLM protestors. The costume that caught the most media attention was the bizarre face-paint, fur-hat, and horns ensemble worn by the "QAnon Shaman" Jacob Chansley.[9] There were also superhero costumes (such as Captain America or the Punisher), as well as a variety of presumably patriotic costumes, including protestors dressed as eagles or as Abraham Lincoln. There was even at least one Guy Fawkes mask. Reporting on these costumes for the *New York Times*, fashion critic Vanessa Friedman noted how the costumes at first seemed comical, until the whole event became deadly: "Somebody who had been hiding under a rock could have been forgiven for thinking that they had wandered into a postponed Halloween parade, not the beginnings of an out-of-control melee egged on by a sitting president." She then, tellingly, specifically cites the Joker character (with a link to Ware's article about *Joker* and white supremacy) as a reminder that "there's a fine line between comedy and horror."

The rioters who attacked the Capitol on January 6 did not appear to have been doing a great deal of sophisticated political analysis. Many did not even seem to have a good idea of what they were trying to achieve, other than a vague notion of disrupting the certification of the recent presidential election. But even this motivation seemed confused, driven by a dedication to the notion that government in general (and the federal government in particular) was basically a bad thing, a notion that had partly been instilled in them by the rhetoric of Donald Trump, despite the fact that he was the sitting president and thus literally the chief executive of the federal government that they so despised. This contradiction, of course, did not originate with the Trump phenomenon, but goes back at least to the Reagan administration, when one of Reagan's greatest PR successes was to be able to sell himself as an anti-government crusader, even while he was the head of the government. Indeed, anti-government rhetoric provides one of the clearest links between the politics of the Reagan years and the politics of the Trump years, links that are also, as I have argued throughout this study, implied in a number of ways by the politics of *Joker*. In the next chapter I will explore this suggestion more thoroughly.

Notes

1 These scenes, in fact, recall Kristeva's description of the carnival, as theorized by Bakhtin: "The laughter of the carnival is not simply parodic; it is no more comic than tragic; it is both at once, one might say that it is serious" (Kristeva, "Word" 50).

2 However, it is also the case that Donald Trump seems to have found Bane a compelling figure. In his 2017 inaugural address, for example, Trump famously paraphrased part of one of Bane's speeches from *The Dark Knight Rises*. In this speech, which the "Kill the Rich" protestors might have greeted warmly, Trump declared that he was "transferring power from Washington, DC, and giving it back to you, the people." Then, during his re-election bid, Trump even adopted music from *The Dark Knight Rises* to accompany one of his campaign ads, causing Warner Bros to threaten legal action. On Trump's "obsession" with Bane, see Child.

3 An excellent such survey can be found in Hobsbawm's *Echoes of the Marseillaise*, which reviews two centuries of reactions to the revolution.

4 This denunciation of the French Revolution was, meanwhile, partly a rejoinder to Marxist thinkers, who also characterized the French Revolution as a forerunner of the Russian Revolution, but in a positive way, seeing it as the most important event in world history and as a crucial step toward the modernization of Europe. For Marxist historians, the French Revolution became "a bourgeois precedent for the coming triumph of the proletariat" (Hobsbawm 8).

5 For a compelling account of American economic inequality from the 1970s to the present, attributing the growing wealth gap primarily to wage suppression, see Lance Taylor.

6 This quote, attributed to a "former senior White House official," appears in Acosta and LeBlanc.

7 See Poniewozik.

8 Ben Sixsmith, discussing the carnivalesque aspects of the insurrection, added a sarcastic link to the French Revolution: "This riot is a peculiarly American combination of the storming of the Bastille and *Animal House*."

9 Continuing the constellation of connections between the insurrection and the Joker, Elena Sheppard suggested that Chansley's transformation into the QAnon Shaman via costuming was similar to Jack Napier's transformation into the Joker in *Batman* (1989).

CHAPTER TEN

The Politics of *Joker* and the Age of Trump

As I have already pointed out several times in this study, one of the most important qualities of *Joker* is its clear ability to suggest connections between the time of its action and the time of its production. Among other things, these connections suggest to the film's initial audiences at the end of the 2010s (perhaps in the mold of the—now old—new historicists) that they cannot possibly view the 1980s in a way that is not influenced by their own situation in the 2010s. We cannot, in short, view the Reagan era in a way that is disconnected from our experience of the Trump era. Seeking utopian solace, many in the Trump era have nostalgically attempted to envision the Reagan era as a kindly and gentler time free of the rancor and divisiveness of Trumpist politics. I would suggest, however, that the difference between the two periods is mostly a matter of style and that the neoliberal substance of the Reagan era is not fundamentally different from that of the Trump era, the former era leading directly to the other along the road to global neoliberal power.

The connections that *Joker* establishes between these two crucial eras in modern American history come with very high stakes attached, which I explore in this chapter. For one thing, as I noted in the last chapter, this aspect of *Joker* casts new light on the nostalgic fascination with the 1980s that has been so prominent in recent popular culture. For another, to suggest parallels between the Reagan era and the Trump era suggests that we re-evaluate both the Reagan and the Trump presidencies, which seem, on the surface, so radically different, despite the fact that both Reagan and Trump were Republican presidents who espoused neoliberal pro-market, anti-government policies as keys to their supposedly conservative agendas.

Whether or not the makers of *Joker* intentionally constructed the film to suggest links between Reagan and Trump, many strong connections between Reagan and Trump do exist, and *Joker*, as a film unusually strongly rooted in its own 2019 context as well as in the 1981 context of the action, almost inevitably reflects these important historical connections. Moreover, these parallels suggest that Trump is not quite the rogue outsider and untraditional paradigm shatterer that he has often been seen to be but is instead a quite natural and mainstream product of the American conservative tradition. The racism, the corruption, the appeal to grievance, and the revisions of reality, I would argue, were there all along—but were typically less foregrounded because they were also of less fundamental importance than the neoliberal emphasis on free markets and on limiting the ability of government to regulate those markets. Trump primarily differed from predecessors such as Reagan (or even Nixon), not so much in terms of substance as in terms of style. Indeed, using *Joker* as a lens through which to view the parallels between Reagan and Trump helps to illuminate this point, while also suggesting that this stylistic difference can be largely described within the context of a cultural transition from modernism to postmodernism or from film to television as dominant media, transitions that are themselves the products of larger developments in the evolution of capitalism itself—or, put differently, in the evolution of the society of the spectacle and of neoliberalism.

Much was said in early reviews of *Joker* about the ways in which the film comments on conditions in the Trump era, even as the film is so firmly rooted in the time period of its action at the beginning of the 1980s. For example, writing in *Vanity Fair*, Joanna Robinson calls the film's version of its title character "the perfect clown prince to haunt the Trump era," while noting the remarkable ability of the Joker character as a whole to shift and change over time in order to reflect the eras in which the works containing him were produced. While placing the film in the company of a number of other works that have questioned the ethos of the mainstream superhero film, Robinson notes that *Joker* stands apart because of its "feeling of untethered free fall into moral bankruptcy," a feeling that she identifies as "its most Trump-era quality."

What Robinson does not note (but what films such as *Wall Street* have vividly detailed) is that moral bankruptcy was a big part of the texture of the 1980s as well. On the other hand, Aaron Freedman, writing for the left-leaning *Jacobin Magazine*, notes how clearly *Joker* could be taken as commentary on the present-day of 2019, but emphasized that the film's most important commentary might be aimed at the Reagan era:

> There's no doubt that *Joker*'s allusions to Reaganism are more subtle than its mirroring of contemporary far-right violence. But, by invoking the politics of *The King of Comedy*, Phillips's film can serve as a powerful reminder that the use of comedy, performance, and

celebrity by right-wing populists today is far from novel. Today's jokers may frighten, but they are mere copycats of the original chuckling and smiling king.

That "smiling and chuckling king," of course, is Reagan himself, and Freedman is surely correct that *Joker* ultimately suggests Reagan as Trump's greatest predecessor.

Despite the film's numerous important connections to the Reagan era (as outlined in Chapter 3), there are a number of signs that the makers of *Joker* might have had Trump on their minds when conceiving and making the film. For example, the original plan was to cast actor Alec Baldwin as Thomas Wayne, before Baldwin withdrew due to "scheduling issues." Baldwin, of course, has played a number of roles in a long career, but the role that would seem to identify him as a candidate to play Wayne is surely his Emmy-nominated performance as Trump in a series of skits of *Saturday Night Live*, both during the 2016 presidential campaign and during the Trump presidency. Noting the legacy of representing Wayne as a paragon of virtue, Kit and Couch suggest that Baldwin might have been considered for the role in *Joker* because of the representation of Wayne in that film as "a cheesy and tanned businessman who is more in the mold of a 1980s Donald Trump."

It would, in fact, be difficult to watch the Thomas Wayne of *Joker* and not think of Trump, although there are more general ways in which the film evokes Trump and all that goes with him. Declaring *Joker* a "cinematic masterpiece," filmmaker Michael Moore describes the film's connection to Trump thusly:

> This movie is not about Trump. It's about the America that gave us Trump—the America which feels no need to help the outcast, the destitute. The America where the filthy rich just get richer and filthier. Except in this story a discomfiting question is posed: What if one day the dispossessed decide to fight back?

In *Joker*, of course, the dispossessed (or at least those who believe themselves to have been dispossessed) do indeed fight back. However, as I noted in the previous chapter, it does not at all appear obvious to me that this response is depicted positively in the film or that we are particularly meant to sympathize with the film's rebels, whose portrayal has a great deal in common with negative Cold War depictions of the French Revolution, while their grievance-fueled revolt seems to anticipate the pro-Trump rioters of January 6, 2021, more than it anticipates any sort of emancipatory rebellion *against* the forces represented by Trump and his ilk.

It should also be pointed out that Arthur Fleck himself might very well be read as one of the "deplorables" who supported Trump, rather than as some sort of proletarian leader opposing the forces of official authority in Gotham. Thus, while de Semlyen notes that "Gotham's fat cat Thomas Wayne (Brett Cullen) has more than a hint of Donald Trump," he also complicates this identification by going on to note that "surely the Joker is nothing if not an accidental populist himself," that is, that Fleck himself might be seen as a sort of inadvertent Trump figure. "Inadvertent," though, is a key word here, and the political implications of *Joker* are clearly impacted by the title character's seeming lack of any coherent political agenda other than pure grievance.

At the same time, the very fact that Fleck is motivated by a vaguely defined sense of grievance rather than by a detailed political complaint against the social structure of Gotham would also put him very much in the same position as many Trump supporters. Indeed, numerous elements of *Joker* seem to place Arthur Fleck in the position of the embattled white male of the Trump era. In the film's first dramatic scene, Fleck is both attacked and humiliated by a gang of nonwhite youths, who mock him for his weakness as they beat and kick him in a key moment that does a great deal to establish Fleck's status as a victim. In other early parts of the film, he is apparently required (as a condition of his release from Arkham Hospital) to report to a social worker who is a black woman. He appears to resent this situation substantially, berating her for what he sees as her lack of real concern for his condition. And, at the end of the film, he is apparently once again in Arkham and once again under the supervisory care of a black woman (identified in the credits as a psychiatrist), who presumably has some sort of authority to determine exactly what will happen to Fleck. Of course, it is possible that he has been in Arkham all along and that the social worker is merely a projection of the psychiatrist. In any case, Fleck is less than fully forthcoming with both of these black women, seeming to assume that they could not possibly understand his situation (Figure 13). Thus, when he laughs during his interview with the woman at the end of the film, apparently at a joke he has thought of, he refuses to share the joke with her, simply declaring that she "wouldn't get it." Then he starts to mouth the words to "That's Life," followed by that final sequence implying that he might have murdered the woman, although it is clearly possible that he is only fantasizing about murdering her.

Joker implies that Fleck has issues with these two black women, although the film does not indicate how much of his resentment toward

The Politics of *Joker* and the Age of Trump

Figure 13. The pained face of Arthur Fleck.

them arises because they are black, how much because they are women, or how much because they are figures of authority. Meanwhile, between these two black women, who bookend the film, there is an additional black woman, Sophie Dumond, who serves as the lead female character in the film, although this film is so dominated by Fleck and his point of view that she remains quite secondary in overall importance. In fact, we barely get to know her, except as she is viewed by Fleck, whose own view is seriously distorted by the fact that she becomes a central object of his fantasies.

The film implies that Arthur and Sophie barely know each other (if at all) before that first meeting in the elevator. Within a few minutes of run time (perhaps the next morning), he is seen stalking her, following her as she drops her daughter off at school and then travels by train to the Gotham Savings Bank, where she is presumably employed, perhaps as a teller. There is no indication in the film that this stalking sequence is merely imagined, but it seems a safe bet that Arthur is merely fantasizing his next encounter with her, in which she comes to his apartment to ask him if he has been following her. When he admits that he has, she says, good-naturedly, "I thought that was you. I was hoping you would come in and rob the place." He responds with, "I have a gun. I could come by tomorrow." She laughs and tells him how funny he is (as she might be expected to do if this is Arthur's fantasy), whereupon he invites her to come see his stand-up act some time, and she agrees.

What follows is that sequence of incel dream outings in which Sophie seems to have become Arthur's girlfriend, but which are later revealed merely to be Arthur's fantasies. Indeed, in the scene in which he apparently really comes to her apartment and sits on the couch, it is clear that she still barely knows him and that she is absolutely terrified to discover him sitting in her living room—so much so that some viewers have concluded (wrongly, I think) that he probably murdered her before leaving the apartment. There is really no way to reach a definitive conclusion concerning Arthur's attitude toward Sophie, although one cannot help but wonder whether part of the reason he becomes so fascinated with her is that she is a black woman: by making her his fantasy object, he is in a position to seize control of his relationship with her as a sort of compensation for his problematic relationship with his social worker, in which he clearly feels so disempowered. Of course, if Fleck has been in Arkham throughout the film, then Sophie might be a sort of projection of the psychiatrist, modified to put him in a more empowered position.

In addition, after that first chance meeting in the elevator, Arthur's only other actual interactions with Sophie involve stalking her and breaking into her apartment, which hardly suggests a healthy attitude. Even his first fantasy interaction with her involves an offer to rob her place of employment at gunpoint. The (imaginary) offer is made in jest, but, like most of Arthur's jokes, this one isn't funny. In fact, it would seem to suggest a thinly veiled hostility and, again, a desire to exert power in the relationship.

Whether the filmmakers meant anything by it or not, it is impossible not to wonder why all of the women (other than his mother) with whom Fleck interacts are black. Again, if he is in Arkham all along and simply projecting the social worker and Sophie as figures of the psychiatrist, then it would make sense that all of them are black, complicating any reading of this situation. Still, given that he also murders (or fantasizes about murdering) his mother, I would think that the central implication in all of these relationships is that Fleck's feelings of hostility and disempowerment are based principally on gender and that he resents all of these women primarily because they are *women*, with the fact that all of these women other than his mother are black perhaps serving as a secondary irritation. Indeed, his mother is surely a key figure here, and the prominent place given to her in the film suggests the extremely important role she must have played in Fleck's psychological development. Everything we learn in the film (interpretive uncertainties aside) suggests that this role was largely a negative one, so it would hardly be surprising were Fleck to have a problematic (or even downright misogynistic) attitude toward women. But the sense of white male grievance to which Trump so centrally appealed as a base for his political ambitions was always based at least as much on a sense of being displaced (and unappreciated) by women as on a sense of racial threat, so Fleck's attitude toward women would also appear to align him with Trumpist forces.

This aspect of Fleck's character was reflected in the numerous early critical discussions of whether or not he might become an inspiration to incels—or to the general category of lonely white men who ultimately become mass killers. It also suggests that, in many ways, it is not Thomas Wayne who serves in *Joker* as a figure of Trump so much as it is Fleck. By this reading, Wayne becomes primarily a Reaganite image, while Fleck becomes primarily a Trumpian one—with the implication that these two types of images are closely related, rather than fundamentally different. But I use the adjective forms of the presidential names here in order to emphasize that Wayne does not serve as some sort of stand-in for Reagan himself so much as he stands in for the wealthy corporate interests served by Reagan—and that helped Reagan to gain power. In the same way, it is quite clear that the lowly Arthur Fleck cannot be read directly as a figure of Donald Trump (who is, after all, himself a representative of corporate interests, populist rhetoric aside). Instead, Fleck must be read as a figure of some of the forces that swept Trump into power on a wave of populist white male grievance, very much in line with Moore's observation that *Joker* is not directly about Trump but is instead about "the America that gave us Trump."

The America that gave us Trump is, in a very real sense, the America of Ronald Reagan and the 1980s, where forces were set in motion that led directly to the Trump presidency. Keeping this fact in mind, one is tempted here to note the possibility suggested in *Joker* that Wayne might be the illegitimate father of Fleck, which (symbolically) could potentially position Trump as a sort of bastard offspring of Reagan. Indeed, while most evidence within *Joker* might point to Wayne *not* being the biological father of Fleck, he is not unequivocally ruled out as the father, and the very fact that the film raises the possibility suggests that we should at least consider the possibility of a symbolic genealogical connection between Reagan and Trump.

That Trump at least has important predecessors in the American conservative tradition seems clear, despite the efforts of some conservatives to distance themselves from his unconventional antics. Indeed, Trump's stylistic differences from his predecessors—his bombastic and sarcastic speaking style, his unprecedented crassness, vulgarity, venality, and mendacity—have a tendency to obscure the similarities between Trump and the other Republican presidents who have made the biggest imprint on the American psyche in the past 50 years. The parallels with Reagan are particularly obvious, starting with the fact that both men were best known as entertainers before entering politics. In addition, once in power, both Trump and Reagan governed in a manner that might be expected of entertainers, depending more on the charismatic power of carefully cultivated personae than on actual executive management to further their agendas. One might say that both ruled primarily as entertainers, but it might be equally accurate (and more indicative of their fundamentally neoliberal worldviews) to say that both ruled primarily by effective marketing.

Moreover, despite their stylistic differences, Trump numbered Reagan among the numerous individuals from whom he borrowed his own rhetoric. It was, for example, Reagan who used the slogan "Make America Great Again" as part of his 1980s presidential campaign, a slogan that Trump would famously resurrect in his successful campaign 36 years later, making it one of the most effective campaign slogans in American history, despite its retrograde connotations.[1] Both Reagan and Trump also employed their personal popularity in the interest of policies as president that were marked by pro-business, anti-government attitudes that intentionally worked to the disadvantage of many of their most enthusiastic working-class constituents—although both also pursued neoliberal policies that were inadvertently to the detriment of the capitalist system they both so claimed to revere. There are also more specific parallels, as when Reagan's Star Wars project, however much it was rooted in the rhetoric of the Cold War, clearly served as a kind of symbolic predecessor to Trump's Space Force, although the latter was perhaps received with more popular derision. In addition, both Reagan and Trump failed to respond vigorously to deadly diseases that threatened the lives of American citizens, preferring instead to focus on paranoid visions of the dangers posed by foreign enemies. Thus, both presidents preferred to focus on bogeymen such as the evil Soviets or the evil Chinese (or the evil U.S. government), while AIDS and Covid ran rampant in America. Finally, both the Reagan and the Trump administrations were unusually shot through with corruption, leading to the indictment of many associates of both presidents on criminal charges.[2]

Of course, none of these connections between Trump and Reagan is particularly surprising, given that Trump himself was very much a product of Reaganite America. After all, the Trump Organization was first registered as a corporation in 1981, the same year that Reagan became president, marking what some would see as the birth of neoliberalism. It is thus perhaps doubly fitting that *Joker* is ostensibly set in this year. That Trump is very much a product of the Reaganite 1980s is well captured in the documentary series *Empires of New York*, which aired on the CNBC cable network in November and December of 2020. This series begins by detailing the embattled condition of New York City in the 1970s and early 1980s but notes that the city emerged into a new era of capitalist glitter in the course of the 1980s. Meanwhile, the series focuses on five New Yorkers it sees as central to this remarkable (if highly problematic) comeback. Trump himself is front and center among these individuals, as is his fellow hotel developer Leona Helmsley. Another focus of the series is future Trump lawyer Rudy Giuliani, prominent in the 1980s as an ambitious young U.S. attorney who set his sights on battling organized crime. Conversely, a fourth key figure in this series is famed mob leader John Gotti. Finally, also emblematic of New York in the 1980s was the intrepid investor Ivan Boesky, a key inspiration for *Wall Street*'s Gordon Gekko, who would ultimately become the best-known pop cultural representative of the cutthroat capitalism of the Reagan years.

Interestingly, Giuliani's anti-mob crusades failed to convict Gotti of any crime during the 1980s, earning the mob leader the nickname of the "Teflon Don" because no charges would stick to him. Giuliani did, however, win a conviction of Boesky for insider trading and of Helmsley for tax evasion, highlighting the extent to which shady deals of various kinds were, in fact, a crucial component of the high-flying capitalism of the 1980s. Trump, of course, was no stranger to shady deals. For example, Trump Tower, perhaps his signature development, was completed in 1983 with the aid of tax breaks that were originally intended to support the development of low-income housing, a category into which Trump Tower decidedly did not fall. Giuliani, of course, worked directly for the Reagan administration as the U.S. Attorney for the Southern District of New York from 1982 to 1989 and then would famously go on to become the mayor of New York City from the beginning of 1994 to the end of 2001. Giuliani gained significant national attention as the New York mayor at the time of the 9/11 bombings in 2001. Prior to that, though, his tenure as mayor had been marked by a controversial turn toward gentrification in key parts of the city (such as Greenwich Village), a move that could be seen as a sign of the increasingly neoliberal nature of life in the city. Meanwhile, Trump not only escaped Giuliani's scrutiny in the 1980s but would ultimately employ the former mayor as his personal lawyer and questionable henchman during the years of the Trump presidency.

The notorious partnership of Trump and Giuliani is thus, among other things, one of many links between Trump and the Reagan era, links that Trump himself has sometimes sought to emphasize. In the summer of 2020, for example, the re-election campaign for then President Trump began raising money by selling commemorative coin sets that featured images of Trump and Reagan. Trump, of course, is well known for being willing to do virtually anything to collect cash from his admirers, but in this case the implication seemed to go beyond the obvious cash grab to include a suggestion that Trump and Reagan were companion figures in American presidential history—two sides of the same coin, as it were. On the other hand, the Reagan Foundation (the organization charged with the oversight of Reagan's legacy) immediately rejected the comparison and demanded that the Trump campaign cease selling the coin sets.

Perhaps the most important thing that Trump, Giuliani, and the other "imperialists" who rose to prominence in New York in the 1980s had in common was that they were showmen (and one show-woman) above all else. Trump, for example, was far better at performing the role of a vastly successful, high-rolling businessman than he was at actual business, where he frequently lost money hand over fist. (And now, of course, he has styled himself as a genius politician, despite the fact that he has never in his life won a popular election.) Giuliani, meanwhile, was far more successful at playing an anti-mob crusader in the media than he was at curbing actual mob activity in New York—as the case of Gotti demonstrates. Indeed, the element of style over substance, the element of *marketing*, that was so critical to the activities of all of these figures can be seen to mark the 1980s as the decade when New York once and for all succumbed to the Debordian spectacle, making *Joker*, a film so shot-through with spectacle, the perfect film to capture this aspect of 1980s New York, even if it captures the city at a time just before the superficial economic boom of the decade would plaster over deep-seated social problems with a thick coat of glamor and glitz, so that the film keeps those problems in full view.

Of course, Trump's political predecessors include some who came before Reagan. Overtly racist demagogues such as Strom Thurmond or George Wallace immediately come to mind, but, even among presidents, Trumpian predecessors go back at least as far as Nixon, another president whose administration was plagued by corruption scandals and abuses of power. The parallels between Nixon and Trump are a bit less direct than those between Reagan and Trump, but they have certainly been noticed. For example, these parallels provide an important subtext to Aaron Sorkin's *The Trial of the Chicago Seven* (released on the Netflix platform after a pandemic-shortened theatrical run), one of the most talked-about films of 2020. Based on one of the most famous political trials in American history (though occasionally playing fast and loose with the historical details), Sorkin's film provides an important reminder that this trial only happened at all due to the politicization of the Justice

Department under a Nixon administration, whose hostility toward anti-war and civil-rights demonstrators would ultimately be matched by Trump's dismissive attitude toward the demonstrators who cried for social justice in the streets of American cities during the last year of the Trump administration.

Perhaps such parallels are again not surprising. Trump corresponded with Nixon in the 1980s, when the latter was a disgraced ex-president in California and the former was a brash, young, up-and-coming real estate developer in New York (Associated Press). Meanwhile, during his presidency, Trump sometimes cited Nixon as a key predecessor as he attempted to sell himself as the law and order candidate in his failed 2020 re-election campaign. Thus, *The Trial of the Chicago Seven* dramatises certain similarities between the late 1960s and the time of its own production, just as *Joker* suggests parallels between its early 1980s setting and the time of *its* production.

The parallels between Trump and Nixon and between Trump and Reagan suggest that Trump is really a more conventional conservative (or neoliberal) than he at first appears, a suggestion that has been pointed out before, of course. For my purposes, the most relevant and convincing argument about Trump's place within the American conservative tradition is that put forth by Corey Robin, who locates Trump within a long line of conservative thought that stretches back not just to Reagan and Nixon, but even, interestingly enough, to Edmund Burke's reaction to the French Revolution. And "reaction" is the key word here, because, for Robin, what ties the entire conservative tradition together is that the things that are being conserved are the power and privileges of its adherents, who are reacting to perceived threats to this power and those privileges. In Robin's view, Burke's perception of the French Revolution as a threat to civilization as he knew it thus becomes the prototype for all subsequent conservative thought, with thinkers such as Nixon, Reagan, and Trump (who might otherwise appear to be quite distinct from one another) all following very much in this reactionary tradition.

For Robin, "conservatism invariably arises in response to a threat to the old regime or after the old regime has been destroyed" (44). And this sense of being embattled drives numerous key elements of conservative thought. As Robin puts it,

> Far from being an invention of the politically correct, victimhood has been a talking point of the right ever since Burke decried the mob's treatment of Marie Antoinette. The conservative, to be sure, speaks for a special type of victim: one who has lost something

of value, as opposed to the wretched of the earth, whose chief complaint is that they never had anything to lose. (*Reactionary Mind* 55)

Joker's Arthur Fleck, of course, would appear to be a classic example of the latter. His case, though, illustrates the extent to which Republican politicians from Nixon, to Reagan, to Trump were remarkably successful in convincing working-class white males to accept them as champions of their embattled predicaments. Thus, these conservatives were speaking for a "special type of victim," as Robin notes, but it is also the case that these victims were largely invented, obscuring the fact that the main threat to working-class white American men is not women or minorities, but rich white men. Conversely, Reagan was able to convince Christians, a dominant force in American culture, that they were being threatened with extinction by the forces of secularism and that he was their champion, despite the fact that he was also able to convince them that the U.S. government, which he himself headed, was the main secular threat (and despite his long career in the Hollywood film industry, often viewed by evangelicals as Satanic).

This fictional victimhood has extended beyond the followers of politicians such as Nixon and Reagan and Trump to include the politicians themselves, which is, in fact, a key to its success as a political strategy. Thus, even when occupying the White House or other positions of power and privilege, conservatives have quite often succeeded in depicting themselves as victims or mistreated underdogs. One of the best-known examples of this phenomenon is Nixon's famous declaration, after losing the 1962 California gubernatorial election, that the media would no longer have Dick Nixon to "kick around," suggesting that he had been victimized by the media, perhaps leading to his loss. It was, though, Trump who perfected this rhetoric of victimhood, going beyond his own Nixonian complaints about the media attacking him via "fake news" to claim that virtually every criticism leveled against him during his presidency was part of some sort of unfair "witch hunt" carried out by mysterious powerful actors (such as the members of the "deep state") opposed to his populist agenda.

That agenda, of course, was key to the way in which the womanizing born-rich billionaire Trump was able to portray himself as a champion of the oppressed, extending Reagan's appeal to the religious right, while appealing in particular to a sense of grievance felt by working-class white males, who have (especially since the 1960s) felt their once supposedly unchallenged hegemony gradually eroding in the face of a steady onslaught conducted by feminists, communists, intellectuals, immigrants, minorities, gays, Muslims, and anyone else differing from what they perceived as the white male norm. Thus, while Trump's actual policies seemed designed primarily to benefit the very wealthy, he enjoyed significant support among groups that were not helped (or that were even hurt) by his policies.

The rhetoric of victimhood that underlies so much of the rhetoric of American conservative politicians is not, of course, a simple appeal for sympathy. It is, instead, an appeal for identification. In the case of Nixon, this argument was fairly straightforward, given his own relatively humble beginnings, despite the fact that he was almost entirely lacking in the folksy charm of a Reagan or the rabble-rousing bluster of a Trump. For example, Nixon was often very effective at presenting himself as an ordinary man who had managed to achieve great things, despite being looked down upon by the elite forces in American society that he connected to things such as inherited wealth and Ivy League (especially Harvard) educations. Indeed, while Nixon first came to political prominence by styling himself as a stalwart protector of the American way from the incursions of communism, the real threat to which he symbolically opposed himself was the snobbishness of America's own upper classes.

Nixon's "little man" persona was perhaps most famously projected in his 1952 "Checkers speech," in which he very successfully established the notion that he was an ordinary, humble public servant, working to serve his constituents and free of all hints of avarice or immorality. The speech has become almost legendary in American political history. At the time a senator from California and the Republican candidate for vice-president, Nixon (who had styled himself a fierce enemy of corruption in government) came under suspicion that improprieties were involved in a fund that had been established by his backers to reimburse him for political expenses. The charges were serious enough that Nixon's place on the Republican ticket seemed in jeopardy. But Nixon responded in a half-hour televised address (perhaps the first truly important use of television in American politics) in which he was able to market himself as virtuous champion of ordinary people who was under attack by moneyed interests who wished to see him fail. Famously, Nixon called attention to his humble lifestyle and to the modest cloth coat worn by his wife Pat (as opposed to the mink coats favored by the elites). Most importantly, he was able to shift the focus to one gift related to the fund that was to give the speech its name: a cocker spaniel named "Checkers" that had been given to the Nixons and that was now a beloved pet to his two young daughters. By calling attention to how devoted his daughters had become to this pet—and by insisting that he would not give up the dog regardless of the political consequences—Nixon was able to make himself appear the victim of charges that were petty, overblown, and spiteful. But he was also able to present himself as a courageous father who would not allow his enemies to deprive his innocent children of their adorable dog.

The speech was a tour de force of political rhetoric (and of marketing) that diverted attention from the very real questions about Nixon's character that this fund had raised. Referred to by Carl Freedman as a "masterpiece of *ressentiment*," the speech nicely illustrates a career-long Nixon strategy (85). In particular, the sense of persecution and victimhood embedded in the speech was central to Nixon's success in gaining the support of ordinary people because he shared their sense of exclusion from the privileges enjoyed by the elites, who later somehow became conflated with the entire 1960s and 1970s counterculture (often led, after all, by college students whom Nixon was able to depict as spoiled rich kids). One only thinks, for example, of those waves of working-class "hardhats" who turned out in droves to support Nixon in his battle in support of "American values" and against the long-haired youth of the counterculture, despite the fact that Nixon's anti-union policies ran directly counter to the real interests of his working-class supporters.

Daraiseh and Booker note the way in which the Nietzschean notion of *ressentiment*, which Freedman sees as a key to understanding Nixon, is a key to understanding Arthur Fleck as well. However, they note that, although he follows in the footsteps of literary predecessors such as Dostoevsky's Underground Man and Eliot's Prufrock (and cinematic predecessors such as the earlier protagonists of Scorsese), Fleck is no longer able to sustain a full-fledged *ressentiment*, because his postmodern psyche is too fragmented to support such strong feelings. For Daraiseh and Booker, although Fleck "is a character of the 1980s, he is a character in a work of the twenty-first century, and it shows in the way that his psychic fragmentation has advanced well beyond that of his ostensible near contemporaries, Travis Bickle and Rupert Pupkin."

By the time of Reagan, the Republican rhetoric of victimhood had already shifted significantly. Reagan, like Nixon, had also come from relatively modest beginnings and had received a significantly less prestigious education than had Nixon. While Nixon often touted the fact that he had not had the resources to attend an Ivy League law school, he did, in fact, attend law school at Duke University on a full scholarship. Reagan, on the other hand, graduated from tiny Eureka College and didn't attend law school at all. As a sportscaster and then movie star, Reagan gradually improved his economic status but was hardly a member of the elites so despised by Nixon. He employed a great deal of the rhetoric of siege that was so important to Nixon's success, overtly opposing many of the same threats (communists, criminals) as had Nixon, while also utilizing a more subtle rhetoric of racism. But, reflecting the rise of neoliberalism, Nixon's true bête noire, the liberal elites, were for Reagan replaced by government itself, making his true mission to protect Americans (and American capitalism) from the ravages of government regulation, even while he himself was the head of a government that greatly expanded during his presidency. In the same way, Reagan, a former union leader, was staunchly opposed to unions as a force that inhibited capitalist competition. For Reagan, the free market was all, and Thomas Wayne's stated belief that people who have "made something of themselves" are inherently superior to the "clowns" who have failed to do so is a Reaganite idea indeed.

A former minor movie star and television personality, Reagan was also emblematic of an important turn in American politics and society toward a more spectacular (in the Debordian sense) form. Reagan's success was far more tied to his style than his substance, and his comfort with the camera was crucial to his ability to win over large portions of the electorate to his cause. This turn was a crucial element of American life in the 1980s; it is reflected in *Joker* in the emphasis placed on the mediatization of reality through television and on other aspects of Gotham City of *Joker* as a spectacular society.

I have already pointed out several times in this study how saturated *Joker*'s Gotham is with media coverage, which is one of the key ways in which the city resembles 1980s New York—and 1980s America in general. Indeed, one reason why the 1980s has become such an object of nostalgia in our own contemporary culture surely has to with the fact that the 1980s was the first decade to see the emergence of the full-blown media culture that has dominated American life ever since. That decade saw the rapid expansion of both cable television and satellite television in the United States It also saw the rapid expansion of home video through the videocassette recorders that had been introduced in America in the late 1970s and that became, in the course of the 1980s, a staple of American home entertainment. All of this media expansion, of course, eventually led to today's Internet, the technological foundations for which were laid in the 1980s as well.

The media explosion that began in the Reaganite 1980s also led directly to the Trump presidency, despite the fact that Trump has often seemed to be something completely new. To this point, Robin notes that the continuity of conservative thought has been obscured by the ways in

233

which shifting historical conditions have forced conservatives to adapt by changing their rhetoric. Thus, while a strain of racism seems to run through all American conservatism, American conservative politicians beginning with Nixon had to couch their racist attitudes in various forms of code. However, Robin argues that, by the time of the Trump era, the situation had changed. Despite the fact that it was groups such as African Americans who were suffering the heaviest economic and social losses during this period, white Americans were feeling more and more threatened by the growing nonwhite population in America, exacerbated by the "tormenting symbolism of a black president and the greater visibility of black and brown faces in the culture industries." Under such circumstances, according to Robin, "Racial dog whistles no longer suffice; a more brazen sound is required. Trump is that sound" (243).

I believe Robin is correct that the differences among conservative figures such as Nixon, Reagan, and Trump are more a matter of appearance than reality. Put differently, one could say that these differences are more a matter of style than of substance. As such, these differences can, to some extent at least, be captured through analogy to cultural forms. Nixon, I would argue, was a sort of "realist" politician, who pursued a relatively conventional road to the White House. Having graduated from law school and then served as a naval officer in World War II, he began a political career that saw him become a congressman and a U.S. senator before serving as the Vice President of the United States from 1953 to 1961. His credentials, in short, were very much what one might (at the time) have expected of a U.S. president, his career arc making perfectly logical, cause-and-effect sense. Nevertheless, as Carl Freedman has argued, Nixon essentially "invented the modern media campaign" in his 1968 run for president (192). In that sense he was very much the direct predecessor to Reagan, who used his skills as an actor to perfect that kind of campaign.

Nixon, Freedman argues, "was the first important American politician to grasp and use the political possibilities of TV, and to appreciate the major role it was destined to play in the country's future" (189). It was, though, Reagan—the "great communicator"—who fulfilled that destiny in the 1980s. And, while Freedman is surely correct that Nixon preceded Reagan as a pioneering media campaigner, Reagan was genuinely new in his ability to carry over the style of a media campaign into the presidency itself. Reagan, one might say, took the presidency in a more modernist direction, with much more attention to performance and style than Nixon had ever managed as president.

Trump, then, extended Reagan's approach to its natural (although perhaps not logical) postmodern conclusion, literally attempting to destroy the federal government that Reagan so often reviled, as in his infamous deployment of high-level appointees who had already established themselves as dedicated opponents of the departments they were selected to head. For example, Betsy DeVos, a longtime foe of the whole idea of public education, became the Secretary of Education, while the anti-environmentalist lobbyist Andrew Wheeler became the administrator of the Environmental Protection Agency (EPA), which had, oddly enough, been established in 1970 by Nixon.

And, of course, the January 6, 2021, attack on the U.S. Capitol building was the ultimate culmination of this assault on the federal government, its performative aspects (as discussed in the previous chapter) serving as an extension of the four-year period in which Trump had performed the role of president, without any real interest in governing. The basic policies of the Trump administration, I would argue, were not that different from those of the Reagan administration. The unrestrained style of the Trump presidency, however, with the total abandonment of any conventional idea of political propriety, differed substantially from that of the Reagan presidency.

This difference can perhaps best be seen in the rhetoric of Otherness that both Reagan and Trump employed in order to establish specific bogeymen against which they could oppose themselves as defenders of the American way on the global stage. For Reagan, of course, this enemy was the Soviet Union, which had occupied that role since the immediate postwar years, when a young Nixon (among others) had helped to establish an atmosphere of anti-communist hysteria as a prevailing tone of American politics. Reagan's overt characterization of the Soviet Union as an "evil empire"—first delivered, tellingly, to a very receptive audience at the 1983 annual convention of the National Association of Evangelicals—brought this rhetoric to a new and more theatrical level. But Trump's ongoing rhetorical war with China took this strategy even farther, topped off with his overtly racist attempts to displace the blame for his own mishandling of the U.S. response to the Coronavirus pandemic by characterizing the virus essentially as a Chinese plot and by repeatedly referring to the virus, in his own inimitable mocking style, as the "China virus," which thus became a new form of the old "yellow menace."

Trump's anti-China rhetoric, however divorced from reality in itself, would eventually lead to a wave of very real violence against innocent Asian Americans, demonstrating that, even in the society of the spectacle, images can have very real material consequences. Nevertheless, Trump's campaign against China with regard to the Coronavirus pandemic was never intended as a description of material reality, just as so much of his language was intended purely to stir the emotions of his political base, with very little concern for the actual veracity of his statements. In many ways, then, the historical arc from Nixon, to Reagan, to Trump can be described, first, as a gradual movement away from what had long been considered to be conventional political behavior and careers and, second, as a gradual disengagement of political rhetoric from material reality.

The movement from Nixon, to Reagan, to Trump can, then, usefully be compared with the movement from realism (Nixon), to modernism (Reagan), to postmodernism (Trump) that has become a common (if problematic) narrative of the evolution of Western culture since the nineteenth century. Perhaps even more useful in this case, however, is the somewhat different (although not entirely unrelated) narrative of cultural history that would focus on dominant media over roughly the same historical period, moving from the novel, to film, to television. From this point of view, I would note Carl Freedman's suggestion that the myth of American upward mobility as epitomized by the popular cultural memory of the nineteenth-century novels of Horatio Alger[3] was "crucial to the formation of Nixon's political personality and was in turn used by him to major political effect" (54). Meanwhile, I have already discussed in some detail in Chapter 3 the ways in which the political style of the former film actor Reagan was heavily influenced by the movies, including the movies in which he himself appeared. And Trump, prior to his run for the presidency, was best known to the American public as the host of the reality television series *The Apprentice* for 14 seasons that spanned the period from 2004 to 2015.

Given these facts, it is perhaps not surprising that the styles of these three presidents might be described as novelistic (in the case of Nixon), cinematic (in the case of Reagan), and televisual (in the case of Trump), even if the time scales for the dominance of those three media do not precisely match up with the rise to power of each medium.[4] In fact, it seems reasonable to expect the media to be leading indicators in this sense. Film could not produce a cinematic president until it had been a powerful force for enough decades to help mold such a person, and Reagan (born in 1911) was exactly the right age to have been among the earliest Americans shaped by film in their young years, while Trump (born in 1946) was similarly a member of the first generation to have been powerfully shaped by television.

I also do not think that it is entirely unfair to point out that the novels of Horatio Alger, the films of Ronald Reagan, and *The Apprentice* are not particularly good examples of the arts they represent. Alger wrote one highly successful young adult novel (*Ragged Dick*, published in 1868), then produced dozens of knock-offs of the same novel, before moving into more lurid material late in his career when those knock-offs ceased to sell. Reagan the actor is perhaps best remembered for the sappy and dishonest *Knute Rockne, All American* (1940) and the ludicrous *Bedtime for Bonzo* (1951). Even the few solid films in which he appeared—such as the sentimental melodramas *Dark Victory* (1939) and *King's Row* (1942)—would never be mistaken for *Citizen Kane*. Finally, *The Apprentice*, an unabashed celebration of capitalist greed that was at the same time a thinly disguised celebration of Donald Trump, was not even a very good version of reality TV, one of the lowliest of all television genres and one of the cultural phenomena that most clearly marks the dissolution of reality itself in American life.

Reality television, I would argue, plays somewhat the same role in the culture of the 2010s as the talk show had in the 1980s. Granted, talk shows are still an important part of our contemporary mediascape, and indeed there are now more talk shows than ever before. But the proliferation of talk shows can be taken as a sign of the increasingly postmodern (read, increasingly multiple and fragmented) nature of this mediascape, which means that no one talk show of today has the cultural power of, say, the *Tonight Show* of the Johnny Carson years. Reality television, however, has become a powerful phenomenon, with shows such as *Survivor* (2000–) leading the way. What these shows—along with singing competitions such as *American Idol* (2002–)—have in common is the addition of a key element of competition, suggesting the extent to which the ideological underpinnings of capitalism have come more and more overtly to dominate American (and global) television in the era of neoliberalism.

One key aspect of such programming is that there are always more losers than winners, while the losers often suffer considerable humiliation and abuse. Trump's famous "You're fired" might be the quintessential example of this abuse, the prominence of which can be seen in the reality programs that have been featured in two of the most insightful satirical films of the twenty-first century, Mike Judge's *Idiocracy* (2006) and Boots Riley's *Sorry to Bother You* (2018), both of which, amid thoroughgoing critiques of American society, include mock reality television programs based primarily on the abuse of contestants: *Ow, My Balls!* and *I Got the S**@ Kicked Out of Me*, respectively. Both of these programs, however, are based on physical abuse, while the nature of the abuse meted out by Trump in *The Apprentice* makes overt the particularly capitalist nature of the competition in this program. All three of these programs, while either lampooning or (in the case of *The Apprentice*) exemplifying the debased level to which television programming has already sunk, also rely upon the notion that audiences, accustomed to a variety of forms of abuse in their daily lives, enjoy seeing someone else be abused for a change. But this phenomenon also suggests that such programming subtly conditions television audiences to endure abuse without protest when it occurs to them in their own lives, making them pliable dupes of the capitalist system.

It is certainly the case that the novels that shaped Nixon, the films that were such a big part of Reagan's very identity, and the television series that made Trump into Trump are all, in one way or another, unapologetically commercial attempts to cash in on the marketability of certain American myths, with very little concern for aesthetic quality or artistic integrity. All thus provide key signposts along the historical way to the society of the spectacle—or along the way to the complete commodification of culture that Jameson associates with postmodernism and Fisher with capitalist realism, but that might be better associated in a more general sense with neoliberalism. Meanwhile, this narrative of historical change also corresponds to changes in presidential style, a notion that is relevant to *Joker* because so much of this same narrative is built into the texture of the film. As I noted in Chapter 3, *Joker*, while showing the strong influence of films roughly contemporary with its own action (such as the early films of Scorsese), also establishes a strong connection with the films of the past, including showing us actual segments of two films from the 1930s, when Reagan was just beginning his career in Hollywood. But *Joker* also makes it clear that, by the 1980s, television had already become the dominant force in the mediascape of Gotham City, just as it had become the dominant medium in real-world America during the Reagan years. Moreover, just as television paved the way for the Trump presidency, so too did it pave the way for the making of *Joker*, a film that perhaps could only have been made in the Trump era, however rooted in the Reagan era its actual events might be.

Notes

1 Science fiction novelist Octavia E. Butler understood these connotations well when she had one of her characters, the demagogic Andrew Steel Jarret, adopt this slogan in her 1998 dystopian novel *Parable of the Talents*, sweeping to the presidency amid a tide of bigotry and religious intolerance.
2 Numerous commentators during the Trump years have noted the parallels between Trump and Reagan. More detailed studies of these parallels have begun to emerge as well. Daniel S. Lucks, for example, notes the strain of

racism that was central to Reagan's policies, identifying that strain as leading directly to Trump. Jack Rasmus, meanwhile, has noted the Reagan and Trump administrations as two important markers along the historical path of neoliberalism, and journalist Gerald Seib notes how Reagan's conservative policies laid the unfortunate groundwork for Trump. Trump enthusiasts, such as Nick Adams, have also attempted to connect Reagan with Trump, apparently feeling that this connection lends Trump some sort of legitimacy.

3 This cultural memory, I should note, does not entirely mesh with the novels themselves. The popular version of the "Horatio Alger myth" has largely to do with success through hard work, while Alger's actual novels emphasized virtuous behavior more than industriousness.

4 One could argue, of course, that the Internet (including such phenomena as social media) is the central medium for both Trumpism and neoliberalism. It would have been virtually impossible to reflect this medium in *Joker*, although it could be argued that some of the more jarring cuts that are central to this film effect sudden changes in context that are reminiscent of the hypertextual shifts that one encounters on the Internet and that are not typically found in films of the 1980s.

Conclusion

Joker is a film about which virtually nothing definitive can be said but about which virtually unlimited speculative conclusions can be drawn. The film is overtly set in Batman's Gotham City, but it contains no superheroes (including Batman) and none of the spectacular action scenes that have come to be associated with the superhero genre. It is, in fact, a carefully constructed work of postmodern art that generates meaning in highly complex ways. At the same time, one of these complexities involves the fact that, despite its postmodern self-consciousness, *Joker* is a film whose texture seems grittily realistic, providing a vivid picture of life in "Gotham City" at the beginning of the 1980s. But Gotham City, of course, has long been widely regarded as a stand-in for New York City, so that *Joker* clearly evokes the New York of this time. It also engages in important and extensive dialogues with the United States as a whole during the Reagan era. Because of the nature of *Joker*'s story, one of the aspects of American life during this period it points toward is the unprecedented media attention gained by serial killers during the time in which the film appears to be set. But *Joker*'s dialogue with the past is often more cultural than historical, and many critics have noted the obvious resemblances between *Joker* and the early films of Martin Scorsese (especially *Taxi Driver* and *The King of Comedy*, but also *Mean Streets*). Actually, *Joker* engages in extensive dialogues with a number of other films of the 1970s and 1980s as well, including the slasher films that dominated American horror in the 1980s. *Joker* also intersects extensively with other horror films. In addition, it engages in dialogue with other elements of American culture, including the very effective use of well-known songs on its soundtrack, supplementing the film's Oscar-winning original score by Hildur Guðnadóttir. There is, however, more at stake than postmodern play in *Joker*'s use of its cultural predecessors. For one thing, the film's play with images and media suggests that the society of Gotham City—and, by extension, of New York City and the United States—corresponds well to the vision of society of the spectacle as envisioned by Guy Debord as a description of the dehumanizing consequences of consumer capitalism. *Joker* also includes more explicitly political material, including the fact that a popular class-based rebellion lies at the heart of the plot of the film. However, this rebellion is depicted as anything but heroic and emancipatory. Meanwhile, although much of the political content of *Joker* is especially relevant to the time of the setting of the film, one of the most striking aspects of *Joker* is its ability to engage in such an extensive dialogue both with the historical and cultural context of the time of its action in the early 1980s and with the historical and cultural context at the time of its production and release in the late 2010s, suggesting important connections between those two time periods. The content of *Joker*, as its connections with Scorsese indicate, is rooted in 1981 (and thereabouts), although certain aspects are much more typical of 2019: Arthur Fleck's turn to spectacle, dancing down those stone steps in a colorful costume and full makeup, is a move that would have been unthinkable for Travis Bickle. Moreover, stylistically, *Joker* is a work of fully evolved postmodernism, making it very much a film of 2019, despite gestures back to the 1980s. Ultimately, the film connects these two time periods and suggests that they are part of a single historical phenomenon, which can be described in terms of the evolution of postmodernism, but is perhaps more tellingly described in terms of the evolution of neoliberalism.

The Joker is easily the most important of all of the antagonists who have battled against Batman since his first appearance in the late 1930s. In fact, he is arguably the most important supervillain in all of comics. And, while it is not at all certain that Arthur Fleck is meant to be the same Joker as the one who has long tormented Batman, the fact that Fleck takes on the name "Joker" in a film that is set in Gotham City clearly invites viewers to consider this film as taking place within the world of the Batman franchise. And the fact that a young Bruce Wayne makes a minor appearance in the film, while his father Thomas Wayne makes a more prominent appearance, also seems openly to declare this film to be part of the Batman universe. The film doubtless owes much of its considerable commercial success to the fact that audiences did view it as an example of the superhero film, perhaps the most thoroughly commercialized (i.e., the most neoliberal) of all film genres. On the other hand, *Joker* in this sense does at least mount some resistance to neoliberalism because the actual nature of the film itself potentially asks us to view superhero films themselves in a new light, challenging their reliance on the neoliberal notion that ordinary people need to rely on special heroic individuals to save them.

One of the ways in which *Joker* deviates most dramatically from the typical superhero narrative is in its complex postmodern style, as in the way it evokes the past mostly through cultural texts. *Joker* is particularly postmodern in the way it defeats any attempts at final and definitive interpretation. This interpretive uncertainty comes about primarily because so much of the action of the film is filtered through the unstable consciousness of protagonist Arthur Fleck, played by Joaquin Phoenix in an Oscar-winning role. Fleck lives in a world in which fantasy and reality are often confused, and this confusion carries over into any attempt to interpret the events of the film. But the film is also carefully constructed (for example, through a highly inventive use of cuts) to reinforce this effect. *Joker*, in fact, is a highly self-conscious work of art that employs all of the resources of the filmmaker's art (camera placement and movement, editing, music, and so on) to good effect. Postmodernism itself might be (and, I think, is) largely congruent with the ideology of neoliberalism, but its refusal of final interpretation can be seen as a movement of resistance to neoliberal commodification.

Again, though, *Joker*'s most obvious evocations of the time period of its action involve its dialogue with cultural products, especially films, of that time. The resonances between *Joker* and Scorsese's early films are particularly strong, but they are only part of an extremely rich dialogue between Phillips's film and American film. But *Joker* also resonates with a number of different kinds of American films all the way up to its release in 2019, establishing a particularly rich dialogue with horror films released between the 1970s and the 2010s. *Joker* also established dialogues with other forms of American culture at and just before the time of its action, including television and popular music. In some cases, this dialogue plays a realistic role, as when the familiar songs used in the film (by performers ranging from Charlie Chaplin, to Frank Sinatra, to the British rock group Cream) are mostly from a slightly earlier period than the time of the film's action, suggesting that they might have played a role in the development of the personality of Arthur Fleck, just as such songs have played a crucial role in the evolution of American society.

Meanwhile, *Joker* does a great deal to link its action to the specific historical context of the United States (and especially New York) in and around the year 1981. For example, Fleck's mental illness is depicted as taking place during a period when the U.S. mental health system was beginning to collapse due to the withdrawal of federal support by the Reagan administration. New York itself had been experiencing a decline since the mid-1970s as well, a situation that is evident in *Joker* from the fact that the action of the film takes place against the background of a garbage strike, garbage strikes at that time being a frequent occurrence in New York City.

The serial-killer plot of *Joker* also provides a reminder that serial killing gained unprecedented prominence in American culture roughly from the time of the Manson family killings in 1969 to the end of the career of Jeffrey Dahmer in 1992, with the action of *Joker* located almost exactly at the midpoint of this "Golden Age" of American serial killing—and to this period of the rise of neoliberalism, under which *everything* (even serial killing) becomes a commodity of one kind or another. And *Joker* shows an awareness of its relevance to this real-world phenomenon in the way that Fleck shares many characteristics with well-known American serial killers, such as the "Killer Clown," John Wayne Gacy, who is specifically (but subtly) referred to within the film.

Joker's evocation of the historical past through images from popular culture is part of its construction of a picture of early 1980s America as a society in which images, in fact, reign supreme. For example, the film clearly indicates the growing mediatization of American reality in the early 1980s, as Fleck seems to gain so much of what he knows about the world through watching commercial television. Indeed, one of the most productive ways in which the politics of *Joker* can be understood is through an examination of the ways in which the world it projects corresponds so closely to the description of the late capitalist world contained in Debord's 1967 book *The Society of the Spectacle*. The world of the book is very much a world of images and performances, which, among other things, contributes to Fleck's disengagement from material reality. Fleck's own mental state, in fact, is often conveyed through performance, especially through his dancing performances that have been one of the most widely discussed aspects of the film. But this emphasis on performance indicates a turn toward a vision even of human beings as marketable commodities, marking the beginning of a neoliberal turn that was just beginning to take shape at the time of the action of *Joker* but was fully formed by the time of the film's release.

Other political aspects of *Joker* are more overt, even if they remain resistant to definitive interpretation. By the end of the film, for example, the common people of Gotham have taken to the streets in violent protest against the economic injustices that reign in the city, their grievances so severe that they adopt the slogan "kill the rich" to define their movement. While some have seen this movement as a statement of support for social justice, even comparing it to the Black Lives Matter protests that rocked America in the summer of 2020, my conclusion is that the rebels of *Joker* are depicted as an unruly mob that has much more in common with the

Trump supporters who invaded the U.S. Capitol on January 6, 2021. In any case, their depiction in *Joker* hardly seems to be an endorsement for their position, especially as the film humanizes the rich by showing the killing of Thomas Wayne.

Finally, one of the most striking and important political aspects of *Joker* is its ability to engage so extensively both with the historical context of its action and with the context of its own production and release. Despite the firm placing of the film's action in the early 1980s, this film might tell us as much about the era of Trump as it does about the era of Reagan. This dual historical and cultural dialogue is possible, of course, because these two time periods, in fact, have a great deal in common and can be seen as part of the same historical progression in the growth of neoliberalism. For example, *Joker* itself is part of a wave of fascination with serial killing that has swept through American popular culture in the last years of the 2010s, bringing that phenomenon to a prominence it had not seen since the beginning of the 1990s. The similarities between the 2010s and the 1980s can also be seen in the nostalgic evocations of the 1980s that appeared in American popular culture in the 2010s. *Joker*, by reminding us of some of the uglier aspects of the 1980s (such as the centrality of serial killings to the era), seriously calls this nostalgia into question. Most importantly, *Joker*'s ability to engage in such intense dialogues with different historical periods tells us a great deal about recent American political history and about the continuity of certain tendencies in American politics in the past few decades, especially the continuity in conservative politics from Nixon, to Reagan, to Trump—three president who might, on first view, seem very different. Read through *Joker*, which in so many ways dramatises transformations in American culture (and in neoliberalism) that took place during the half century before its production, we can see that the movement from Nixon, to Reagan, to Trump was very much part of these same transformations and that the differences among these three politicians was more a matter of style than substance (and of a movement toward more style and less substance), paralleling systemic changes in the culture at large in the neoliberal shift toward marketing as the paradigm of all social activity.

Works Cited

"The 200 Greatest Comic Book Characters." *WizardUniverse.com*, October 3, 2009, https://web.archive.org/web/20091003165505/www.wizarduniverse.com/05240810thgreatestcharacters2.html. Accessed 2 October 2020.

"The 50 Greatest Comic-Book Characters." *Empire*, 1 August 2019, www.empireonline.com/movies/features/50greatestcomiccharacters/. Accessed 2 October 2020.

Acosta, Jim, and Paul LeBlanc. "Trump Tells Aides He Thinks He'll Be Acquitted as He Remains Fixated on 'Accountability' for GOP Lawmakers Who Voted to Impeach." 8 February 2021, www.cnn.com/2021/02/08/politics/trump-impeachment/index.html. Accessed 27 March 2021.

Adams, Nick. *Trump and Reagan: Defenders of America*. Post Hill Press, 2021.

Ashton, Will. "Wait, Is Joker A Horror Movie?" *CinemaBlend*, 24 October 2019, www.cinemablend.com/news/2482941/wait-is-joker-a-horror-movie. Accessed 12 November 2020.

Associated Press. "Trump and Nixon Were Pen Pals in the '80s. Here Are Their Letters." *Politico*, 23 September 2020, www.politico.com/news/2020/09/23/donald-trump-richard-nixon-pen-pals-420567. Accessed 2 December 2020.

Augustine, J. B. "Toby Emmerich: Warner Bros. Didn't Expect Success or Violence Out of *Joker*." *Bounding into Comics*, 31 October 2019, https://boundingintocomics.com/2019/10/31/toby-emmerich-warner-bros-didnt-expect-success-or-violence-out-of-joker/. Accessed 29 September 2020.

Ayres, Jackson. "The Joker." *Comics through Time: A History of Icons, Idols, and Ideas*, vol. 3, *1980–1995*, edited by M. Keith Booker, Greenwood Press, 2014, pp. 1097–1098.

———. "The Joker." *Comics through Time: A History of Icons, Idols, and Ideas*, vol. 4, *1995–Present*, edited by M. Keith Booker, Greenwood Press, 2014, pp. 1577–1578.

Bainbridge, Caroline. "Cracking Up: *Joker* and the Mediatisation of the Arse-end of the World." *New Review of Film and Television Studies*, vol. 19, no. 1, 2021, pp. 54–64.

Barsanti, Sam. "*Batman* Prequel *Pennyworth* Feels Like a Comic Book, Just Not the One It's Actually Based on." *AV Club*, 25 July 2019, https://tv.avclub.com/batman-prequel-pennyworth-feels-like-a-comic-book-just-1836671224. Accessed 4 October 2020.

Baudrillard, Jean. *The Gulf War Did Not Take Place*. Translated by Paul Patton, Indiana University Press, 1995.

—. *Simulacra and Simulations*. 1981. Translated by Sheila Faria Glaser, University of Michigan Press, 1994.

Belton, John. *American Cinema/American Culture*. 5th edition. McGraw-Hill Education, 2017.

Biskind, Peter. *Easy Riders, Raging Bulls: How the Sex-Drugs-and-Rock 'n' Roll Generation Saved Hollywood*. Simon & Schuster, 1998.

Blunden, Fred. "The 25 Greatest Comic Book Supervillains of All Time, Ranked." *Screen Rant*, 10 March 2017, https://screenrant.com/comic-book-supervillains-ranked-all-time/. Accessed 2 October 2020.

Board of Governors of the Federal Reserve System. "Distribution of Household Wealth in the U.S. since 1989," 19 March 2021, www.federalreserve.gov/releases/z1/dataviz/dfa/distribute/table/. Accessed 21 March 2021.

Booker, M. Keith. *Alternate Americas: Science Fiction Film and American Culture*. Praeger, 2006.

—. *Postmodern Hollywood: What's New in Film and Why It Makes Us Feel So Strange*. Praeger, 2007.

Booker, M. Keith, and Isra Daraiseh. *Consumerist Orientalism: The Convergence of Arab and American Popular Culture in the Age of Global Capitalism*. I. B. Tauris, 2019.

—. "'This is the Bloody Twenty-first Century!': The (Post)Modern Vampires of Jim Jarmusch's *Only Lovers Left Alive*." *Spoofing the Vampire*, edited by Simon Bacon, McFarland, 2002, pp. 213–27.

Bremer, Arthur. *An Assassin's Diary*. Harper's Magazine Press, 1974.

Brody, Richard. "*Joker* Is a Viewing Experience of Rare, Numbing Emptiness." *New Yorker*, 3 October 2019, www.newyorker.com/culture/the-front-row/joker-is-a-viewing-experience-of-rare-numbing-emptiness. Accessed 22 August 2020.

Brown, Jeffrey. "A City without a Hero: *Joker* and Rethinking Hegemony." *New Review of Film and Television Studies*, vol. 19, no. 1, 2021, pp. 7–18.

Bugliosi, Vincent, and Curt Gentry. *Helter Skelter: The True Story of the Manson Murders*. W. W. Norton, 1974.

Bundel, Ani. "'Joker,' Starring Joaquin Phoenix, Sparked an Incel Controversy Because It's Hopelessly Hollow." *NBC News.com*, 5 October 2019, www.nbcnews.com/think/opinion/joker-starring-joaquin-phoenix-sparked-incel-controversy-because-it-s-ncna1062656. Accessed 1 December 2022.

Burke, Edmund. *Reflections on the Revolution in France*. 1790. Oxford University Press, 2009.

Works Cited

Burton, Tara Isabella. "A 'Joker'—and a World—Gone Mad from Nihilism." *Religion News Service*, 17 October 2019, https://religionnews.com/2019/10/17/a-joker-and-a-world-gone-mad-from-nihilism/. Accessed 28 August 2020.

Burwick, Kevin. "Memorable Joker Scene Was Improvised by Joaquin Phoenix in One Take." *Movieweb*, 24 October 2019, https://movieweb.com/joker-movie-improvised-fridge-scene-joaquin-phoenix/. Accessed 1 September 2020.

Butler, Octavia E. *Parable of the Talents*. 1988. Grand Central Publishing, 2019.

Carlyle, Thomas. *The French Revolution*. 1837. Modern Library, 2002.

Child, Ben. "Why is Donald Trump Obsessed with Bane in *The Dark Knight Rises*?" *Guardian*, 11 April 2019, www.theguardian.com/film/filmblog/2019/apr/11/donald-trump-thomas-hardy-the-dark-knight-rises-christopher-nolan-batman. Accessed 23 March 2021.

Clover, Carol J. *Men, Women, and Chain Saws: Gender in the Modern Horror Film*. Updated edition, Princeton University Press, 2015.

Coletta, Charles. "The Joker." *Comics through Time: A History of Icons, Idols, and Ideas*, vol. 1, *1800–1960*, edited by M. Keith Booker, Greenwood Press, 2014, pp. 195–197.

—. "The Joker." *Comics through Time: A History of Icons, Idols, and Ideas*, vol. 2, *1960–1980*, edited by M. Keith Booker, Greenwood Press, 2014, pp. 650–652.

Collins, Jim. *Uncommon Cultures: Popular Culture and Post-Modernism*. Routledge, 1989.

Collura, Scott. "*The Dark Knight*: Heath Ledger Talks Joker." *IGN*, 7 November 2006, www.ign.com/articles/2006/11/08/the-dark-knight-heath-ledger-talks-joker. Accessed 29 September 2020.

Crary, Robert. *24/7: Late Capitalism and the Ends of Sleep*. Verso, 2013.

Curran, Brad. "*Joker* Does Have One Connection to *Batman v Superman*." *ScreenRant*, 9 September 2019, https://screenrant.com/joker-batman-v-superman-connection-excalibur-poster/. Accessed 25 October 2020.

Daraiseh, Isra, and M. Keith Booker. "Jokes from Underground: The Disintegration of the Bourgeois Subject and the Progress of Capitalist Modernization from Dostoevsky to Todd Phillips's *Joker*." *Literature/Film Quarterly*, vol. 48, no. 3, 2020. https://lfq.salisbury.edu/_issues/48_3/jokes_from_underground_the_disintegration_of_the_bourgeois_subject_and_the_progress_of_capitalist_modernization_from_dostoevsky_to_todd_phillips_jokcr.html. Accessed 23 August 2020.

—. "Unreal City: Nostalgia, Authenticity, and Posthumanity in 'San Junipero.'" *Through the* Black Mirror: *Deconstructing the Side Effects of the Digital Age*, edited by Terence McSweeney and Stuart Joy, Palgrave Macmillan, 2019, pp. 151–163.

De Semlyen, Phil. "*Joker.*" *Time Out*, 26 September 2019, www.timeout.com/movies/joker-1. Accessed 28 March 2021.

Debord, Guy. *Comments on the Society of the Spectacle*. 1990. Translated by Malcolm Imrie, 3rd edition, Verso, 2011.

—. *The Society of the Spectacle*. 1967. [3rd French edition] Translated by Donald Nicholson-Smith, Zone Books, 1994.

Dickens, Charles. *A Tale of Two Cities*. 1859. Penguin Classics, 1985.

Dietsch, Drew. "7 Horror Movies to Watch Before You See *Joker* This Weekend." *Bloody Disgusting*, 30 September 2019, https://bloody-disgusting.com/editorials/3586465/7-horror-movies-watch-see-joker-weekend/. Accessed 12 November 2020.

—. "The Horrors of *Joker*: How the Controversial Comic Book Film Earns a Place in the Genre." *Bloody Disgusting*, 8 October 2019, https://bloody-disgusting.com/editorials/3588016/horrors-joker-controversial-comic-book-film-earns-place-genre/. Accessed 12 November 2020.

Doctorow, E. L. *Ragtime*. Random House, 1975.

Dominguez, Noah. "*Joker* Director Talks Film's '70s Influence." *CBR.com*, 2 September 2019, www.cbr.com/joker-director-talks-films-70s-influence/. Accessed 8 November 2020.

Donagan, Colleen T. *Consuming Dance: Choreography and Advertising*. Oxford University Press, 2018.

Douglas, John E., and Mark Olshaker. *Mindhunter: Inside the FBI's Elite Serial Crime Unit*. 1995. Gallery Books, 2017.

Ebert, Roger. "Batman." *Roger Ebert.com*, 23 June 1989, www.rogerebert.com/reviews/batman-1989. Accessed 28 September 2020.

—. "Henry: Portrait of a Serial Killer." *RogerEbert.com*, 14 September 1990, www.rogerebert.com/reviews/henry-portrait-of-a-serial-killer-1990. Accessed 1 August 1990.

Eghian, Shant. "Making Gotham Great Again, Part 1: The Media—Considering Frank Miller's *The Dark Knight Returns* as a Mirror to Today's Politics." *Liberty Island Magazine*, 18 December 2018, https://libertyislandmag.com/2018/12/18/making-gotham-great-again-part-1-the-media/. Accessed 26 September 2020.

—. "Making Gotham Great Again, Part 2: Law and Order—Considering Frank Miller's *The Dark Knight Returns* as a Mirror to Today's Politics." *Liberty Island Magazine*, 3 January 2019, https://libertyislandmag.com/2019/01/03/making-gotham-great-again-part-2-law-and-order/. Accessed 26 September 2020.

—. "Making Gotham Great Again, Part 3: Ronald Reagan and the Republican Establishment—Considering Frank Miller's *The Dark Knight Returns* as a Mirror to Today's Politics." *Liberty Island Magazine*, 7 January 2019, https://libertyislandmag.com/2019/01/17/making-gotham-great-again-part-3-ronald-reagan-and-the-republican-establishment/. Accessed 26 September 2020.

—. "Making Gotham Great Again, Part 4: Mitt Romney, Man of Steel—Considering Frank Miller's *The Dark Knight Returns* as a Mirror to Today's Politics." *Liberty Island Magazine*, 24 January 2019, https://libertyislandmag.com/2019/01/24/making-gotham-great-again-part-4-mitt-romney-man-of-steel/. Accessed 26 September 2020.

Evangelista, Chris. "*Joker* Review: Joaquin Phoenix Is Phenomenal in This Nihilistic Nightmare." */Film*, 10 September 2019, www.slashfilm.com/joker-review/. Accessed 12 November 2020.

Fisher, Mark. *Capitalist Realism: Is There No Alternative?* Zero Books, 2009.

Flood, Maria. "*Joker* Makes for Uncomfortable Viewing—It Shows How Society Creates Extremists." *Conversation*, 8 October 2019, https://theconversation.com/joker-makes-for-uncomfortable-viewing-it-shows-how-society-creates-extremists-124832. Accessed 11 March 2021.

Freedman, Aaron. "It's Morning in Joker's America." *Jacobin Magazine*, 1 October 2019, https://jacobinmag.com/2019/10/joker-reagan-1981-martin-scorsese-king-comedy. Accessed 5 April 2021.

Freedman, Carl. *The Age of Nixon: A Study in Cultural Power*. Zero Books, 2012.

Friedman, Vanessa. "Why Rioters Wear Costumes: As Star-Spangled Superheroes and Militiamen, the Rioters of D.C. Dressed with a License for Mayhem." *New York Times*, 7 January 2021, www.nytimes.com/2021/01/07/style/capitol-riot-tactics.html. Accessed 24 March 2021.

Gonzaga, Elmo. "The Cinematic Unconscious of Slum Voyeurism." *Cinema Journal*, vol. 56, no. 4, 2017, pp. 102–125.

Gough, Charlotte. "The Ballerina Body-Horror: Spectatorship, Female Subjectivity and the Abject in Dario Argento's *Suspiria* (1977)." *Irish Journal of Gothic and Horror Studies*, vol. 17, 2018, pp. 51–69.

Guinn, Jeff. *Manson: The Life and Times of Charles Manson*. Simon & Schuster, 2013.

Hajdu, David. *The Ten-Cent Plague: The Great Comic-Book Scare and How It Changed America*. Picador, 2009.

Harvey, David. *The Condition of Postmodernity: An Enquiry into the Origins of Cultural Change*. Blackwell, 1990.

Hobsbawm, Eric. *Echoes of the Marseillaise: Two Centuries Look Back on the French Revolution*. Rutgers University Press, 1990.

Howard, Dylan, and Andy Tillett. *The Last Charles Manson Tapes: Evil Lives Beyond the Grave*. Skyhorse, 2019.

Jackson, Nicholas A. "Neoliberalism as Spectacle: Economic Theory, Development and Corporate Exploitation." *Human Geography*, vol. 4, no. 3, 2011, pp. 1–13.

James, David. "Batman and Joker Spotted at George Floyd Protests over the Weekend." *Wegotthiscovered.com*, 1 June 2020, https://wegotthiscovered.com/movies/batman-joker-spotted-national-protests-weekend/. Accessed 15 March 2021.

James, Oliver. *The Selfish Capitalist: Origins of Affluenza*. Vermilion, 2008.

Jameson, Fredric. *The Political Unconscious: Narrative as a Socially Symbolic Act*. Cornell University Press, 1981.

—. "Postmodernism and Consumer Society." *The Anti-Aesthetic: Essays on Postmodern Culture*, edited by Hal Foster, New Press, 1983, pp. 111–125.

—. *Postmodernism, or, The Cultural Logic of Late Capitalism*. Duke University Press, 1991.

"John Wayne Gacy." *Biography*, 9 September 2019, www.biography.com/crime-figure/john-wayne-gacy. Accessed 9 August 2020.

Jürgens, Anna-Sophie. "The Pathology of Joker's Dance: The Origins of Arthur Fleck's Body Aesthetics in Todd Phillips's 2019 *Joker* Film." *Dance Chronicle*, vol. 43, no. 3, 2020, pp. 321–337.

Kaur, Harmeet. "In Protests around the World, One Image Stands Out: The Joker." *CNN.com*. 3 November 2019, www.cnn.com/2019/11/03/world/joker-global-protests-trnd/index.html. Accessed 15 March 2021.

Kay, Andrew. "In Review: *Maniac*." *New Empress Magazine*, 13 March 2013, https://web.archive.org/web/20141006075902/http://newempress-magazine.com/2013/03/in-review-maniac/. Accessed 28 November 2020.

Kenny, Glenn. "*Joker*." *Roger Ebert.com*, 30 September 2019, www.rogerebert.com/reviews/joker-movie-review-2019. Accessed 28 August 2020.

Keppel, Robert D., and William J. Birnes. *The Psychology of Serial Killer Investigations: The Grisly Business Unit*. Academic Press, 2003.

Kerins, Mark. "Hearing Reality in *Joker*." *New Review of Film and Television Studies*, vol. 19, no. 1, 2021, pp. 89–100.

Kimber, Shaun. *Henry: Portrait of a Serial Killer*. Palgrave Macmillan, 2011.

Kit, Borys, and Aaron Couch. "Alec Baldwin Exits 'Joker' Movie." *Hollywood Reporter*, 29 August 2018, www.hollywoodreporter.com/heat-vision/alec-baldwin-exits-joker-movie-says-he-wont-play-trump-like-role-1138384. Accessed 28 March 2021.

Kohut, Heinz. *The Analysis of the Self: A Systematic Approach to the Psychoanalytic Treatment of Narcissistic Personality Disorders*. 1968. Reprint edition, University of Chicago Press, 2013.

Kristeva, Julia. *Powers of Horror: An Essay on Abjection*. Translated by Leon S. Roudiez, Columbia University Press, 1982.

—. "Word, Dialogue, and Novel." *Desire in Language: A Semiotic Approach to Literature and Art*. Translated by Thomas Gora, Alice Jardine, and Leon S. Roudiez, edited by Leon S. Roudiez, Columbia University Press, 1980, pp. 64–91.

Works Cited

Leach, William. *Land of Desire: Merchants, Power, and the Rise of a New American Culture*. Vintage Books, 1993.

Lesnick, Silas. "Christopher Nolan on *The Dark Knight Rises*' Literary Inspiration." *Comingsoon.net*, 8 July 2012, www.comingsoon.net/movies/news/92305-christopher-nolan-on-the-dark-knight-rises-literary-inspiration. Accessed 19 March 2021.

Lickona, Matthew. "*Joker.*" *San Diego Reader*, 2019, www.sandiegoreader.com/movies/joker/. Accessed 22 August 2020.

Lucks, Daniel S. *Reconsidering Reagan: Racism, Republicans, and the Road to Trump*. Beacon Press, 2021.

McHale, Brian. *Postmodernist Fiction*. Methuen, 1987.

Marx, Karl, and Friedrich Engels. *The Marx–Engels Reader*. 2nd edition, edited by Robert C. Tucker, W. W. Norton, 1978.

Mendelson, Scott. "Box Office: *Joker* Becomes the Most Profitable Comic Book Movie Ever." *Forbes*, 8 November 2019, www.forbes.com/sites/scottmendelson/2019/11/08/box-office-dc-films-joker-tops-955-million-to-become-more-profitable-than-deadpool-venom-and-batman/#7a70982a18ff. Accessed 22 September 2020.

Moore, Alan (w), and Brian Bolland (a). *Batman: The Killing Joke, The Deluxe Edition*. DC Comics, 2008.

Moore, Michael. "'Joker': Michael Moore Writes Tribute to Todd Phillips' 'Cinematic Masterpiece.'" *Variety*, 18 December 2019, https://variety.com/2019/film/awards/michael-moore-todd-phillips-joker-1203446280/. Accessed 28 March 2021.

Morton, Robert J., and Mark A. Hilts, editors. "Serial Murder." Official FBI Website. www.fbi.gov/stats-services/publications/serial-murder#ack. Accessed 10 August 2020.

Mumford, Lewis. *The City in History: Its Origins, Its Transformations, and Its Prospects*. Harcourt, Brace Jovanovich, 1961.

Newcott, Bill. "Review: *Joker.*" *Saturday Evening Post*, 3 October 2019, www.saturdayeveningpost.com/2019/10/review-joker-movies-for-the-rest-of-us-with-bill-newcott/. Accessed 22 August 2020.

Nilsson, Johan. "Rictus Grins and Glasgow Smiles: The Joker as Satirical Discourse." *The Joker: A Serious Study of the Clown Prince of Crime*, edited by Robert Moses Peaslee and Robert G. Weiner, University Press of Mississippi, 2016, pp. 165–178.

O'Neil, Dennis. "The Dynamic Duo Swinging into Adventure." Text insert inside front and back cover of the millennium issue reprint of *Batman* #1. DC, 2001.

Patterson, Clayton, and Jeff Ferrell, editors. *Resistance: A Social and Political History of the Lower East Side*. Seven Stories Press, 2006.

Pearson, Roberta E., and William Uricchio. "'I'm Not Fooled By That Cheap Disguise.'" *The Many Lives of the Batman: Critical Approaches to a Superhero and His Media*, edited by Roberta E. Pearson and William Uricchio, Routledge, 1991, pp. 182–213.

Peaslee, Robert Moses, and Robert G. Weiner, editors. *The Joker: A Serious Study of the Clown Prince of Crime.* University Press of Mississippi, 2015.

Phillips, Kendall R. *Projected Fears: Horror Films and American Culture.* Praeger, 2005.

Picchi, Aimee. "50 Years of Tax Cuts for the Rich Failed to Trickle Down, Economics Study Says." *CBSNews.com*, 17 December 2020, www.cbsnews.com/news/tax-cuts-rich-50-years-no-trickle-down/. Accessed 21 March 2021.

Pinedo, Isabel Christina. *Recreational Terror: Women and the Pleasures of Horror Film Viewing.* State University of New York Press, 1997.

Poniewozik, James. "The Attack on the Capitol Was Even Worse Than It Looked." *New York Times*, 11 January 2021, www.nytimes.com/2021/01/11/arts/television/capitol-riot-graphic-videos.html? Accessed 23 March 2021.

Poole, Steven. "The Great Clown Panic of 2016: 'A Volatile Mix of Fear and Contagion.'" *Guardian*, 31 October 2016, www.theguardian.com/culture/2016/oct/31/the-great-clown-panic-of-2016-a-volatile-mix-of-fear-and-contagion. Accessed 21 November 2020.

Rasmus, Jack. *The Scourge of Neoliberalism: US Economic Policy from Reagan to Trump.* Clarity Press, 2020.

Redmond, Sean. "The Loneliness of *Joker*." *New Review of Film and Television Studies*, vol. 19, no. 1, 2021, pp. 65–77.

Riesman, David, with Reuel Denney and Nathan Glazer. *The Lonely Crowd: A Study of the Changing American Character.* Yale University Press, 1950.

Risen, James. "Only the Rich Got Richer in '80s, Fed Concludes during Reagan Era, Poor Lost Ground." *Baltimore Sun*, 7 January 1992, www.baltimoresun.com/news/bs-xpm-1992-01-07-1992007010-story.html. Accessed 22 March 2021.

Robin, Corey. *The Reactionary Mind: Conservatism from Edmund Burke to Donald Trump.* 2nd edition, Oxford University Press, 2017.

Robinson, Joanna. "This Is the Joker the Trump Era Deserves—But Not the One We Need Right Now." *Vanity Fair*, 4 October 2019, www.vanityfair.com/hollywood/2019/10/joker-joaquin-phoenix-trump-era. Accessed 5 April 2021.

Rogers, Ginger. *My Story.* HarperCollins, 1991.

Rogin, Michael. *Ronald Reagan, the Movie and Other Episodes in Political Demonology.* University of California Press, 1987.

Rosewood, Jack, and Rebecca Lo. *The Big Book of Serial Killers.* LAK Publishing, 2017.

Works Cited

Rothenberger, Joshua. "Lower East Side Class War and the Subversive Media Spectacle." *Resistance: A Social and Political History of the Lower East Side*, edited by Clayton Patterson and Jeff Ferrell, Seven Stories Press, 2006, pp. 350–358.

Rottenberg, Josh. "*Joker* Ending Explained: Director Todd Phillips on Fan Theories and Open Questions." *Los Angeles Times*, 4 October 2019, www.latimes.com/entertainment-arts/movies/story/2019-10-04/joker-ending-explained-todd-phillips. Accessed 16 September 2020.

Scherer, Jenna. "Clowns, Cults and Trump: Why New 'American Horror Story' Is a Missed Opportunity." *RollingStone.com*, 6 September 2017, www.rollingstone.com/tv/tv-news/clowns-cults-and-trump-why-new-american-horror-story-is-a-missed-opportunity-201631/. Accessed 25 March 2021.

Seib, Gerald F. *We Should Have Seen It Coming: From Reagan to Trump—A Front-Row Seat to a Political Revolution*. Random House, 2020.

Senesi, Lucia. "Swept Away by Inequality: *Joker* as Neorealism." *Film International*, vol. 18, no. 1, 2020, pp. 7–11.

Sharf, Zack. "*Joker* Cinematographer Says Warner Bros. Passed on Original Plan for 70mm Shoot." *IndieWire*, 12 November 2019, www.indiewire.com/2019/11/joker-warner-bros-turned-down-70mm-film-shoot-1202189137/. Accessed 9 October 2020.

—. "*Joker*: Here's the Original Bathroom Scene Joaquin Phoenix Threw Out with His Improvisation." *IndieWire*, 10 October 2019, www.indiewire.com/2019/10/joker-bathroom-dance-todd-phillips-cut-scene-1202180584/. Accessed 30 August 2020.

Shaviro, Steven. "*Only Lovers Left Alive*." *Pinocchio Theory*, 10 April 2014, www.shaviro.com/Blog/?p=1205. Accessed 1 June 2020.

Sheppard, Elena. "Pro-Trump Capitol Rioters Like the 'QAnon Shaman' Looked Ridiculous—by Design." *NBC News.com*, 13 January 2021, www.nbcnews.com/think/opinion/pro-trump-capitol-rioters-qanon-shaman-looked-ridiculous-design-ncna1254010. Accessed 25 March 2021.

Simmel, Georg. "The Stranger." *The Sociology of Georg Simmel*, edited by K. H. Wolff, Free Press, pp. 402–408.

Sims, David. "Netflix's Ted Bundy Movie Is a Study in True Crime's Most Troubling Questions." *Atlantic*, 3 May 2019, www.theatlantic.com/entertainment/archive/2019/05/extremely-wicked-shockingly-evil-and-vile-review-ted-bundy-zac-efron/588493/. Accessed 15 July 2020.

Sixsmith, Ben. "The Carnival in the Capitol." *Spectator*, 7 January 2021, https://spectator.us/topic/carnival-capitol-camp-larping/. Accessed 23 March 2021.

Slotkin, Richard. *Gunfighter Nation: The Myth of the Frontier in Twentieth-Century America*. University of Oklahoma Press, 1998.

Smaczylo, Mike. "Inside Hildur Guðnadóttir's Haunting Score for Todd Phillips' *Joker*." *Muse by Clio*, 12 June 2020, https://musebycl.io/music-film/inside-hildur-gudnadottirs-haunting-score-todd-phillips-joker. Accessed 6 December 2020.

Steven, Mark. *Splatter Capital: The Political Economy of Gore Films*. Repeater Books, 2017.

Tangcay, Jazz. "Make-Up Artist Nicki Ledermann on the Stages of 'Joker' Face." *Variety*, 23 January 2020, https://variety.com/2020/artisans/awards/todd-phillips-nicki-ledermann-joker-makeup-1203477928/. Accessed 2 May 2021.

Taubin, Amy. *Taxi Driver*. 2nd edition, BFI Film Classics/Palgrave Macmillan, 2012.

Taylor, Brandon. *Modernism, Post-modernism, Realism: A Critical Perspective for Art*. Winchester School of Art Press, 1987.

Taylor, Lance, with Özlem Ömer. *Macroeconomic Inequality from Reagan to Trump*. Cambridge University Press, 2020.

Thiher, Allen. *Words in Reflection: Modern Language Theory and Postmodern Fiction*. University of Chicago Press, 1984.

Thomas, Alexander R. "Ronald Reagan and the Commitment of the Mentally Ill: Capital, Interest Groups, and the Eclipse of Social Policy." *Electronic Journal of Sociology*, vol. 3, no. 4, 1998, pp. 1–13, https://web.archive.org/web/20200713054302/http://www.sociology.org/ejs-archives/vol003.004/thomas.html. Accessed 10 September 2020.

Torrey, E. Fuller. *American Psychosis: How the Federal Government Destroyed the Mental Illness Treatment System*. Oxford University Press, 2013.

Vachss, Andrew. *Batman: The Ultimate Evil*. Warner Books, 1995.

Vronsky, Peter. *Serial Killers: The Method and Madness of Monsters*. Penguin, 2020.

Ware, Lawrence. "The Real Threat of 'Joker' Is Hiding in Plain Sight." *New York Times*, 9 October 2019, www.nytimes.com/2019/10/09/movies/joker-movie-controversy.html. Accessed 1 December 2022.

Wertham, Fredric. *Seduction of the Innocent*. Rinehart and Co., 1954.

West, Alexandra. *Films of the New French Extremity: Visceral Horror and National Identity*. McFarland, 2016.

Williams, Linda. "Discipline and Distraction: *Psycho*, Visual Culture, and Postmodern Cinema." *"Culture" and the Problem of the Disciplines*, edited by John Carlos Rowe, Columbia University Press, 1998, pp. 87–120.

Wills, Gary. *Ronald Reagan's America: Innocents at Home*. Open Road, 2017.

Wood, Robin. *Hollywood from Vietnam to Reagan and Beyond*. Revised and expanded edition, Columbia University Press, 2003.

Works Cited

Zacharek, Stephanie. "The Problem with *Joker* Isn't Its Brutal Violence. It's the Muddled Message It Sends About Our Times." *Time*, 2 October 2019, https://time.com/5688305/joker-todd-phillips-review/. Accessed 22 August 2020.

Žižek, Slavoj. "More on *Joker*: From Apolitical Nihilism to a New Left, or Why Trump Is No Joker." *Philosophical Salon*, 11 November 2019, https://thephilosophicalsalon.com/more-on-joker-from-apolitical-nihilism-to-a-new-left-or-why-trump-is-no-joker/. Accessed 28 March 2021.

—. "The Politics of Batman." *New Statesman*, 23 August 2012, https://archive.ph/n2LTU. Accessed 1 December 2022.

Zollo, Paul. "Behind The Song: "Smile" by Charlie Chaplin with Turner & Parsons, and, Most Likely, Raksin." *American Songwriter*, March 2020, https://americansongwriter.com/smile-charlie-chaplin-david-raskin-turner-parsons-behind-the-song/. Accessed 8 December 2020.

Zullo, Valentino L. "What's Diagnosis Got to Do With It?: Psychiatry, Comics and *Batman: The Killing Joke*." *Inks: The Journal of the Comics Studies Society*, vol. 2, no. 2, 2018, pp. 194–214.

Films and Television Series Cited

31, dir. Rob Zombie, 2016.
All Hallow's Eve, dir. Damien Leone, 2013.
American Horror Story: Cult, created by Ryan Murphy and Brad Falchuk, 2017.
American Horror Story: Freak Show, created by Ryan Murphy and Brad Falchuk, 2014–2015.
American Idol, created by Simon Fuller, 2002– .
American Psycho, dir. Mary Harron, 2000.
The Apprentice, created by Mark Burnett, 2004–2015.
Batman, dir. Tim Burton, 1989.
Batman (television), executive producer William Dozier, 1966–1968.
Batman: Mask of the Phantasm, dir. Eric Radomski and Bruce Timm, 1993.
Batman & Robin, dir. Joel Schumacher, 1997.
Batman Begins, dir. Christopher Nolan, 2005.
Batman Forever, dir. Joel Schumacher, 1995.
Batman Returns, dir. Tim Burton, 1992.
Birds of Prey (and the Fantabulous Emancipation of One Harley Quinn), dir. Cathy Yan, 2020.
Black Christmas, dir. Bob Clark, 1974.
Black Mirror, created by Charlie Brooker, 2011–2019.
Blade Runner, dir. Ridley Scott, 1982.
Breathless (*À bout de souffle*), dir. Jean-Luc Godard, 1960.
Buck Rogers in the 25th Century, developed by Glen A. Larson and Leslie Stevens, 1979–1981.
Bundy: An American Icon, dir. Michael Feifer, 2008. Also known as *Bundy: A Legacy of Evil*.
The Cabinet of Dr. Caligari, dir. Robert Wiene, 1920.
The Capture of the Green River Killer, dir. Norma Bailey, 2008.
Carnival of Souls, dir. Adam Grossman, 1998.
Charlie Says, dir. Mary Harron, 2018.
Chernobyl, created by Craig Mazin, 2019.
Circus Kane, dir. Christopher Ray, 2017.

Cléo from 5 to 7, dir. Agnès Varda, 1962.
Climax, dir. Gaspar Noé, 2018.
A Clockwork Orange, dir. Stanley Kubrick, 1971.
Clown, dir. Jon Watts, 2014.
Clown Motel: Spirits Arise, dir. Joseph Kelly, 2019.
Clown Motel Massacre, dir. Tom Newth, 2018.
Clownado, dir. Todd Sheets, 2019.
Clowntergeist, dir. Aaron Mirtes, 2017.
Conversations with a Killer: The Ted Bundy Tapes, dir. Joe Berlinger, 2019.
Crepitus, dir. Haynze Whitmore, 2018.
Crispy's Curse, dir. John Williams, 2017.
The Dark Knight, dir. Christopher Nolan, 2008.
The Dark Knight Rises, dir. Christopher Nolan, 2012.
The Deliberate Stranger, dir. Marvin J. Chomsky, 1986.
Detroit, dir. Kathryn Bigelow, 2017.
The Devil's Rejects, dir. Rob Zombie, 2005.
Do the Right Thing, dir. Spike Lee, 1989.
Don't Go in the House, dir. Joseph Ellison, 1980.
Don't Look, dir. Luciana Faulhaber, 2018.
Drown the Clown, dir. Justin Viggiano, 2020.
Easy Rider, dir. Dennis Hopper, 1969.
The Eiger Sanction, dir. Clint Eastwood, 1975.
E.T. the Extra-Terrestrial, dir. Steven Spielberg, 1982.
Extremely Wicked, Shockingly Evil, and Vile, dir. Joe Berlinger, 2019.
Frankenstein, dir. James Whale, 1931.
Friday the 13th, dir. Sean S. Cunningham, 1980.
Gacy, dir. Clive Saunders, 2003.
Gags the Clown, dir. Adam Krause, 2018.
Get Out, dir. Jordan Peele, 2017.
Ghostbusters, dir. Ivan Reitman, 1984.
The Godfather, dir. Francis Ford Coppola, 1972.
Goodfellas, dir. Martin Scorsese, 1990.
Gotham, executive producers Bruno Heller, et al., 2014–2019.
The Great Gatsby, dir. Baz Luhrmann, 2013.
The Guest, dir. Adam Wingard, 2014.
Halloween, dir. John Carpenter, 1978.
Happy Death Day, dir. Christopher Landon, 2017.
Haunt, dir. Scott Beck and Bryan Woods, 2019.
The Haunting of Sharon Tate, dir. Daniel Farrands, 2019.
Helter Skelter, dir. Tom Greis, 1976.
Helter Skelter, dir. John Gray, 2004.
Helter Skelter: An American Myth, dir. Lesley Chilcott, 2020.

He-Man and the Masters of the Universe, executive producer Lou Scheimer, 1983–1985.
Henry: Portrait of a Serial Killer, dir. John McNaughton, 1986.
Hereditary, dir. Ari Aster, 2018.
House of 1000 Corpses, dir. Rob Zombie, 2003.
The House that Jack Built, dir. Lars von Trier, 2018.
The Hunger Games, dir. Gary Ross, 2012.
Hush, dir. Mike Flanagan, 2016.
I Knew Her Well (*Io la conoscevo bene*), dir. Antonio Pietrangeli, 1965.
I Love Melvin, dir. Don Weis, 1953.
Idiocracy, dir. Mike Judge, 2006.
I'm Still Here, dir. Casey Affleck, 2010
It, dir. Tommy Lee Wallace, 1990.
It, dir. Andy Muschietti, 2017.
It Chapter Two, dir. Andy Muschietti, 2019.
It's Always Fair Weather, dir. Stanley Donen and Gene Kelly, 1955.
The Jack in the Box, dir. Lawrence Fowler, 2019.
The Killing of America, dir. Sheldon Renan, 1981.
The Last Circus (*Balada triste de trompeta*), dir. Álex de la Iglesia, 2010.
Lovers Rock, dir. Steve McQueen, 2020.
The Machinist, dir. Brad Anderson, 2004.
Man Bites Dog, dir. Rémy Belvaux, André Bonzel, and Benoît Poelvoorde, 1992.
Maniac, dir. William Lustig, 1980.
Maniac, dir. Franck Khalfoun, 2012.
Memento, dir. Christopher Nolan, 2000.
Mindhunter, executive producers Joe Penhall, David Fincher, et al., 2017–2019.
Modern Times, dir. Charles Chaplin, 1936.
A Most Violent Year, dir. J. C. Chandor, 2014.
Moulin Rouge!, dir. Baz Luhrmann, 2001.
Mr. Majestyk, dir. Richard Fleischer, 1974.
Mulberry Street, dir. Jim Mickle, 2006.
My Life to Live (*Vivre sa vie*), dir. Jean-Luc Godard, 1962.
The Nest, dir. Sean Durkin, 2020.
Network, dir. Sidney Lumet, 1976.
News from Home, dir. Chantal Akerman, 1977.
Night of the Living Dead, dir. George Romero, 1968.
A Nightmare on Elm Street, dir. Wes Craven, 1984.
On Halloween, dir. Timothy Boyle, 2020
Once Upon a Time in Hollywood, dir. Quentin Tarantino, 2019.
Pennyworth, executive producers Bruno Heller and Danny Cannon, 2019– .
The People Under the Stairs, dir. Wes Craven, 1991.
Poltergeist, dir. Tobe Hooper, 1982.

Poltergeist, dir. Gil Kenan, 2015.
Psycho, dir. Alfred Hitchcock, 1960.
Ragtime, dir. Miloš Forman, 1981.
Ready Player One, dir. Steven Spielberg, 2018.
Rent-A-Pal, dir. Jon Stevenson, 2020.
Revenge, dir. Coralie Fargeat, 2017.
The Riverman, dir. Bill Eagles, 2004.
The Searchers, dir. John Ford, 1956.
Shall We Dance, dir. Mark Sandrich, 1937.
The Silence of the Lambs, dir. Jonathan Demme, 1991.
Slumdog Millionaire, dir. Danny Boyle, 2008.
Society, dir. Brian Yuzna, 1989.
Sometime Sweet Susan, dir. Fred Donaldson, 1975.
The Sopranos, executive producers David Chase, et al., 1999–2007.
Sorry to Bother You, dir. Boots Riley, 2018.
Spider-Man: Far from Home, dir. Jon Watts, 2019.
Spider-Man: Homecoming, dir. Jon Watts, 2017.
The Spirit of the Beehive (*El espíritu de la colmena*), dir. Víctor Erice, 1973.
Stand By Me, dir. Rob Reiner, 1986.
Star Wars, dir. George Lucas, 1977.
The Sting, dir. George Roy Hill, 1973.
Stranger Things, executive producers the Duffer Brothers, et al., 2016– .
Suicide Squad, dir. David Ayer, 2016.
Summer of Sam, dir. Spike Lee, 1999.
Survivor, created by Charlie Parsons, 2000– .
Suspiria, dir. Dario Argento, 1977.
Suspiria, dir. Luca Guadagnino, 2018.
Ted Bundy, dir. Matthew Bright, 2002.
Ted Bundy: Falling for a Killer, dir. Trish Wood, 2020.
Ted Bundy: Natural Porn Killer, dir. Sascha Olofson, 2006.
Terrifier, dir. Damien Leone, 2016.
Terrifier 2, dir. Damien Leone, 2021.
The Texas Chain Saw Massacre, dir. Tobe Hooper, 1974.
Us, dir. Jordan Peele, 2019.
The Voices, dir. Marjane Satrapi, 2014.
Wall Street, dir. Oliver Stone, 1987.
Wrinkles the Clown, dir. Michael Beach Nichols, 2019
The X-Files, executive producers Chris Carter, et al. 1993–2002.
Yankee Doodle Dandy, dir. Michael Curtiz, 1942.
You Were Never Really Here, dir. Lynne Ramsay, 2017.
You're Next, dir. Adam Wingard, 2011.
Zelig, dir. Woody Allen, 1983.
Zodiac, dir. David Fincher, 2007.

Index

31 (2016 film) 93

Acosta, Jim 218n6
Adams, Nick 239n2
alienation 41, 183, 185, 187, 199
All Hallow's Eve 93
American Horror Story: Cult 90
American Horror Story: Freak Show 107n1
American Idol 237
American Psycho (2000 film) 89, 95, 96, 173n11
The Apprentice 236, 237
Ashton, Will 89
Astaire, Fred 140–44, 161, 178, 179, 187
Augustine, J. B. 30n11
Avengers: Endgame 26
Ayres, Jackson 19, 29n2

Bainbridge, Caroline 186, 200
Baldwin, Alec 221
Barsanti, Sam 31n13
Batman 1–4, 28, 34, 63, 84n1, 127, 131, 158, 202, 203, 241
    comics featuring the Joker 4, 8, 11, 16–22, 25, 26, 28
    films featuring the Joker 23–29
    Thomas Wayne and 11–16
Batman (1960s television series) 4
Batman (1989 film) 4, 12, 23, 24, 34, 218n9
Batman: The Animated Series 24

Batman: Mask of the Phantasm 30n9
Batman & Robin 61n1
Batman Begins 12, 25
Batman Forever 61n1
Batman Returns 23–24
Batman v. Superman 27, 65
Baudrillard, Jean 34, 175, 180, 195, 196, 196n2
Belton, John 85n13
Berkowitz, David 85n12
    see also serial killers
Birds of Prey 30n10
Birnes, William J. 152
Biskind, Peter 71
Black Christmas (1974 film) 97
Black Mirror 193
Blade Runner 39, 40, 195
Blunden, Fred 16
Bolland, Brian 21, 22
Booker, M. Keith 39, 64, 191, 200, 232
    Alternate Americas 40
    Consumerist Orientalism 178
    Postmodern Hollywood 42, 85, 146
Breathless (*À bout de souffle*) 47
Bremer, Arthur 74
Brody, Richard 38
Brown, Jeffrey 202, 203, 208
Buck Rogers in the 25th Century 61n8
Bugliosi, Vincent 165, 172n7–8
Bundy, Ted 153, 168, 169, 173n10, 173n11, 173n12
    see also serial killers

263

Burke, Edmund 210, 229
Burton, Tara Isabella 47
Burwick, Kevin 61n3
Butler, Octavia E. 238n1

The Cabinet of Dr. Caligari 100
capitalism 5, 59, 88, 107n6, 110, 112, 162, 180, 182, 185, 188, 200, 226, 227, 233, 237
   and modernization 4, 195, 220
   and postmodernism 35–46
   see also consumerism; neoliberalism; spectacle
Carlyle, Thomas 210
Carnival of Souls 93
Chaplin, Charles 2, 48, 49, 114, 115, 140, 142, 143, 144, 159, 177, 179, 207, 243
   see also Modern Times
Charlie Says 169
Chernobyl 2, 109
Child, Ben 218n2
Circus Kane 94
Cléo from 5 to 7 54, 55
Climax 197n7
A Clockwork Orange (1971 film) 74
Clover, Carol J. 108n9
Clown (2014 film) 93
Clown Motel: Spirits Arise 94
Clown Motel Massacre 94
Clownado 94
Clowntergeist 94
Coletta, Charles 29n2
Collins, Jim 57, 58
Collins, Judy 50, 113
Collura, Scott 25
consumerism 59, 116, 181, 194, 196n4, 242
Couch, Aaron 221
Crary, Robert 59
Crepitus 94
Crispy's Curse 94
Curran, Brad 84n3

Daraiseh, Isra 39, 64, 178, 191, 200, 232
The Dark Knight 19, 20
The Dark Knight Rises 207–10, 218n2
De Semlyen, Phil 88, 222
Debord, Guy 7, 8, 175, 177, 180–85, 187, 188, 194, 195, 196, 196n5, 197n6, 199, 228, 233, 242, 244
   see also spectacle
The Deliberate Stranger 168
Detroit (2017 film) 215
The Devil's Rejects 93
Dickens, Charles 208, 209, 210
Dietsch, Drew 89
Do the Right Thing 215
Doctorow, E. L. 116
Dominguez, Noah 66
Donagan, Colleen T. 55
Don't Go in the House 99
Don't Look 94
Douglas, John E. 172n1
Drown the Clown 94

E. T. the Extra-Terrestrial 191
Easy Rider 163
Ebert, Roger 30n8, 102
Eghian, Shant 21
The Eiger Sanction 73
Engels, Friedrich 182
Evangelista, Chris 88

Ferrell, Jeff 149n2
Finger, Bill 11
Fisher, Mark 36, 238
Flood, Maria 184
Frankenstein (1931 film) 107n7, 211
Freedman, Aaron 220, 221
Freedman, Carl 166, 232, 234, 236
French Revolution 208–11, 214, 218n4, 218n8, 221, 229
Friday the 13th 98
Friedman, Milton 6, 35
Friedman, Vanessa 217

INDEX

Gacy (2003 film) 107n3
Gacy, John Wayne 7, 91, 152–55, 160–62, 172n2, 172n3, 244
  See also serial killers
Gags the Clown 94
Gein, Ed 162
  see also serial killers
Gentry, Curt 165
Get Out 88, 106
Ghostbusters 191
Glitter, Gary 53, 111, 112, 120, 189
The Godfather 66, 68, 70, 117
Gonzaga, Elmo 190
Goodfellas 70
Gotham (2010s television series) 4, 12
Gough, Charlotte 197n7
The Great Gatsby (2013 film) 179
Guðnadóttir, Hildur 2, 38, 50, 55, 109, 110, 113, 117, 119, 120, 187, 211, 241
The Guest 101
Guinn, Jeff 165, 166

Hajdu, David 30n5
Halloween (1978 film) 66, 97, 98–100, 122
Happy Death Day 101
Harvey, David 46, 60
Haunt (2019 film) 94
The Haunting of Sharon Tate 169
Hayek, Friedrich 6
He-Man and the Masters of the Universe 193
Helter Skelter (1976 film) 168
Helter Skelter (2004 film) 168
Helter Skelter: An American Myth 170
Henry: Portrait of a Serial Killer 89, 102–5
Hereditary 88
Hilts, Mark A. 151
Hobsbawm, Eric 218n3, 218n4
House of 1000 Corpses 93
The House that Jack Built 101

Howard, Dylan 168
The Hunger Games 215
Hush 101

I Knew Her Well (*Io la conoscevo bene*) 110
I Love Melvin 143
Idiocracy 237
I'm Still Here 196n3
It (1990 miniseries) 92
It (2017 film) 92, 94
It Chapter Two 107n5
It's Always Fair Weather 143

The Jack in the Box 219
Jackson, Nicholas A. 196n1
James, David 203
James, Oliver 36
Jameson, Fredric 36, 45, 58, 59, 60, 84, 175, 180, 182, 195
  The Political Unconscious 65
  Postmodernism 4, 35–42, 45, 46, 47, 193, 196
January 6 insurrection 8, 90, 216, 217, 221, 235, 245
Jürgens, Anna-Sophie 197n8

Kane, Bob 11, 61n2
Kaur, Harmeet 205
Kay, Andrew 100
Kenny, Glenn 47
Keppel, Robert D. 152
Kerins, Mark 122n1
Kimber, Shaun 104
Kit, Borys 221
Kohut, Heinz 172n5
Kristeva, Julia 186, 190, 217n1

The Last Circus (*Balada triste de trompeta*) 89, 94
Leach, William 196n4
LeBlanc, Paul 218n6
Lesnick, Silas 209

265

Lickona, Matthew 38, 39
Lovers Rock (2020 film) 111
Lucks, Daniel S. 238n2

McHale, Brian 103
The Machinist 95, 96
Man Bites Dog 89
Maniac (1980 film) 89
Maniac (2012 film) 89
Manson, Charles 6, 69, 90, 152, 153, 162–71, 172n7–9, 244
    see also serial killers
Marx, Karl 180–83
Memento 42
Mendelson, Scott 37
mental health system in the U.S. 106, 118, 132–35, 138, 139, 194
Mindhunter 170, 171
Modern Times 2, 48, 49, 114, 115, 140, 142, 143, 144, 159, 177, 179, 207, 243
    see also Chaplin, Charles
Moore, Alan 21, 22, 214
Moore, Michael 221, 225
Morton, Robert J. 151
Most Violent Year, A 131
Moulin Rouge! 179
Mr. Majestyk 73
Mulberry Street 106
My Life to Live (*Vivre sa vie*) 110

neoliberalism 3, 6, 7, 8, 33–36, 55, 87, 88, 106, 128, 153, 163, 167, 175, 196n1, 200, 212, 219, 220, 226–29, 233, 237, 238, 239n2, 239n4, 242–45
The Nest 87, 88
Network 146
Newcott, Bill 38
News from Home 129
Night of the Living Dead 163
Nightmare on Elm Street, A 98
Nilsson, Johan 17

Nixon, Richard 3, 8, 74, 135, 137, 144, 162–66, 172n8, 214, 220, 228–36, 238, 245
nostalgia (1980s) 25, 87, 92, 191–94, 233, 245

Occupy Wall Street 208, 209
Olshaker, Mark 172n1
On Halloween 94
Once Upon a Time in Hollywood 169, 170
O'Neil, Dennis 17, 19

Patterson, Clayton 149n2
Pearson, Roberta E. 203
Peaslee, Robert Moses 30n4
Pennyworth 30
The People Under the Stairs 106
Phillips, Kendall R. 163
Picchi, Aimee 213
Pinedo, Isabel Christina 104
Poltergeist (1982 film) 91
Poltergeist (2015 film) 107n4
Poniewozik, James 90, 218n7
Poole, Steven 107n2
postmodernism 2, 4, 5, 7, 29, 33–61, 63–67, 72, 78, 83, 84, 85n13, 95, 103, 104, 121, 127–29, 146, 148, 151, 153, 175, 179, 182, 193, 195, 200, 220, 232, 234, 236–38, 241–43
    loss of historical sense in 58–60, 127, 128
    pastiche in 5, 45–47, 85, 191
    psychic fragmentation in 41, 42, 46, 47, 58, 137, 183, 232
    see also Jameson, Fredric
Psycho (1960 film) 95, 97, 99, 102, 103, 122, 162

Ragtime (1981 film) 116
Rasmus, Jack 239
Ready Player One 92, 193

Index

Reagan, Ronald 6, 8, 25, 43, 74, 87, 88, 91, 96, 127–49, 163, 173n10, 191–93, 212, 214, 217, 220, 221, 241, 243
   in *The Dark Knight Returns* 20–25
   and Donald Trump 133, 219–20, 225–38, 238n2, 245
   see also mental health system in the U.S.
Redmond, Sean 200
Rent-A-Pal 88
Revenge (2017 film) 106
Riesman, David 183
Risen, James 213
Robin, Corey 229, 230, 233, 234
Robinson, Jerry 11
Robinson, Joanna 220
Rogers, Ginger 140–44, 149n5
Rogin, Michael 136, 139
Rothenberger, Joshua 149n2
Rottenberg, Josh 149n3

Scherer, Jenna 90
The Searchers 68, 69, 75, 77, 78, 84n4
Seib, Gerald F. 239n2
Senesi, Lucia 110, 111
serial killers 6, 7, 37, 69, 87–108
Shall We Dance 111, 140–44, 147, 149n4, 161, 187
Sharf, Zack 2, 50
Shaviro, Steven 191
Sheppard, Elena 218n9
The Silence of the Lambs 97, 98, 162
Simmel, Georg 200
Sims, David 173n12
Sinatra, Frank 2, 49, 53, 61n4, 110, 112–14, 117, 120, 121, 123n2, 188, 189
Sixsmith, Ben 218n8
slasher films 68, 69, 73, 87, 89, 93, 94, 97–107

Slumdog Millionaire 190
Smaczylo, Mike 110
Society (1989 film) 106
Sometime Sweet Susan 73
The Sopranos 70
Sorry to Bother You 237
spectacle 7, 8, 33, 54, 55, 167, 175, 197, 238, 242
   see also Debord, Guy
Spider-Man: Far from Home 27, 93
Spider-Man: Homecoming 93
The Spirit of the Beehive (*El espíritu de la colmena*) 107n7
Stand By Me (1986 film)
Star Wars (1977 film) 26, 66, 68, 135, 136, 176, 180, 215
Steven, Mark 107n6
The Sting 116
Stranger Things 191–93
Suicide Squad (2016 film) 30n10
Summer of Sam 123n2, 167, 168
Survivor 237
Suspiria (1977 film) 197n7
Suspiria (2018 film) 197n7

Tangcay, Jazz 129
Taubin, Amy 75, 77, 84n4
Taylor, Lance 218n5
Terrifier 93, 101
Terrifier 2 93
The Texas Chain Saw Massacre 66, 73, 97, 122, 162
Thiher, Allen 45
Thomas, Alexander R. 133
Tillett, Andy 168
Torrey, E. Fuller 134, 135
Trump, Donald 3, 8, 14, 21, 30n6, 43, 90, 107n1, 128, 130, 137, 163, 177, 213, 214, 216, 217, 218n2, 219–39, 245
   and Ronald Reagan 133, 219–20, 225–38, 238n2, 245
   see also January 6 insurrection

Uricchio, William 203
Us (2019 film) 106

Vachss, Andrew 61n2
The Voices 89, 96, 97
Vronsky, Peter 152, 153, 157

Wall Street (1987 film) 25, 220, 227
Weiner, Robert G. 30n4
Wertham, Fredric 30n5
West, Alexandra 108n11
Williams, Linda 95
Wills, Gary 135
Wood, Robin 79, 106
Wrinkles the Clown 94

The X-Files 191

Yankee Doodle Dandy 179
You Were Never Really Here 29, 30n14
You're Next 101

Zacharek, Stephanie 38
Zelig 42
Žižek, Slavoj 28, 85n7, 208
Zodiac 107n1, 167
Zodiac killer 166, 167
  see also serial killers
Zollo, Paul 123n3
Zullo, Valentino L. 22